tear here

The Complete Idiot's Reference Card

Top 10 Hints on Buying Fabrics

1. Pick out your color scheme.

2. Buy 100 percent cotton or cotton/polyester blend fabrics.

3. Don't buy fabric with nap or a one-way design.

4. Pick out fabrics with variety in the scale of the patterns.

5. First choose a blender fabric that contains all the colors of your color scheme in a medium to large pattern.

6. Select a dominant color and a contrasting color fabric.

7. Choose at least two other fabrics that are lighter or darker values of the dominant and contrasting fabrics.

8. Pick a background or ground fabric that is a solid or a solid print.

9. Line up all the fabrics in the store and use the squint method to make sure the colors blend.

10. Purchase quality fabrics and wash them as soon as you go home.

Mattress Sizes

Twin	39" × 75"
Full	52" × 75"
Queen	60" × 80"
King	72" × 84"

Finished Size of Quilt Tops

Lap	40" × 56"
Twin	68" × 94"
Full	80" × 103"
Queen	83" × 103"
King	100" × 116"

alpha
books

How to Make a Template

1. Choose a block.

2. Copy each pattern of the block by tracing or carefully photocopying the page.

3. Rubber cement medium-weight sandpaper to cardboard.

4. Then rubber cement the copied quilt patterns onto the cardboard side of this sandpaper/cardboard.

5. Carefully cut through all three layers and around the outer edges of the pattern.

6. Test for accuracy and size by placing the template over the pattern in the book.

7. Be sure all important information is written on the template: the name of the block, the straight-of-grain arrow, and the number of pieces needed to cut.

8. Don't mix quilt block templates—store templates for each block in an envelope or plastic zip-lock bag.

How to Calculate Yardage for One Specific Pattern Template

1. Count the number of pattern shapes needed for one quilt block.

2. Determine how many pattern pieces are needed for the entire quilt. (Multiply the number of shapes in the block by the number of blocks in the quilt.)

3. Calculate the size of the pattern shape you need to cut. Add on $1/4$-inch seam allowance all around the outside of the shape. (If it's a four-inch square, then the size including seam allowances will be $41/2$ inches.)

4. Measure the width of your fabric.

5. Find out how many fabric pieces fit into the width of your fabric (fabric width divided by the size of the pattern with seam allowances). This will form a row.

6. Figure the length of fabric needed (total number of fabric pieces needed for a quilt divided by how many can fit across in a row).

7. Multiply the number of rows by the length of the pattern pieces, including the seam allowances (number of rows multiplied by the size of the pattern pieces).

8. Add on a fudge factor of four or five inches to the length of rows.

9. Calculate the yardage (total length of inches of the rows divided by 36 inches in a yard).

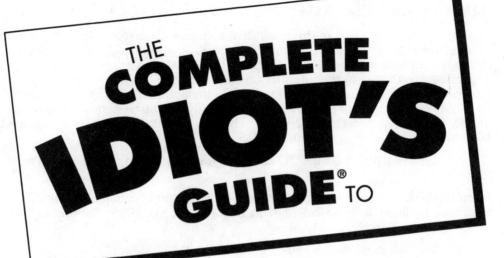

THE COMPLETE IDIOT'S GUIDE® TO

Quilting

by Laura Ehrlich

alpha books

A Division of Macmillan General Reference
A Simon & Schuster Macmillan Company
1633 Broadway, New York, NY 10019

Macmillan Publishing books may be purchased for business or sales promotional use. For information please write: Special Markets Department, Macmillan Publishing USA, 1633 Broadway, New York, NY 10019.

International Standard Book Number: 0-02862411-4
Library of Congress Catalog Card Number: 98-86764

00 99 98   8 7 6 5 4 3 2 1

Interpretation of the printing code: the rightmost number of the first series of numbers is the year of the book's printing; the rightmost number of the second series of numbers is the number of the book's printing. For example, a printing code of 98-1 shows that the first printing occurred in 1998.

Printed in the United States of America

ALPHA DEVELOPMENT TEAM

Publisher
Kathy Nebenhaus

Editorial Director
Gary M. Krebs

Managing Editor
Bob Shuman

Marketing Brand Manager
Felice Primeau

Senior Editor
Nancy Mikhail

Development Editors
Phil Kitchel
Jennifer Perillo
Amy Zavatto

Editorial Assistant
Maureen Horn

PRODUCTION TEAM

Development Editor
Joan Paterson

Production Editor
Christy Wagner

Copy Editor
Susan Aufheimer

Cover Designer
Mike Freeland

Photo Editor
Richard H. Fox

Illustrator
Jody P. Schaeffer

Designer
Glenn Larsen

Indexer
Sandra Henselmeier

Layout/Proofreading
Angela Calvert
Mary Hunt

Contents at a Glance

Contents

Foreword

Welcome to the world of quilt making! It's a wonderful world with a distinguished history that has risen from humble beginnings to a multi-million-dollar industry. As Laura explains in her first chapter, the idea of stitching two or three layers of fabric together is certainly not new. Ancient Egyptians did it to create covers for extra warmth, and bits of fabric sewn together to form a whole cloth are found in early Oriental, Middle Eastern, and European textiles. Today, quilt making, a cherished part of our own country's heritage, is as popular around the world as it was centuries ago.

One reason for its popularity lies in the intrinsic beauty of the quilt itself. The exciting color combinations, the intriguing patterns, the textural surface designs—just feast your eyes on the quilts in this book! Another reason quilt making has remained so popular is that a quilt is easy to make, especially when you have Laura by your side every step of the way. Believe it or not, the aptitude to shop for fabric (a most pleasant experience), the talent to cut the fabric into pieces (you know how to use scissors so this step is a cinch), and the ability to sew pieces together (a simple straight stitch by hand or machine does it) are really all the technical skills needed to create a quilt.

As you begin to create your first quilt, you begin your exciting journey into the wonderful world of quilt making. And with Laura as your personal guide, you'll explore every realm from planning your quilt to displaying it on your bed or wall. On each page, Laura shares many years of quilt making and teaching experience so you can learn everything you need to know about making a quilt, including things you didn't know enough to ask about.

By the end of the book and upon the completion of your first quilt, you will have learned the most important lesson of all: Quilt making is not just another craft. It's a means of creative expression. It's an art form. It's a quiet street you stroll along to savor solitude. It's a bustling boulevard along which you encounter the friendliest folks. It's the adventure of a lifetime. It's a lifetime of adventure. It's everything you are now and everything you can be. It's a state of mind. It's a wonderful world, and you are part of it. Welcome!

Jan Burns
Editor, *Creative Quilting* magazine

Introduction

I always get a comfortable feeling when I look at a room that has a quilt in it. There is nothing like a quilt to add warmth and beauty to a room. Quilts have an appeal that has lasted through centuries. Some people regard quilts as an investment and collect antique quilts. Nowadays we are valuing quilts more and more as works of art. You can see quilts displayed in museums and art galleries as the new textile art. Most people, however, just like quilts because they are beautiful to have around.

If you are someone who loves quilts and has decided to join your heritage and create your own quilt, you have many decisions to make. Quilts come with a variety of different names, designs, and options that make the quilting process complicated enough, without throwing in the dilemma of choosing colors. Where do you begin?

I began by looking through quilt books for inspiration. Then I walked through craft stores and linen departments to see what I liked. Finally, my friend Linda twisted my arm and I took a class in beginner quilting. I loved the class—especially the creativity and productivity! At the end of 10 weeks, I had lots of squares of quilt block designs but did not know what to do with them. It bothered me that putting these blocks together into a quilt was only briefly discussed in the class. That is where the idea for offering my own class and writing this book came into being.

This book will take you from start to finish in making a quilt. It will give you a basic understanding of quilts—their history, types, and names. You'll learn about quilt components and quilt construction. I will take you step-by-step through all the decisions you have to make. You will learn how to plan the quilt, buy the materials, piece the quilt top, quilt, and sign your work of art.

What You'll Find in This Book

Beginners need to be realistic. Quilts vary in size, and the designs range from easy to very challenging. I encourage beginners to experiment with a variety of simple designs for a small project. The best way to learn quilting is to make a Sampler quilt. The Sampler quilt combines different designs, both pieced and appliquéd. You can pick and choose blocks, starting with the easy ones and then, as you become more accomplished, go on to make more challenging ones. Here's how you do it: Follow this book from Part 1 all the way to the end and you will have a quilt you're proud to display.

Part 1, "Let's Get Ready to Quilt!" gives you a general understanding about types of quilts and how our ancestors developed them. There are many decisions to make, so first take some time to look at the quilt patterns throughout this book and choose the quilt you would like to make. We'll take the mystery out of planning the size and selecting colors to make your quilt one that you will want to live with for a lifetime.

In **Part 2, "Get Set,"** you'll learn about equipment and materials. There are certain supplies that you will need to get started. I have listed the necessities—you'll find many of them around the house, but there are some neat gadgets that could help you in your quest for the perfect quilt. Probably the scariest part in making a quilt is purchasing the fabric. There are so many choices it boggles the brain. Knowing the type of fabric and how much you need will help put your mind at ease.

Part 3, "Hands On: It's Time to Start," provides you with a general knowledge of fabric characteristics. Templates or quilt patterns must be made and transferred onto the fabric. You'll discover how to cut your fabric and put the pieces of the quilt together. There are certain stitches that will help your quilt be durable and hold up to everyday usage. Don't forget the quickness and practicality of machine-made quilts. Careful ironing will help your quilt look professional.

The chapters in **Part 4, "Choose a Pattern for Your Quilt,"** include step-by-step instructions and pictures of each quilt design arranged by degree of difficulty—I don't want a beginner to bite off more than you can sew. Helpful hints will ease you into patching the pieced, appliqué, and machine-sewn blocks. The patterns for each design are full-size so you will not have to enlarge them. All the blocks are 12-inch squares.

By **Part 5, "Let's Put It All Together and Quilt,"** you will have constructed many quilt blocks. It's time to put them all together and frame them out to form the quilt top. In addition, you need the filling batting and a backing. How much and what type to purchase for your quilt is examined. Holding this quilt sandwich together in wrinkle-free layers is imperative—basting is your key to success. Can you believe we are almost at the end of the book and just starting to quilt? Decide how to give your quilt the three-dimensional life it deserves by tying, hand quilting, or machine quilting.

Part 6, "Your Finished Quilt," addresses the finishing touches. You'll find out how to eliminate all those frayed edges. Artists sign their creations and so should quilters. Sometimes you only want to make a small project. I'll explain how to make a pillow and wall hanging from start to finish. After all the time, work, and love you have put into your quilt, you'll learn how to take care of it with tender loving care. Happy quilting!

Extras

There are many steps involved in making a quilt. This book is designed to make it as easy as possible and help you avoid any problems. Sidebars are scattered throughout the book and will highlight things I feel are important for all quilters to know.

Scraps and Pieces

This box offers a variety of different quilt stories, historical tidbits, or just interesting information about quilting.

Quilt Talk
Quilters seem to have a language of their own. Any new and unusual words will be explained.

Quilting Bee
Sometimes there is an easy way of doing something, and these tips are ones that you would learn at a quilting bee.

Don't Get Stuck!
Throughout my many years of teaching beginner quilters, I have discovered many different pitfalls that may occur. Hopefully the hints in these boxes will help you avoid these problems.

Acknowledgments

Many people have contributed to this quilting guide. I first of all would like to thank my husband Elliott, and my girls, Jamie, Jessica, and Amanda, for encouraging me, helping me with all my computer glitches, and putting up with me in general. Here's to all the times you've forgiven me when you've stepped on runaway pins while I was working on a quilting project. I'll always be grateful to my mother, Tony Mangano, for giving me an appreciation of fabrics and taking me all over the state looking for fabric when I first started sewing. Thanks especially to Linda Mayer, my wonderful friend who twisted my arm and made me take my first quilting class, and to Debra for allowing me to teach quilting in her store. Thank you, Dr. Linda Meyer, for sending me to a computer class to overcome my computer phobia.

I am especially appreciative of all my "quilting ladies" who have given me insight and taught me as much as I taught them. Thanks for all the wonderful years of finding new and unusual quilts for me to draft, create, or figure out how to assemble. It has always been fun.

A special thanks to Joan Paterson, my editor, for making sense out of my words; Nita Munson, my technical editor, for her vast knowledge of quilt history, exquisite antique quilt collection, and making sure I was technically accurate and counted all parts of the quilt blocks correctly; Phil Valcarcel for being so gracious and taking such wonderful color photographs of the quilts; and Marie Varner, quilter and friend who supported me throughout the writing process and was so helpful during the photography by carrying and holding all the quilts.

Special Thanks to the Technical Reviewer

The Complete Idiot's Guide to Quilting was reviewed by an expert who double-checked the accuracy of what you'll learn here to help us ensure that this book gives you everything you need to know about quilting. Special thanks are extended to Nita Munson.

Part 1
Let's Get Ready to Quilt!

There are many decisions for all beginner quilt makers to make, and I suggest you first acquire a general understanding about types of quilts and how our ancestors developed them. Then take some time to look at the quilt patterns throughout this book and choose the quilt you would like to make. We'll take the mystery out of planning the size and selecting colors to make your quilt one that you will want to live with for a lifetime.

Chapter 1

Quilts Through the Ages

In This Chapter

➤ Understanding what a quilt is

➤ Learning about quilts through the ages

➤ Exploring the alphabet of quilt names

When I first took a quilting course, I had no idea what quilts were or how they have affected people's lives. I just knew that I wanted to learn how to make a cover for my bed! Little did I know that I was about to embark on a life-long quest for new and different projects with each new quilt book I read or quilt show I attended. There is always a new idea or technique to be learned. As a beginner, I learned that there are three basic components involved in making a quilt: putting together small pieces of fabric to make the quilt top, attaching the fluffy inside layer, and then securing the backing fabric that holds the quilt together.

In the process of making my quilt, I learned something about the background of the people who have made quilts, especially the pioneer women whose lives centered on quilting and quilting bees. I read interesting and beautiful books that discuss this important part of our American heritage, and I encourage you to read them too. Now let's add to your knowledge of types of quilts, from Amish to Yo-yo.

What Is a Quilt?

A quilt consists of three layers: the quilt top, which is the right side displaying the pattern designs; the batting or filling substance; and the backing, most often one solid piece of fabric and usually considered the wrong side.

Since America's bicentennial there has been a revival of interest in crafts, especially quilt making. Today's quilts have many different uses—they're no longer found just in the bedroom. You can find quilts throughout the house, on chairs, on the backs of sofas, and on walls. Besides in houses, quilts are used as works of art, hanging on walls in doctors' offices, corporate headquarters, art galleries, and museums. Some of my students started by making quilted placemats that ended up as a queen-size bed cover. Quilts are accommodating—all it takes is your imagination and a plan.

Quilts Through the Ages

It is believed that quilted fabric dates back to the Egyptians. Do you think that Cleopatra might have worn a quilted vest? Then there is a theory that knights on the Crusades liked the idea of wearing quilted garments under their armor for comfort. (Wouldn't you want some padding under that heavy metal suit?) Another theory is that quilting was brought back from China by Marco Polo! Europeans have used bed quilts for warmth since the 14th century. But American quilters have expanded the purpose of quilts: Quilts not only are utilitarian but add beauty and individuality through the creative patterns of the quilt top. Quilting has become a craft that spans the world—Hawaiian quilts, Hmong needlework (quilting popular in southeast Asia), and Japanese Sashiko quilts are just some of the Asian innovations.

American Quilts: Necessity and Creativity

In colonial America, women were in charge of making bedcovers. In winter, houses were cold and drafty and quilts provided warmth. The first quilts were *whole cloth* quilts.

Scraps and Pieces

Colonial women would sandwich and stitch together one large length of fabric (either a woolen fabric, cotton, or a chintz); a layer of cotton, wool, or even rags, feathers, or newspapers for the stuffing; and another large length of fabric for the backing—thereby derives the name *whole cloth* quilt. As quilting developed, the large fabric was divided into smaller and smaller pieces, evolving into patchwork.

The solid color of the quilt top was a perfect showcase for displaying their quilting ability and creativity. Quilting stitches in intricate designs adorned these solid-colored quilts, often white stitches on a white background, hence the name "White on White." Other whole cloth quilts used *chintz* (a patterned, glazed cotton often in floral designs) fabrics, allowing the women to stitch around the flowers or paisley designs.

Lengths of fabric was at a premium, coming all the way from Europe, and necessity became the mother of invention. It was easier and more economical to use smaller pieces of fabric. That's how *patchwork* was born—pattern shapes developed from leftover scraps and pieces cut from old clothing and leftover fabrics. It always amazes my husband that quilters take a large length of material, cut it up into small pieces, and then spend a lot of time sewing the small pieces of fabric together to make a large piece of fabric!

As patchwork became popular, American women showed their inventiveness in designing new patterns. The fact that specific types of quilts evolved in different places indicates that women in various regions may have had strong rivalries. Names for their quilts like Lone Star, Amish, Hawaiian, and Baltimore Album are examples of this competitive attitude.

> **Quilt Talk**
> *Patchwork* refers to fabric cut into various shapes and sizes (drawn from patterns) and sewn together like a jig-saw puzzle to form a larger piece called a square or block. The finished block is generally an 8-, 9-, 12-, or 15-inch square, depending on the size of the finished wall hanging or quilt. However, a block can be any size the quilter desires.

Quilts from A to Y

The quilt alphabet ends at Y because I couldn't think of any Z quilt names. Each of the quilts has a different name. Let's learn some interesting names of quilt patterns and de-mystify how these names came into being. We will get into the spirit of our quilting ancestors. This section deals with types of quilts or specific patterns that quilters admire and create. Many of these quilts are not for beginners, but you can appreciate them for their detail and workmanship. There are many outstanding books that picture and explain the construction of these quilts so that you can assemble and appreciate the intricate patterns and colorful designs. For a novice quilter, a Sampler quilt is best to learn the basics. But beginner or expert, we all recognize and enjoy beautiful quilts.

Album Quilts

Album quilts are also known as friendship quilts and are made by a group of friends. Each person made one or more blocks, which were then combined to make the quilt.

The blocks could be signed using India ink or embroidered with the signature of the maker. An Album quilt was given to a special person, a bride perhaps, or to a friend or pastor as a going-away or retirement gift. Anyone who wanted to be represented signed a small section of the fabric. Sometimes the members of entire families would fill a block. The quilt would be dated with the name of the town and reason for the celebration. It is now an excellent way of tracing family lines or important events.

During the 1800s, Baltimore, not New York, was the main seaport in the United States. Affluent women in Baltimore were able to purchase magnificent fabrics imported from England. Each square of an Album quilt is exquisitely designed with appliquéd baskets, flowers, birds (especially eagles), and cornucopias. The petals and leaves of a flower, animals, and figures could be made to look real by painting details with different fabrics. Each square of an Album quilt is a work of art in itself. They are truly amazing.

Baltimore Album quilt.

Amish Quilts

Members of the Amish and Mennonite communities in Pennsylvania, Ohio, and Indiana made these quilts, which are characterized by solid dark and bright colors with lots of beautiful quilting. The Amish are known for their quilting technique. Intricate designs are executed with tiny running stitches that hold together all three layers of the quilt. Amish and Mennonite women, because of the dictates of their religion, used black, dark brown, or other solid dark fabrics for their clothing. Quilts used scraps left over from making clothing for their family, or pieces cut from worn clothes.

Scraps and Pieces

Since Amish women have to follow so many rules concerning their religion, clothing, hairstyles, housework, and behavior, it is believed that quilting is one of their creative outlets. Although quilts were considered strictly utilitarian bed clothes, and being "prideful" was a sin, there was and continues to be great competition among Amish women as to the choice of quilting patterns, number of spools of thread used, and the number of stitches counted to the inch.

Be sure to look at the color photo insert for the picture of the Amish Square quilt in a square design to see the dramatic coloration that Amish quilts are known for.

Crazy Quilts

Crazy quilts became popular around the time of the American centennial. Made of velvet and silk fabrics, they are pieced together in random designs. The quilter's embroidery stitches are showcased along the seams joining each piece of fabric. It is believed that the term "crazy" came from the haphazard placement of the pieces of fabric, not from the state of mind of the quilter. As the crazy quilts became more popular, the makers became more artistic, embroidering birds, flowers, and initials, dates, and locations directly on the fabrics.

Crazy quilts are made from random pieces of fabric with intricate embroidery, as illustrated in this pillow.

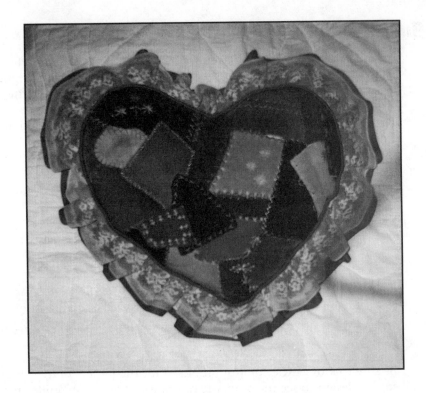

Hawaiian Quilts

A Hawaiian quilt is made by cutting one large length of fabric into an overall design of leaves or flowers and then appliquéing it onto a background fabric. Hawaiians love nature, and one huge design is made by following the "snow flake" method of folding paper in half and then diagonally again and again to form eight layers. A pattern is made incorporating stylized fruit, flowers, and leaves. The small running quilting stitches follow the outline of the outside of the design. The quilting covers the entire background of the quilt. It's worth a trip to Hawaii to see these amazing quilts.

Hawaiian quilt patterns. Look at the flower, leaf, and pineapple motifs.

Log Cabin Quilts

Log Cabin quilts have a series of strips that are placed around a central square, which is usually red. Half of each block has light-colored fabrics and the other half has dark-colored fabrics. The blocks are small, some only six inches in size. These quilts can be put together by rotating the diagonal dark and light sides in a variety of ways, making specific designs that look totally different. Some of these designs have their own names: Barn Raising, Sunshine and Shadows, and Straight Furrows. See if you can find the Log Cabin quilt in the color photo section. These quilts are versatile, blending with either country or modern decor.

Scraps and Pieces

The Log Cabin quilt became popular in the 1860s and the belief is that the center square depicts Abraham Lincoln's log cabin. The traditionally red center represents the fire in the hearth of the cabin; a yellow center depicts a lantern in the window. The quilt could also be created as a tribute to Abraham Lincoln after his assassination.

Lone Star Quilts

The Lone Star quilt, also called the Star of Bethlehem, became popular in the 1820s. It has many, many tiny fabric diamonds making up a larger diamond; then eight of these larger diamonds are put together to form a star. There can be thousands of diamonds in a quilt, a truly wondrous sight. See the red, white, and blue Lone Star quilt in the color photo section.

Sampler Quilts

Sampler quilts combine blocks of different types of patterns. Each block is often framed by a strip of fabric called a *lattice* or sashing. Quilters have developed thousands of block designs. Some are easy, others are more advanced. A Sampler quilt is perfect for beginners to practice their craft. Since each block is different, you can start with easy ones and then choose blocks that are more difficult as you gain confidence. There is a challenge to combining the variety of different patterns and colors. You can admire the Sampler quilts in the color photo section.

Trip Around the World Quilts

This quilt is made up of many squares of similar colors pieced on the diagonal around a central square. The lines of similar-colored squares surround one center square and the contrasting light and dark fabric squares give the impression of orbiting the world. See this quilt pictured in the color photo section.

Wedding Ring Quilts

The Wedding Ring quilt was first seen around the beginning of the 1900s and grew more popular during the Depression. Wedges are put together to form an interlocking pattern of circles. It is challenging piecing together curves, so beginners beware! Patterns for this quilt were even found in newspapers. Friends and relatives usually pieced this quilt for young women who were engaged and, of course, the quilt had to be completed before the wedding date. A bride hoped that her friends were quick quilters! Find the Wedding Ring quilts in the color photo section.

Yo-Yo Quilts

Yo-yo quilts are novelty quilts. Technically, they are not really quilts because there is no second and third layers—no filling or backing. Individual yo-yos are made from small, round pieces of fabric that have been gathered around the outside edge. Quilts are usually made from left-over fabric, so they are good to the last scrap. The thread is pulled to form a flat circle of fabric that resembles a yo-yo. The yo-yos are then invisibly stitched together to form a "quilt," leaving open spaces between the circles. The completed yo-yo spread is used over a solid-color blanket or sheet and is made purely for decoration, not warmth.

Pictured is a section of a Yo-yo quilt. The round, gathered pieces of fabric are whipstitched together.

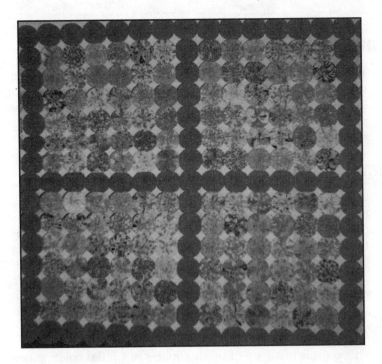

I have a friend who started to make a Yo-yo quilt and cut one hundred two-inch circles. After gathering many of them into yo-yos, she decided that they were too small and went on to cut several hundred three-inch squares. She has been making them ever since. But she's not upset about her unfinished project—she has all of her yo-yos sitting in a pretty basket in her living room where they look very decorative indeed.

How Did They Get That Name?

One of the most interesting, but also one of the most bewildering, aspects of quilting is the multitude of quilt names. There are books with hundreds of patch diagrams and names that can be very confusing for beginners. The names of the patchwork designs follow the story of our forefathers. Let's wander through a history of quilt names and see how they mirror pioneer wanderings.

Starting in England, the colonists began their trip to America. They named quilt blocks after their experiences: London Road, Ocean Waves, Mariner's Compass, and, after settling in America, Log Cabin, Virginia Star, or Ohio Star. The frontier surroundings were also inspirational in naming the Honey Bee, Bear's Paw, and thousands of floral blocks. Religion was an important part of colonial America as quilt patches such as Jacob's Ladder, Church Steps, or Star of Bethlehem exemplify. Quilters even entered the political arena by designing quilts named Tudor Rose, Clay's Choice, and 54-40 or Fight. Even more confusing is that similar patterns have different names in various regions of the country; for example, in the north a quilt was known as the Star of Bethlehem but in Texas it was called the Lone Star. How perplexing!

Quilters have used their lives and surroundings to name quilt blocks. It's not important to remember all the names, but it is fun to get into the quilters' minds and understand how they devised the making of their quilts.

Scraps and Pieces

When frontier women settled down after their travels across America, they sought out each other to quilt. These meetings were called   and only later became known as quilting bees. Quilts were made and completed by a group of women while their families socialized with dinner and square dancing. The quilting group would make quilts for special occasions such as engagements and weddings. Or they would construct freedom quilts for young men who, when they turned 21, were to leave home.

The Least You Need to Know

➤ A quilt is composed of three layers—a quilt top, a fluffy filling, and a backing fabric—which are secured by small running stitches.

➤ People have made quilts throughout the ages in different regions of the world.

➤ Patchwork consists of small pieces of fabric that are sewn together to form a larger piece, called a square or block.

➤ Discovering the names of quilt blocks and how they evolved can be fun and educational!

Chapter 2

Quilt Construction: Block by Block by Block

In This Chapter

➤ Learning the difference between piecing and appliqué

➤ Finding out how quilt tops can be designed and assembled

➤ Learning different piecing methods—from whole cloth, to medallion, to blocks

Let's examine the various methods for constructing quilt tops. A patch, or a portion of a quilt, can be made either by piecing or appliquéing the top, or face, of the quilt into designs using a variety of different-size pieces. Quilters can then assemble these sections of the quilt, starting with a single length of material, and work their way up to creating overall designs using thousands of pieces of one shape. Don't stop reading when you see "thousands of pieces" because beginners start with the building blocks of quilting.

Piecing and Appliqué

We're going to use fabric to create your quilt top. Just as women apply lipstick or blush to their faces, we're going to apply our fabrics to the quilt face by sewing together pieces of fabric with different colors and designs. You can choose to sew quilt tops together by piecing or appliqué. Each uses a different technique and stitch and the resulting quilts have a distinctive look. We'll learn how to make the stitches in Chapter 11, "Do Be a Sew and Sew"—right now, let's look at quilts in each of the different techniques.

Quilt Talk
Piecing is the cutting out of fabric shapes and sewing them together two pieces at a time with a small running stitch. Then they are combined to another shape to form a larger section until the block or square is completed.

See if you can find all the different geometric shapes in this pieced patch.

Pieced Quilt: Geometry Lesson

In a *pieced* quilt block, the pattern is divided into geometric shapes—usually squares, rectangles, triangles, and diamonds. When various shapes are sewn, it is like putting a fabric jigsaw puzzle together.

In more challenging patches, you can use hexagons, pentagons, and weirdly shaped rhomboids. Doesn't this sound like a high school Geometry class? Drafting your own patchwork patch uses geometric skills to get the pattern pieces to fit together like an intricate puzzle. If one pattern piece is cut slightly wrong, the alignment of the entire quilt will be off.

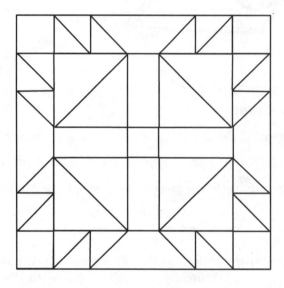

Quilt Talk
Appliqué is the technique of applying a shaped piece of fabric onto a larger contrasting piece of base or background fabric. The edges of the applied design are turned under and sewn down.

Appliqué Quilt: Drawing Pictures

Appliqué quilts always seem more feminine than the angular pieced patchwork quilts. The pattern pieces of an *appliqué* block may be free-form or portray a specific object.

Some of my students make quilts with appliqué shapes in the form of hearts, flowers, birdhouses, roosters, moose, and Santa Claus. Traditionally, the oldest appliqué quilts are of flowers. Other quilters have appliquéd historically important buildings, churches, and even family crests. The shaped pieces can be attached using a special appliqué stitch, a hemming blind stitch, or by machine zigzagging. You can also use a black embroidery thread to decorate the design with a blanket stitch. (These stitches will be discussed in Chapter 11.)

Notice the rounded, pictorial pieces of the Tudor Rose appliqué block.

If you love the hearts-and-flowers look of appliqué patches but are leery of making an appliquéd quilt, don't be afraid of appliqué. Getting a flower to look like a flower can be intimidating but if you follow the step-by-step directions in Chapter 14, "Combination Pieced and Appliqué Blocks," your fabrics will lay down perfectly. Beginners should experiment with both techniques in pieced and appliqué blocks in order to become a well-rounded quilter.

Cutting Your Quilt Top into Designs

Another method of categorizing quilts is by the way a quilt top is designed. Examine quilts and notice if there is one central design, several smaller repeated designs, or many small shapes that form an overall pattern. Quilters can start by planning a quilt top with one large piece of fabric or by cutting the material smaller and smaller until the quilt top is composed of thousands of fabric pieces.

Examine how these five quilt tops are divided into smaller and smaller pieces.

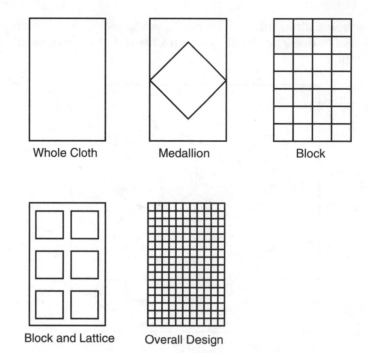

Whole Cloth   Medallion   Block

Block and Lattice   Overall Design

When designing a quilt, a quilter can start with the whole cloth quilt, discussed in the first chapter. As the name implies, you use only one length of material for the quilt top. Now I know you're saying, "Wow, what a great quilt, no sewing little pieces together." Before you start one of these quilts, however, be aware that they usually involve elaborate quilting designs that can be very tedious for beginners.

The medallion quilt has one large central pieced or appliquéd design with strips of fabric or borders to finish out the top. A Lone Star is a good example of a medallion quilt.

The quilt face can also be divided into squares or blocks of patterns. This is the most popular method of designing or planning a quilt. The pieced or appliquéd blocks can be attached together or framed out with a piece of fabric called a lattice or sashing. Because the block method is the easiest for beginners, the patterns I have included in this book are all 12-inch blocks of designs.

Scraps and Pieces

Blocks developed and flourished because they were easy for our pioneer ancestors to carry from house to house to work on at quilting bees. Each individual would make a square block and then all the blocks were assembled to create the quilt top. That's what you call teamwork.

The last way a quilt top can be drafted is with an overall design. A quilt top can consist of all squares, as in the Trip Around the World quilt; or hexagons, for example, like Grandmother's Flower Garden; or diamonds, exemplified by the Baby Block quilt. You can realistically have a thousand pieces all of the same fabric in one quilt top.

This Trip Around the World quilt illustrates an overall design using hundreds of squares.

After examining and drafting many entire quilt tops using each of these categories, I have found the easiest for a beginner is definitely the block method. Blocks are the building blocks of many quilts. They can have all the same design with one block repeated throughout the quilt, or you can assemble a Sampler quilt where each block or square has a different design. It's great fun.

The Least You Need to Know

➤ Quilt tops are constructed by either the piecing or appliqué technique.

➤ Pieced patchwork quilts have a geometric or angular look.

➤ Appliqué quilts are made by sewing small pieces of fabric onto a background or base fabric.

➤ Appliqué quilts can picture a specific object.

➤ When designing, the quilt top layout can be categorized into the classifications of whole cloth, medallion, blocks, or individual shapes to create an overall design.

Chapter 3

Time to Plan Your Quilt!

In This Chapter

➤ Understanding the decisions you will make in planning your quilt

➤ Learning how the quilt top is set up

➤ Surveying pattern designs and choosing your pattern

Where do you start? After learning about our quilting ancestors and how they developed their quilts, it's your turn. There are many questions to ask yourself in order to determine what type of quilt you should make. Once you've decided, your decision is not written in stone. One of my students wanted to make a small crib quilt and started piecing blocks together. She enjoyed the process so much that her crib quilt ended up as a queen-size quilt! That's the beauty of the block method—you can add or subtract squares to suit your need.

When you have decided on the size of quilt you intend to make, you have to pick out the quilt patterns you want to tackle. I have drawn out all the designs for the patterns that are included in this book at the end of this chapter. Look at the patterns and start to recognize them in the quilts pictured in the color section.

This is where we really begin!

Decisions, Decisions, Decisions!

There are several things you have to think about before starting your quilt. Let's take them one by one.

Quilt Talk
A *lap quilt* is a small quilt put together with six to nine blocks, usually 60 by 60 inches square. I like to drape one over a sofa or at the base of a bed.

What's Your Quilt's Use?

First of all: What do *you* want to make? Almost everyone wants to make a bed-size quilt to show off their workmanship. I do *not* suggest you do this. A quilt of that size is a huge undertaking and could take more than a year to complete. I have found that beginners are much happier working on a project that they can finish quickly. You need the positive reinforcement of accomplishment—a wall hanging or *lap quilt* is a perfect small project.

This baby quilt features hearts constructed with pastel fabrics.

Another important question is: "Who will use this quilt?" If you want to make a crib quilt or a quilt for a young child, you may have to change your ideas about colors and patterns. Children love colors and bold patterns. Be sure to use fabrics that are durable and totally washable. Don't make something that is so difficult and time-consuming that you will be offended if something happens to it—kids will be kids.

Will Your Quilt Be the Center of Attention?

Look around the room that your quilt will live in. Do you want it to be the focal point of the room or blend with the surroundings? Bright dynamic colors will ensure that

20

everyone's eyes are on your masterpiece. While a Scrap quilt fits in with your colonial decor, a Danish Modern may not. Look through quilt books. Check out the room decor— a dramatic quilt can pull together an eclectic room.

See how the Pineapple table cover pulls the elements of the room together?

What Do You Like?

Everyone has preferences. Do you like rounded shapes or angular? Flowers or geometrics? Many men do not like the floral motifs of appliqué quilts (and not just men—several of my women students hate those rounded, fussy patterns). Quilts can look either modern or traditional, masculine or feminine. Find out the names of quilt patterns that you are drawn to. I hope you will find many of the patterns you like in this book. When I started quilting, I wanted to make a Dresden Plate quilt with all pastel colors. I didn't start with that block, but took a class to learn about quilt basics.

Be Realistic

Once you have tried a variety of patches in a small quilt, you can tackle a large project. The Sampler quilt is a challenge to coordinate; that's part of the fun.

A quilt isn't meant only for a bed. Here is an example of a beginner's Sampler quilt made by Marie Varner. She uses it as a wall hanging in her living room.

Here are several suggestions that I have found to be helpful in avoiding problems that beginners have. Make sure you know the parts of the quilt and the terminology. Be realistic about your abilities. Check out the difficulty of the quilt patterns. A hint: The smaller the pieces in a block, the more time-consuming to make; the larger the number of pieces in a block, the more work you have to do. The 12-inch square block of the Churn Dash pattern has 17 pieces, while the Bear's Paw has 53. That's a big difference! Creating a quilt using only one quilt pattern may be aesthetically pleasing but may also become monotonous. Piecing 20 patches that are all the same is not as challenging or as creative as stitching 20 different blocks.

The Quilt Setup

It's important to understand the language of quilting. Before you start planning your quilt, look at the diagram of a quilt top and learn the parts of the quilt. Understanding these terms is important because I will be discussing their construction for the quilt top throughout the rest of the book.

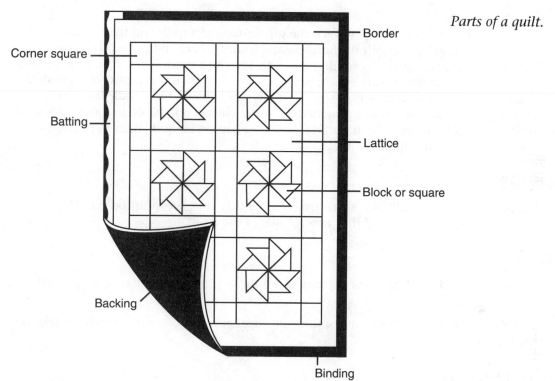

Parts of a quilt.

Block

A block is a square of pieced or appliquéd patchwork, also called a square, that is put together with other blocks to make a quilt.

Lattice

A lattice is a strip of fabric that frames each block in a quilt. The strip can be a solid strip or it can have small squares at the corner of each block. The lattice is also sometimes called sashing. I will discuss this part of a quilt in Chapter 17, "Setting It All Together."

Border

A length of fabric that frames the outside edge of the quilt top is the border. Borders can be as simple as solid strips of fabric or as complex as intricate geometric patterns or appliqués. We'll learn about borders in Chapter 17.

Batting

The batting is the inner lining between the top, or face, of a quilt and the bottom layer, or backing, that gives the quilt its fluffiness and warmth. Back in the "good old days," stuffing or filling was anything to fill the middle layer in a quilt. It could be cotton picked in the fields and stuffed into the quilt, or the cotton could have been carded or combed to smooth it out. Sometimes old, worn-out quilts were used as the middle layer, or old, discarded men's suits were cut up and used. Cotton batting purchased in a store was used for many years in the early 20th century. Polyester batting bought either in packages or from a giant roll dates from the 1970s.

Backing

The bottom part of a quilt that sandwiches the batting with the quilt top is called the backing. It is often considered the "wrong" side of the quilt.

Binding

The binding is the folding of the backing or a long strip of bias fabric that finishes off the edge of a quilt.

Now you know about all the parts of the quilt top. Let's start planning which designs to create for your quilt.

Quilt Designs

Now that you know the parts that make up a quilt top, find the blocks that appeal to you. Pattern blocks are divided by method of piecing and arranged in the order of difficulty. Just remember to match your capabilities to the difficulty of the block.

The first set of blocks are where a beginner should start—I know I did. Easy pieced blocks have few fabric pieces, and the shapes are easy to assemble. Full-size patterns and instructions are found in Chapter 12, "Easy Pieced Patchwork Blocks." The easy pieced blocks are: Double Nine Patch, Churn Dash, Ohio Star, Eight Point Star, Dutchman's Puzzle, Weathervane, and the Rolling Star.

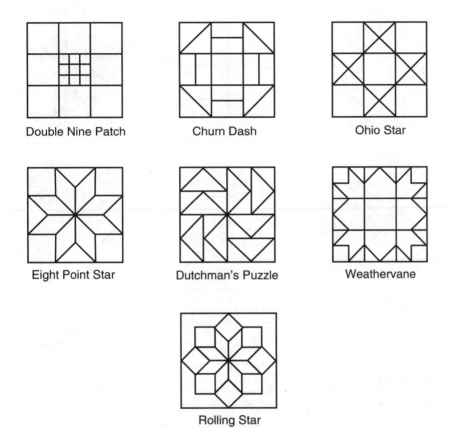

Beginners should start with one of the easy pieced blocks.

Double Nine Patch   Churn Dash   Ohio Star

Eight Point Star   Dutchman's Puzzle   Weathervane

Rolling Star

Examine the challenging pieced blocks on the following page. You can see that there are many pieces and the designs are more elaborate. Before a beginner tackles one of these blocks, you should read Chapter 13, "Challenging Pieced Patchwork Blocks," to learn special cutting and piecing know-how. Challenging blocks are: Drunkard's Path, Pinwheel, Virginia Star, Mexican Star, 54-40 or Fight, Flying Geese, Clay's Choice, and Bear's Paw.

Our quilting ancestors developed blocks that combine both piecing and appliqué techniques in the same design. In some blocks, pieces of fabric are sewn together and the patch is appliquéd onto a background of fabric, as in the Dresden Plate and Grandmother's Fan. There are also blocks that are made in just the opposite way, by piecing the base of the block and then appliquéing specially shaped fabric pieces, such as with the Honey Bee's wings and the Peony's stem and leaves. Check out Chapter 14, "Combination Pieced and Appliqué Blocks."

These blocks will challenge your cutting and piecing ability.

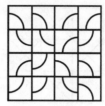

Drunkard's Path

Pinwheel

Virginia Star

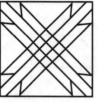

Mexican Star

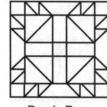

54-40 or Fight

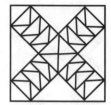

Flying Geese

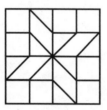

Clay's Choice

Bear's Paw

Blocks that are pieced and appliquéd.

Dresden Plate

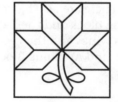

Honey Bee

Grandmother's Fan

Peony

Traditionally appliquéd blocks have separate pieces of fabric that, when positioned in a specific pattern, form a picture or design. The blocks found in this book are Hearts All Around, Tudor Rose, and Tulips. Patterns and instructions are found in Chapter 15, "Traditional Appliqué Block Patterns: Add a Layer to Your Quilt."

Hearts All Around

Tulips

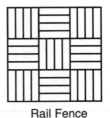

Rail Fence

Appliqué and machine-pieced blocks.

Tudor Rose

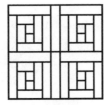

Log Cabin

The last category of blocks in this book are for those people who love and know how to use their sewing machine. The Rail Fence and Log Cabin blocks can be joined by using the hand-piecing method but can be sewn quickly and accurately by using the sewing machine.

These are just drawings of the blocks you can make from the instructions found in this book. It's up to you to add the color and visual texture with your fabric, which brings us to the next stop: shopping!

The Least You Need to Know

➤ Choose a project that will be easy to finish. Be honest about your abilities.

➤ Decide who will use the quilt, what your preferences are, whether you want the quilt to be the focal point of the room, and how you will use it.

➤ The parts that make up the quilt top are blocks, lattice, and border.

➤ Survey the quilt designs in this book and choose patterns that you like and that match up with your know-how.

➤ A sampler quilt is the best learning experience for a beginner.

Chapter 4

Color, Your Wheel of Fortune

In This Chapter

➤ How to use the color wheel

➤ Types of color schemes

➤ Learning how colors affect one another as well as your emotions

➤ Choosing successful color combinations

Color is probably the most important element of a quilt. Whenever my students and I go to quilt shows, our eyes are always pulled to quilts with the most vibrant or pleasing colors. Once we get closer to the quilts, we start looking at the patterns, designs, and technique—but the colors give us a first impression that lasts throughout the show. Even if the pattern is not one of your favorites, you can like a quilt because of its pleasing color combination.

How do you choose these pleasing combinations? Let's explore the science of mixing and matching colors. Examining color schemes and how colors relate to each other will help turn your quilt into the one that has the crowd around it at the quilt show.

The Color Wheel: Scheme of Things to Come

Colors affect our emotions. Attractive color combinations make us happy. Let's examine the facts and the characteristics of color relationships. Color is actually different wavelengths of light. Scientists have found that the colors of the spectrum are at their strongest intensity or brightness. Maybe that's why rainbows are so dramatic and pleasing, since all colors are included to make everybody happy. The color wheel is technically a round rainbow containing each of the seven colors of the rainbow, along with combinations of these colors where they adjoin one another. If you refer to the color wheel found in the color photo section, you can see that the colors progress through the spectrum:

red, red-orange, orange, yellow-orange, yellow, yellow-green, green, blue-green, blue, blue-violet, violet, and lastly, red-violet.

The color wheel is built around three primary colors. These colors cannot be blended from any other pigment. They are red, yellow, and blue. If you look at the color wheel, you find that they are spaced equally apart in a triad. When two of these colors are mixed together they create the secondary colors: Red and blue make purple; blue and yellow make green; and yellow and red make orange.

> **Quilting Bee**
> Bet you didn't know that Sir Isaac Newton developed the color wheel. And you thought he worked with only apples and gravity!

The primary colors form a triangle within the wheel. Locate the secondary colors of green, violet, and orange. The colors between the primary and secondary are the tertiary colors. Arrows show complementary positioning, and analogous color schemes are next to each other.

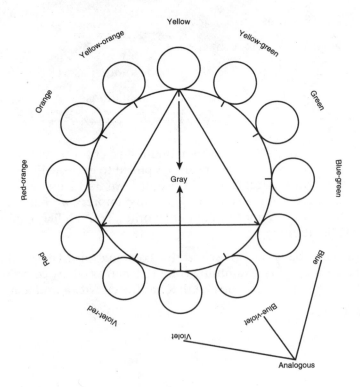

As the hues are arranged in a rainbow sequence, there are still more colors that can be blended together. A primary color, such as red, and its adjacent secondary color, violet, can be combined to form a tertiary color, red-violet. What is the difference between red-violet and violet-red? The answer is the amount of red that is added to violet.

There are some basic principles that you can deduce from the color wheel. Place your hand over half of the color wheel, exposing the yellow, orange, and red colors. These hues are considered warm colors. What sunny, happy colors—they seem to explode right out at you. Now change positions and look at green, blue, and purple. The difference is amazing—now calm and tranquillity prevail. When these colors are combined in a quilt, the warm colors advance at you while the cool ones recede. Knowing this will help you plan the placement of colors throughout your quilt.

Quilting Bee
Time to get out your crayons—the box with at least 24 crayons. Go to the color wheel figure, and let's play. Find the primary and secondary colors. Fill in the circle under each corresponding color and color in all the tertiary colors. This will help you understand how there can be so many types of violets and why some do not quite match each other.

Do You Have Values? Color Values That Is!

We've mentioned approximately 12 colors in the color wheel, but there are thousands more that can be blended by mixing the colors on the wheel with a neutral. A neutral can be either white, black, or gray.

With respect to values, everything is relative. A range of color *values* adds contrast and depth to your quilt patterns. We need to look at a color in comparison to those around it. Fabrics can be divided into lights (*tint*), mediums (*hue*), or darks (*shade*). A light fabric may actually become a medium tone if a white or a lighter-colored fabric is introduced. Our eyes also perceive differences when the background fabric changes. Take a piece of medium-colored green fabric and place it on top of a white fabric. The colors pop out at you. On the other hand, if you place the same piece of fabric on a black fabric, the black sinks away from you.

Quilt Talk
Hue is the name of a specific color, for example, navy blue, or magenta. *Value* is the lightness or darkness of a color. There are either tints or shades. *Tint* is a hue that contains more light or white. Pink is a tint of red. *Shade* is a hue that has been blended with black or a darker color. Cranberry is a shade of red.

Even more mystifying is the effect of *complementary colors*. When these colors are put next to each other, each color seems brighter. Think of a tree with red apples on it. The red apples jump out at you. Red and green colors complement each other, and the brightness of each is brought out.

Don't Get Stuck!
Be very careful about using too much black in your quilt—you don't want your quilt having a too dark or somber look. Remember, black recedes or could look like a hole in your quilt. To brighten it up, use tints or a brightly colored fabric.

Quilt Talk
Complementary colors are those colors found across from each other on the color wheel. *Complementary combinations* are red and green, yellow and purple, blue and orange, or any of these values.

The Color Schemes of Things to Come

Pleasing color harmonies can be created from the color wheel. Decorators and fashion designers have used these tried-and-true combinations for years. At my first quilt class I met a friend who always used this line when she looked at a quilt: "I never would have chosen those colors, but it does looks nice." I was never sure whether it was a compliment or not. Hopefully, understanding and using color schemes will build your confidence to choose quilt colors you love. Look in the color photo section and see if you can identify some of the following color schemes. Here are three of the most popular:

Monochromatic Color Scheme

This is probably the easiest color scheme for a beginner to use. Monochromatic means one color. Your quilt will have only one color, for example blue. But it should not be boring. Think of all the values there are of blue—baby blue, colonial blue, and navy blue. You can use the full range of tints and shades to add contrast.

Analogous Color Scheme

When you look at the color wheel, the analogous colors are the ones next to each other. A good example is blue, blue-violet, and violet. With the addition of two related colors, blue-violet and violet, your quilt top becomes more and more interesting. I made an Amish quilt using this analogous color scheme. Instead of using a white background, the Amish and I used black to give the quilt a jewel quality. See if you can find it in the photo section.

Complementary Color Scheme

Do you remember that complementary colors are on opposite sides of the color wheel? Red is the complement of green; blue the complement of orange; and yellow the complement of purple. When used as the true hue found on the color wheel, these colors are intense. In the '60s, my parents decorated their family room in the complementary colors of blue and orange. These were intense and not toned down with a variety of shades. It was very fashionable but hard on the eyes, and within one or two years this color scheme was changed. Make sure the colors of your quilt are ones you can live with. Don't forget to use shades and tints.

There are many more color schemes that can be created from the color wheel, but it is probably easier for a beginner to choose color schemes from pictures of quilts that they admire.

It's a well-known fact that certain color schemes evoke moods or feelings. A quilt that is predominately yellow will always seem cheerful and sunny. If your colors are red, white, and blue, you can be sure your quilt will feel very patriotic or folksy. A very feminine quilt would result from using all pastel fabrics. Color symbolism can suggest moods or feelings, so be positive your colors suit your taste.

> **Quilting Bee**
> The complementary colors of blue and orange may be too strong for you, but peach and colonial blue are beautiful together. Red and green may look too much like Christmas, but a forest green quilt with cranberry flowers can be used all year.

Dominant or Contrasting: Blending It All Together

Now that we have a color senseand have learned about the color wheel, color schemes, moods and symbolism, tints, and shades and values, it's time to choose your colors. Decide on a color scheme, or find a picture in a catalogue or book that appeals to you. I usually begin with the quilt's surroundings to start this process. Because the walls of my bedroom are blue and the rug is cranberry, that's probably a good color combination to start with. I need to decide on the dominant or main color. Do I want the quilt more blue or more cranberry? I chose blue. That was my dominant color. It should be found in almost every quilt block, and possibly also in the lattice and the border. The contrasting color will then be cranberry. The contrast color is used as an accent and should be in most of the patches and the corner blocks.

Now you have both ends of the color scheme—the dominant and contrasting colors. When purchasing your fabric, choose a large printed fabric that includes both of those colors. It could be floral, paisley, or an abstract design. I call this the *blender fabric*. The blender fabric creates a harmonious bridge between the dominant and contrasting colors. The most important blender fabric is one that has both of the colors from your color scheme. I was able to find a floral fabric that contained cranberry and blue. It was a medium shade

> **Don't Get Stuck!**
> Be sure to choose a color scheme that you want to live with for a while. I have several quilts in avocado green and gold that were popular in the '70s. As a beginner, by the time I finished the quilts, the color combination was passé. So you have to either learn to like it or learn to quilt faster!

of the colors and blended both perfectly. You will notice that fabric manufacturers have developed patterns with quilters in mind, having coordinated combinations of popular colors in the same material. Don't forget to choose a variety of fabrics with different values of each color in your color scheme to add interest to your quilt.

Find blender fabrics in different values. Some fabrics should appear as a tint or lighter color, while a darker-colored blender fabric will give you a full range of values. In my cranberry-and-blue quilt, I was able to find fabrics that blended together but gave the quilt variety in colors. I started by choosing a fabric with an off-white background and small navy-blue-and-cranberry flowers, giving the impression of a light tint. Then I found a navy fabric with an overall design of small white flowers and leaves. Even though this fabric had a navy background, it was a medium value because it contained so much white. When you squint at the fabrics you can see the values. Lastly, looking through the fabric store, I found a cranberry fabric with pin dots (small dots about an inch apart), which I used for my dark color.

At least one fabric should contain your dominant and contrasting colors. Other fabrics should harmonize with your color scheme but do not have to contain all the colors. When these fabrics are put next to one another, they should give you a range of values. Get your value out of your colors!

Now that you have thought about your color scheme, the dominant color, contrasting color, a blender fabric, and approximately three fabrics in a variety of values from tints to shades, it's time to move to the next step: How much to buy?

The Least You Need to Know

➤ The color wheel helps you learn about color relationships.

➤ Value is the lightness (tint) or darkness (shade) of a hue.

➤ A range of values provides contrast and depth in your quilt.

➤ A color will react to its surrounding colors.

➤ Warm colors advance, while cool colors recede.

➤ The dominant color is the most important color in the scheme and should be found in almost all quilt blocks. The accent color creates contrast, and the blender color contains both colors in a pattern.

Part 2
Get Set

Now that you have a general idea of the type of quilt you want to make, it's time to go shopping. Before you go, let's take a moment to talk about what you need. Unlike pioneer women who did not have the advantage of all our craft and quilt stores jam-packed with supplies and fabrics, we can easily go into shopping overload. If you have trouble making decisions, these next chapters will help.

Some supplies can be found around your house. A few will be essential for beginning your project; others can wait until later, when you have a handle on quilting.

"Help!" This is what most beginners say when it's time to buy fabric. Put your mind at ease. Suggestions on types of fabric and tips on what to avoid will make your shopping easier. And I'll provide a chart to help you plan the exact amount of fabric you need.

Chapter 5

Tools of the Trade

In This Chapter

➤ Finding the basic supplies you really, really need

➤ Choosing the materials that best help you

➤ Super cool gadgets to spark creativity

➤ Keeping it all together

Most quilters collect more supplies than they really need. I have many ladies in my quilting class who bring in new gadgets each week. Some are good, some are bad, and some are useless.

This chapter is about the supplies that every quilter needs in order to make a quilt. Some items listed are necessities. But because everyone has different preferences and abilities, I will give you many options and suggestions. Some supplies you will need right now, some you will need at a later time, and others you may want but are never a necessity.

We will start our supply list with things you can find around your own home, then get into the materials that you will need to purchase in a craft store or specialty quilt store. When you go to a quilt store that sells supplies, do not be intimidated by the multitude of "stuff" that is displayed. Start with the basics. Do not be encouraged or persuaded to buy something that a beginner may not need. As you work on your quilt you will discover what will help YOU.

The Necessities: Supplies You Need Right Now

There are many things listed below that you will be able to find right around your house. Look at the list, and see what you can find before you go out to the store. Some things may seem very strange but I will address each item and explain it.

➤ Pencils: Number 2 lead and a variety of colored pencils

➤ Ruler: 12 or l8 inches

➤ Straight pins

➤ Paper scissors

➤ Fabric scissors

➤ Quilting needles: betweens and embroidery needles

➤ Quilting and regular thread

➤ Poster board or oak tag

➤ Rubber cement

➤ Medium sandpaper

➤ Seam ripper

➤ Thimbles

Quilt Talk
A *template* is a pattern of the exact size of each design element, usually made with cardboard or plastic. A block may have several shapes of templates incorporated into the square; for example, the Ohio Star block is composed of two templates—a square and a small triangle.

Pencils

Number 2 lead pencil: Quilters use this type of pencil to draft *templates* and trace these patterns onto the wrong side of the fabric. Do not use a softer pencil because you will be forever sharpening it. This pencil can also be used to lightly mark your quilt designs onto the right side of the quilt top.

Colored pencils: There are many fabrics that are dark in color (navy, red, and especially black) or have a design so busy that a pencil mark does not show. If this is the case, turn your fabric to the wrong side and try whichever colored pencil shows the best. Colored pencils are also helpful in planning the colors of your quilt blocks.

Rulers

I usually have a variety of rulers that I use. The best all-around ruler is one that is see-through plastic, 12 or 18 inches, and has parallel lines running the length, marking every quarter inch. This will be very useful in marking long seam allowances on your fabric and testing to see if your borders or lattices are even. I sometimes also like to use a small plastic six-inch ruler because it is easier to maneuver around the templates. There are other rulers that are optional and will be discussed later.

Straight Pins

I use regular old straight pins (one-inch long pins used by dressmakers) when I am piecing my patches. For pin-basting your quilt top we will discuss other options (see Chapter 18, "The Three Bs: Batting, Backing, and Basting").

Paper Scissors

Paper scissors are necessary when we make the templates. Templates are made from cardboard and sandpaper, or a plastic sheet. If you use good fabric scissors on the template material, they will not be good for long.

Fabric Scissors

There are many different types of scissors or dress-maker shears that you can purchase. Fabric scissors are sharper than paper scissors and are usually made of lighter-weight steel. Prices vary greatly. As a beginner, do not buy really expensive scissors. Eventually, if you become addicted to quilting, you will need scissors that cut through the fabric easily—when working on large projects I've had blisters pop up on my fingers as my scissors got dull. There are also scissors that can cut through several layers of fabric at a time.

> **Quilting Bee**
> My favorite scissors are Ginghers, and they can be purchased at most quilt stores or through dressmaker catalogues.

A pair of small thread-cutting scissors is also useful. The best practice is to hang them on a ribbon around your neck. It makes them easier to find while you are working.

Bent dressmaker shears with a protective nylon sheath and thread nippers are your best bet for scissors.

Needles

Quilters use "between" needles to piece their projects. A between needle is short and has a small round eye. The larger the number, the smaller the needle size. Size 10 is smaller than size 6. I had one student who said that compared to quilting needles, her needle was like a crowbar!

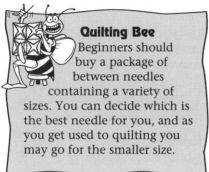

Quilting Bee
Beginners should
buy a package of
between needles
containing a variety of
sizes. You can decide which is
the best needle for you, and as
you get used to quilting you
may go for the smaller size.

*Here is a package
of quilting
betweens size 8,
which is a medium-
size needle.*

When you get experienced, there are also quilting needles that are even shorter than betweens. These are specifically used for quilting. Quilters have learned that the smaller the needle, the smaller and more durable the quilting stitches. Occasionally you will need to use embroidery needles when basting your quilt together, decorating your appliqué block with embroidery stitches, or tying your quilt (sometimes knots can be used instead of quilting stitches to hold together the three layers).

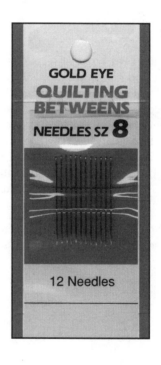

Quilting Bee
Buy beeswax that is
in a holder, because
the holder will make
it easier for you to run
the thread through the
beeswax and will keep it neat
and clean.

Thread

For piecing or quilting, use acotton-covered polyester quilting thread. This thread is superior to the 100 percent polyester thread that is usually on sale. Quilt thread is heavier and does not tangle or knot when used. Try to purchase a color that blends well with your fabrics. For example, if your background fabric is muslin, purchase a thread that is ecru; if your background is white, use a white thread; or if the background is navy, buy a navy quilting thread. If you can't match the color with a quilting thread, you can use a regular cotton-covered polyester thread. In order to keep this thread from tangling, run each length of thread through beeswax.

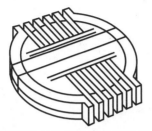

This container of beeswax makes it easy to run your thread through it.

Poster Board or Oak Tag

You can purchase poster board or oak tag paper at stationery, craft, or five-and-dime stores. This weight of cardboard is the best for making templates. I've even used gift boxes in a pinch, just don't use thick cardboard because it is difficult to cut accurately.

Rubber Cement

Rubber cement is used to make templates and for gluing together the poster board and sandpaper. Do not use white school glue or craft glue because it makes your templates ripple and they will not dry flat.

Sandpaper

Not all templates need sandpaper, but it helps beginners trace around the pattern accurately. Buy a medium-weight sandpaper that is approximately 8" by 10" in size. This will be used for the backing of your templates.

Seam Ripper

I hate to even mention ripping seams, but everyone makes mistakes, and seam rippers remove your boo-boos quickly and safely. A seam ripper is a small pen-like tool that allows you to put a sharp point under the "bad" stitches, carefully breaking the thread. Look for a seam ripper that is a medium size. When a seam ripper is too small, it gets lost in the shuffle. If it is too large, it is harder to manipulate under the line of stitches.

Don't Get Stuck!
One of my quilting students has a problem because her dog loves to chew her leather thimble, so she has to buy several! Keep them out of reach and with your sewing equipment.

Thimbles

Most quilters or seamstresses insist on using a thimble. A lot of people do not like the needle pricking their finger every time they take a stitch. Unfortunately, I have never felt comfortable wearing one. Many quilters wear a thimble on the third finger of the hand that holds the needle. Some wear thimbles on both hands. There are many types of thimbles. The most common is the metal thimble. Try one out and see how it feels. If it is uncomfortable, there are newer types of finger guards available. One very popular type is a leather thimble.

These are both thimbles. The right is the traditional, metal thimble and the left is a leather finger guard.

Things You Will Need Later

You will need the items already on this list once your quilt top is completed. You have pieced or appliquéd, then set the blocks together and framed them out with borders.

Certain supplies will be necessary for joining the three layers of the quilt together. Never purchase your batting until the face of the quilt is complete—you may get carried away and your quilt plan may grow.

Quilt Talk
Batting is the middle or filling part of the sandwich that makes up the quilt. It is the material that makes a quilt puffy and adds the warmth.

➤ Batting: The thimblestypes and specific amounts of *batting* needed for your projects will be discussed in Chapter 18.

➤ Marking equipment: Don't buy these yet!

➤ Quilt stencils

➤ Quilt hoop: There are many types and everyone has different dexterity and preferences. Hoops will be discussed in Chapter 19.

Marking and quilting equipment will be discussed in detail in Chapter 19, "Quilting 101." Sometimes you have to see the finished quilt top to decide on the type of quilting you want and the pattern of the quilting stencil. As you learn to handle fabrics, you will discover what equipment will work for you. There are different types of hoops. The hoop is necessary to hold the quilt in place and smooth while you quilt. I suggest purchasing your hoop after you are more experienced, and by the time you're ready to quilt, you will be experienced!

Optional Supplies That Are Neat

Through my years of experience I've found the items on the "neat" list to be helpful. They are not really necessary for a beginner to own, but if you become a serious quilter, these tools and supplies may assist you with certain projects.

➤ Graph paper: four squares to the inch

➤ Quilter's quarter

➤ Rotary cutter

➤ Cutting mat with grids

➤ Ruler with a lip

➤ T-square ruler

➤ Quilting pins

Now for an in-depth discussion of each gadget, and how you use it.

Graph Paper

Graph paper is helpful when making patterns or templates that have right angles: squares, rectangles, and triangles. It will help you see if your template is true to shape. Be sure to purchase graph paper that has four grids to the inch. It is easier to compute enlarging or transferring patterns. One-fourth increments are easier to calculate than $^1/_5$-inch grids. Try to fold anything into five sections!

Quilter's Quarter

A quilter's quarter is a $^1/_4$" by $^1/_4$" by 8" piece of plastic that is used to mark the $^1/_4$-inch seam allowance on your fabric. This tool makes marking very quick and accurate, so beginners like to use it.

Quilting Bee
Be sure to purchase a quilter's quarter that is made of colored plastic. I have searched many an hour trying to find a clear quilter's quarter in my sewing supplies.

Rotary Cutter

A rotary cutter is a great tool for cutting straight lines on your fabric. It looks very similar to a pizza cutter. If you are very careful, it can cut through several layers of fabric at a time. The rotary cutter is used mainly when you are making a quilt that is strip-pieced by machine and can be used when you are cutting lattices and borders. One drawback: You can't cut on curves, and you always need a ruler to guide the rotary blade.

Rotary cutter.

Cutting Mat with Grids

Rotary cutters should always be used with a cutting mat that is "self healing." The plastic mat is strong enough not to be damaged by the sharp blade. These mats are marked with $1/4$-inch hash marks on the sides and also one-inch grids over the whole surface. There should also be two bias diagonals over the grid as well. Buy a mat that is at least 18 by 24 inches. I have just discovered cutting mats that have a handle opening cut right into the plastic. It makes it easier to carry!

A self-healing cutting mat comes in a variety of sizes.

Ruler with a Lip

There are many see-through plastic rulers with grids that are heavy enough to withstand rotary cutters. Rulers come in all sizes and shapes, and the one you purchase will depend on the quilt you are making.

I personally like a plastic ruler with a lip for use with the rotary cutter. It has a clear plastic piece under the ruler that allows you to wedge it against the cutting mat so your cut is accurate.

T-Square Ruler

A metal or heavy-duty plastic T-square is used for squaring off the patches.

Quilting Pins

These pins are $1^3/_4$ inches long and have brightly colored heads. They are really great for pin-basting your quilt top, batting, and backing together, and many quilters feel they are a necessity when assembling a quilt.

Your Supplies: Get Them All Together

Quilters need to keep all their supplies in one place. There is nothing worse than running around your house looking for something. Many people use boxes to store their things. See-through plastic boxes with a lid are probably the most popular. I've also seen cigar boxes or unused pizza boxes filled with supplies going back and forth to class. I personally like fabric bags to hold my tools. You do have to keep certain things, like scissors, in a smaller bag to keep the sharp point from cutting the fabric. Be sure to hide your fabric scissors amongst your supplies so the rest of the family doesn't use them for cutting paper.

The Least You Need to Know

➤ Check over the supply list and look around your house before going shopping.

➤ Get all your necessary materials before starting your project.

➤ Experience piecing blocks before buying specialty gadgets.

➤ Keep all your supplies together.

Chapter 6

Materially Speaking, How Much Do You Need?

In This Chapter

➤ Popular quilt sizes

➤ How to calculate the amount of fabric needed for a pattern piece

➤ Estimating fabric amounts for a particular part of a quilt

➤ Table for computing the amount of fabric to buy for an entire quilt

---

There are two theories in making a quilt: You can either (1) plan, plan, plan, and get all your fabrics before you actually start (which is the preferred method) or (2) let your quilt evolve as you go along. One of my beginning students wanted to make four placemats. After constructing two patches, she was hooked and bought enough fabric for a lap quilt. A few weeks later, she decided to make a full-size quilt, so back to the store she went. At the end of the session, she had made a terrific full-size quilt top. This was a success story, but be warned: If you don't purchase enough fabric at the start, when you go back to get more, it's often gone! Let's figure out how much fabric you need.

This chapter is arranged in four sections. The first segment deals with quilt sizes. So get out your tape measure and calculate the exact size that you need. I still advise you to start small for your first project. In the second section I'll show you a method of calculating fabric amounts for a specific pattern piece of a quilt pattern. If you are making a quilt with only one pattern, there may be hundreds of the same pattern piece. So it would be smart to be able to estimate how much fabric you will need to purchase. I'll explain how to make those calculations. The third section explains two ways to consider fabric amounts. I have developed a table showing how much fabric you will need to buy for your whole quilting project. Lastly, you can purchase material for a specific part of your quilt; for example, you may need to buy fabric just for the borders. If that is the case, I have a table to help you determine that amount. So let's start measuring and discovering how much fabric to buy.

Quilting Bee
Remember that a lattice is the fabric frame around each quilt block. It can also be called sashing. The corner squares are squares where the lattices meet, and the borders outline the entire quilt. If it is very wide, the border may be divided into a border A and B.

Your Quilt's Dimensions

It's important to know the size of a finished quilt. I had a student who made a twin-size quilt but it wasn't quite large enough. She had an antique bed that stood high off the floor, therefore the quilt was too short. Please don't let that happen to you. Choose a quilt size and check your dimensions carefully.

Lap Quilt

A lap quilt can have many purposes. It's a great size for a baby's crib quilt, for hanging on the wall, or, my favorite, for putting over your lap when you're cold.

➤ Finished size: 40 inches by 56 inches
➤ Six blocks (12-inch squares)
➤ Lattice: 3 inches wide
➤ Corner squares: 3 inches
➤ Border: 4 inches wide

Twin Size

➤ Mattress size: 39 inches by 75 inches

➤ Finished size: 68 inches by 94 inches

➤ 15 blocks (12-inch squares)

➤ Lattice: 3 inches wide

➤ Corner squares: 3 inches

➤ Border: One 10-inch border

Full Size

➤ Mattress size: 52 inches by 75 inches

➤ Finished size: 80 inches by 103 inches

➤ 15 blocks (12-inch squares)

➤ Lattice: 4 inches wide

➤ Corner squares: 4 inches

➤ Border: 14 inches, broken down into 6 inches and 8 inches

49

Queen Size

➤ Mattress size: 60 inches by 80 inches

➤ Finished size: 83 inches by 103 inches

➤ 24 blocks (12-inch squares)

➤ Lattice: 3 inches wide

➤ Corner squares: 3 inches

➤ Border: 10 inches wide

King Size

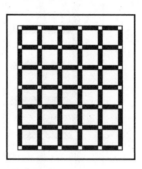

➤ Mattress size: 72 inches by 84 inches

➤ Finished size: 100 inches by 116 inches

➤ 30 blocks (12-inch square)

➤ Lattice: 4 inches wide

➤ Corner squares: 4 inches

➤ Border: 8 inches wide

Estimating Fabrics, or How Many Pieces Can I Get from a Yard?

There will come a time when you will have to calculate how much fabric you need to purchase for a quilt project. One quilt block may have many pattern pieces that fit together to make the 12-inch square. The following strategy will help you calculate the amount you need for each pattern piece in a quilt block. If you are creating a quilt that repeats one type of block you will have many similar pattern pieces, for example, when making a Double Nine Patch lap quilt, pictured below. It has four four-inch squares of the dominant color and four four-inch squares of the accent color. Let's figure out how much fabric you will need of each fabric.

A Double Nine Patch lap quilt.

1. Count the number of pattern shapes you need for one block. Measure and add on the $1/4$-inch seam allowances to get the true size. (For each Double Nine Patch you need four $4^{1}/_{2}$-inch squares of the dominant color and four $4^{1}/_{2}$-inch squares of the accent color.)

2. Determine how many of these pattern pieces you will need for the entire quilt. (There are four squares of dominant colors in each block of the Double Nine Patch, and there are six blocks in the quilt, so you'll need 24 $4^{1}/_{2}$-inch squares.)

3. Measure the width of your fabric. Usually it's 44 inches.

4. Find out how many pattern pieces (with seam allowances added on) will fit across the fabric width. Divide the fabric width by the width of the pattern piece. (Forty-four inches divided by $4^1/_2$ inches of the Double Nine Patch square is 9.7—but wait—you can only fit nine whole square pattern pieces in the width.)

5. To determine the length of fabric needed and how many rows needed to fit all the squares in, first divide the total number of pattern pieces by the number of squares that fit across the width of the fabric. (Remember, we need 24 squares for the lap quilt, and 24 divided by nine is 2.6 rows. You'll have to allow for three whole rows of fabric.)

6. Then multiply that number of rows by the length of the pattern piece, including the seam allowance. (Multiplying the $4^1/_2$ inches of the Double Nine Patch square by three rows yields $13^1/_2$ inches.)

7. To figure out how many yards are needed, divide the total inches by 36 inches (for the yard). Add on a four- or five-inch "fudge factor" to allow for mistakes. (For the Double Nine Patch, $13^1/_2$ inches are needed for the rows plus a four-inch fudge factor to equal $17^1/_2$ inches. So approximately 18 inches divided by 36 inches equals half a yard. You will need half a yard of the dominant color and half a yard for the accent color.)

See how many Double Nine Patch squares will fit on the fabric.

Do Your Math: Calculate the Right Amount

Now that we know the fabric yardage you need to buy for a specific pattern piece or template of your quilt, let me show you how these amounts can be put together. There are ways that you lay out your patterns, dovetailing them with borders and lattices to save fabric. I try to use every scrap of my material. When we get to the chapter about cutting out the templates, I will show you some handy hints to reduce fabric waste. It is difficult to estimate the exact amount of fabric for a sampler quilt, since each patch is different. The following table gives you an educated guesstimate for fabric yardage. Backing and batting are not included, but will be discussed in Chapter 18, "The Three Bs: Batting, Backing, and Basting."

Table 6.1 Fabric Guesstimates to Purchase for Entire Project

Quilt Size	Color	What Is Included	Fabric Yardage*
Lap	Dominant	Blocks, lattice	2
	Contrast	Blocks, borders	2
	Blenders	Blocks (two fabrics)	$1/2$ each
		Blocks and corner squares (one fabric)	$3/4$
	Background	Blocks	1
Twin	Dominant	Blocks, lattice, border B	4
	Contrast	Blocks, border A	$3^1/2$
	Blenders	Blocks (two fabrics)	$3/4$ each
		Blocks and corner squares (one fabric)	1
	Background	Blocks	$1^3/4$
Full	Dominant	Blocks, lattice, border B	$4^1/2$
	Contrast	Blocks, border A	$3^3/4$
	Blenders	Blocks (two to four fabrics)	$3/4$ each
		Blocks and corner squares (one fabric)	1
	Background	Blocks	$1^3/4$
Queen	Dominant	Blocks, lattice, border B	5
	Contrast	Blocks, border A	4
	Blenders	Blocks (two fabrics)	1
		Blocks and corner squares (one fabric)	$1^5/8$
	Background	Blocks	2
King	Dominant	Blocks, lattice, border B	$5^1/2$
	Contrast	Blocks, border A	$4^1/2$
	Blenders	Blocks (two fabrics)	$1^1/4$ each
		Blocks and corner squares (one fabric)	$1^3/4$
	Background	Blocks	$2^1/2$

Remember, these are estimates—NOT everybody cuts wisely.

Sometimes it's necessary to know the amount of fabric to purchase for a specific part of your quilt. I can't tell you how many times I've had to go back to the store and buy a different fabric for a lattice or border because the one that I purchased wasn't quite right. Occasionally some quilters wait to see how the patches look before choosing the border fabric. If that happens to you, I've calculated how much fabric you'll need for each section of your quilt. So get out your pad and pencil and let's see what you'll need.

To use this table, locate the section of the quilt that you need to purchase fabric for, perhaps it's the lattice. Then look for the quilt size you are making, let's say full size, and determine the yardage you should buy.

Table 6.2 Yardage for a Specific Part of a Quilt

Part	Quilt Size	Number Needed and Size	Yardage
Lattice	Lap	17 (3" × 12")	$^3/_4$
	Twin	38 (3" × 12")	$1^1/_2$
	Full	38 (4" × 12")	2
	Queen	58 (3" × 12")	$2^1/_4$
	King	71 (4" × 12")	$2^3/_4$
Corner Squares	Lap	12 (3" × 3")	$^1/_4$
	Twin	24 (3" × 3")	$^1/_2$
	Full	24 (4" × 4")	$^5/_8$
	Queen	35 (3" × 3")	$^5/_8$
	King	42 (4" × 4")	$^3/_4$
Borders	Lap	4"	1
	Twin	10" or	$2^1/_2$
		A: 4"	$1^1/_2$
		B: 6"	$1^3/_4$
	Full	14" or	3
		A: 6"	$1^3/_4$
		B: 8"	$2^1/_2$
	Queen	10" or	$3^1/_2$
		A: 4"	$1^3/_4$
		B: 6"	2
	King	8" or	$3^1/_2$
		A: 3"	2
		B: 5"	$2^1/_2$
Background Fabric	Lap	6 blocks	1
	Twin	15 blocks	$1^3/_4$
	Full	15 blocks	$1^3/_4$
	Queen	24 blocks	2
	King	30 blocks	$2^1/_2$
Blenders	Lap	2 or 3 fabrics	$^1/_2$–$^3/_4$ of each
	Twin	3 fabrics	$^3/_4$–1 of each
	Full	3 to 5 fabrics	$^3/_4$–1 of each
	Queen	3 to 5 fabrics	1 of each
	King	3 to 5 fabrics	$1^1/_2$ of each

In your quilt, you may have several blender fabrics. One blender fabric should include all the colors of your color scheme. Others will be of different values of the dominant and accent colors. You can have as many blenders as you want; I've suggested the minimum.

We've discovered three different methods of calculating fabric yardage. You can determine the fabric requirements of a specific pattern piece or template in a patch, figure out yardage for the entire quilt, or lastly, find the yardage amounts for one particular part of the quilt. Let's decide on your project, do the arithmetic, and calculate the amount you need to purchase before going to the store. Next stop—the fabric store.

The Least You Need to Know

➤ Know the dimensions of the finished size of the quilt.

➤ Measure the width of the fabric in order to calculate the number of templates that will fit.

➤ Check the charts and plan the amount of fabric needed, but remember, you may need more.

➤ Be realistic—start small.

Hmmm.....

Chapter 7

Time to Purchase Your Fabric

In This Chapter

➤ Understanding the type of fabric appropriate for making quilts

➤ Knowing which fabrics to avoid

➤ Choosing fabrics with variety in scale and pattern

➤ Choosing fabric to blend in with your color scheme

➤ Determining the best places to purchase fabrics

Every quilter accumulates a stash of fabrics. Your leftovers will grow with each project. After quilting for 25 years, I have a great fabric collection. One of my students bought me a bumper sticker that said, "The quilter who dies with the most fabric wins." Actually everyone in my class seems to be vying for that title.

Purchasing the appropriate fabric for your project can be intimidating, but this chapter sets out guidelines to follow to make it easier. Today we are fortunate to have a variety of sources to obtain fabric. We take fabric for granted, while our ancestors used their fabric with reverence, using every scrap. Let's start our modern-day quest for the perfect fabric, and you may become a "fabriholic" too.

What Type of Fabric?

Without a doubt, the best type of fabric for beginners to use is 100 percent cotton. Cotton has been proven through the test of time to be easy to work with and also durable. The material shouldn't ravel or stretch, since these characteristics make it difficult to work with. Your fabric should be colorfast and washable. To check out your fabric, look at the end of the *bolt* in the store.

Quilt Talk
A *bolt* is the fabric that is rolled around a cardboard base. The end of the bolt has a great deal of information: fiber content, colorfastness, finish (permanent press), and, of course, the price.

Synthetic fabrics, such as polyester, are more difficult to control. The fibers themselves are slippery and stretchy, and the cloth frays easily—three very problematic factors. Many quilters will use polyester fabrics when the fibers are blended with cotton. Make sure there is an equal or greater percentage of cotton to polyester. The fabric should be called cotton/polyester, not polyester/cotton. The end of the bolt will state the exact percentage of cotton to polyester, so be sure to look. You can also buy fabric from precut yardage found folded on tables in many stores; but be sure to ask a salesperson for the fabric's fiber content.

There are certain fabrics that beginners should avoid. Knits, corduroys, ginghams, stripes, and fabrics with *nap* or one-way designs are all materials that are difficult to handle. Fabrics with tulips all standing in a row are just more complicated to cut and sew together into blocks. If you are not careful, some tulips will be on their sides, upside down, or if you are lucky, they will be standing up straight.

Quilt Talk
Nap has nothing to do with sleeping. It's the short, fuzzy ends of fibers on the surface of cloth. The nap usually falls in one direction, as it does on velvet. When you look at velvet one way it's one color, but turn it around and the color darkens depending on the way the fibers are brushed. I extend this definition to include patterns with one-way designs, such as tulips all in a row.

Even though I tell you to avoid these fabrics, quilters do make quilts using these fabrics with great success. I just feel that beginners should stick with basic cotton. Slippery satins and napped velvets are used beautifully in crazy quilts. Stripes can be extremely effective as borders, or specially cut in your patches, if you know how to "fussy cut" them. It takes experience and extra planning to work with fabrics that aren't cotton or that have special cutting needs.

Where to Get Your Fabric

Where do you get your fabric? There are plenty of ways to acquire your material. Of course the best place for a beginner to go is to a fabric store that specializes in quilting fabric. The shopkeepers are only too anxious to help beginners plan their quilts. I have a favorite fabric store where the staff helps you choose the fabric, cuts swatches from each piece and pins it on a sheet of paper, and lists where you will use it. Now that is service.

Quilt shows offer great selections of fabrics and even have special lengths of fabrics called *fat quarters*, used just for small accents in your quilt.

It's so much fun going to quilt shows and seeing all the booths with new gadgets and fabrics. Many merchants have fabrics that are specially dyed and bundled into coordinated fabrics. That really makes it easier to purchase your material.

Now for some unconventional ways to get fabric. There are catalogues that sell supplies and fabrics, so you can buy from your own home. I love to feel the fabric, so I usually don't use catalogues to buy fabrics. They do have an assortment of selections, and the quality is top-notch. When you need small amounts of a fabric, it's fun to have a swap with your friends. Garage sales and rummage sales are also good sources for fabric, although unfortunately you won't know the fiber content in most cases.

Lastly, before you go fabric shopping look around your house to see what you already have. Remember you can use fabric from old projects or garments as long as the fabric is cotton and is the right weight.

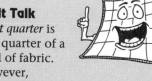

Quilt Talk

A *fat quarter* is one quarter of a yard of fabric. However, instead of the salesperson cutting $1/4$ yard the normal way across the width of the fabric (9 inches by 44 inches), she cuts the yard in half lengthwise and then across the width (18 inches by 22 inches). These pieces are great because you can fit larger pattern templates on them.

Put Your Fabric on a Scale, Then Do a Background Check

There are very few quilts that are created from only solid fabrics. There needs to be patterning to make your quilt visually interesting. Let's examine how you can add variety to your fabrics. One of the most important dimensions, besides the color value of a fabric, is the scale of the design. Prints that are all the same size are dull and boring. Little calico prints are nice in small doses but choosing five calicos of all the same design is monotonous. You should choose small-, medium-, and large-size prints for your quilt. Pin dots and little flowers are examples of small-scale prints—I've even bought fabrics with little spools of thread. Small-scale material appears almost solid. Large-size prints have motifs of three or four inches in size, and the large design patterns can be an overall floral or paisley or any other large figure.

Quilting Bee

A quilter went shopping for fabric at a rummage sale at her church and saw a table of old clothes. She knew shirts are a great weight for quilting fabric, so she purchased some. When she brought them home, her husband remarked that they looked familiar. Upon examination, they noticed the dry cleaner's marking with their name on the collar! She had bought back her husband's shirts!

Look at the variety of scale and how it is more interesting than fabric with a one-size scale.

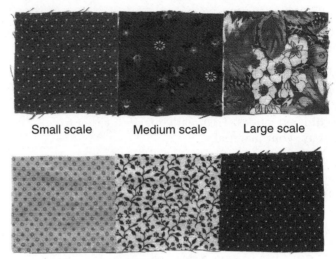

Small scale   Medium scale   Large scale

All one scale

Look at the motif of the fabric and keep in mind who will use the quilt. One of my students spent all her time making patches for a baby quilt. When her quilt top was completed, she found a really cute, colorful, frog fabric for the backing. Of course her nephew loves the back of the quilt, not the front that she toiled over. You can see that fabric patterns are a crucial consideration when buying fabric for your quilt.

There is one more important factor in purchasing your fabric, and that is the background of a fabric. The background or ground color of the material is the hue on which the design is placed. For example, a fabric may have red and pink hearts on a white background, or you may have red and white hearts on a pink color. Same colors, different fabric appearance. Be sure that the background coordinates with all your fabrics. For example, if all of your fabric motifs but one are on an ecru background, a white one will stick out like a sore thumb. The value of the background hue will help blend with your other fabrics.

Blending Your Fabric Together: Dominant and Contrasting

Now it's time to select your fabric. Most fabric stores have their cottons, many times advertised as *calico*, in one section with all similar hues arranged together, almost like a rainbow.

I start by going to the row that has the dominant color I'm looking for. Let's say I've chosen a color scheme of red and blue, with blue being the dominant color. I first try to find a fabric that blends all the colors of my color scheme—in other words, red and blue. It should be in a large-scale overall pattern. This is the blender fabric.

Scraps and Pieces

Be sure the blender fabric is really the color you want. Many times beginners are so close to the fabric that they see one color, but from afar it may appear a different hue. If the fabric design is red and blue flowers with green leaves, be sure the fabric gives a red and blue look, not green. Do what I call the "squint method." Stand back from the fabric bolt, look away, then turn back and squint at it. The first impression of color is how it will appear in your quilt.

Once this blender fabric has been chosen, I then pull out bolts of the dominant- and contrasting-colored fabrics that coordinate with the blender fabric. Next, decide on a lighter or darker value of the dominant and contrasting colors. That brings your fabric total to five, which is perfect for beginners. Lean your bolts of fabric against a wall, one next to another. Step back and do the squint method to evaluate your fabrics. Is there variety in the values of light and darkness of the fabrics? Do you have a good mixture of patterns and scale of designs? Most important, do you like it? This quilt will reflect your personality—can you live with it? If the answers are yes, let's pick out the background fabric.

The background fabric is the material that surrounds the main design of a patch. For example, in the Eight Point star, the star motif is made up of the dominant, contrasting, or blending color and appears to be laying on top of the background. This background fabric traditionally was a solid color so it would not detract from the pattern. You have to decide on the intensity of the background: Do you want a white, ecru *muslin*, or even a hue of the dominant color?

Remember that a plain white fabric makes a strong contrast against your color scheme. Sometimes a neutral-color muslin makes your quilt colors appear softer. Recently quilters have started using a solid print for the background. This material should have a motif so small that from a distance it appears solid, but as you get closer the fabric adds texture to your patch. The white, tan, or gray fabric may have swirls, flowers, or a paisley motif in the same subtle shades of neutral colors. These are known as white-on-white fabrics.

Quilt Talk

The term *calico* today is used to describe quilt fabrics that are 100 percent cotton or cotton/polyester blends. At one time, calico pertained to a process of printing designs on a cotton fabric by using a roller. The patterns were usually small florals.

Quilt Talk

Muslin is a plain weave cotton fabric, generally used as the background fabric for your patches or appliqué. Muslin comes in a variety of different shades of beige (unbleached is ecru or beige) and if the manufacturer bleaches the muslin, it will appear whiter. Today there is even a permanent-press muslin that will not wrinkle. Since muslin comes in a wide range of weights, be sure to buy a good quality.

Notice how each star motif looks distinctive with different background fabrics.

 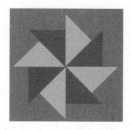 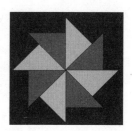

Quilting Bee
If you use a colored fabric with a small white design for your solid print, stand back and squint at it. Be sure the motif is not too bright against the background. A navy fabric with white dots jarred my eyes and I ended up not using it. All colors should flow into one another.

Don't forget you can also use a color or black for the background. Amish quilts with black backgrounds are extremely dramatic.

The salespeople at the fabric stores usually hate to see me coming because I take out bolts and bolts of fabric to get just the right color combinations. Be nice and put back all the bolts that you're not buying.

Now that I've given you some guidelines to help in your quest for the perfect fabrics, choosing your fabrics should be exciting and fun. Buy the best fabric that you can afford. We want this to be a family heirloom and last a lifetime. Now go out and buy.

The Least You Need to Know

➤ Do not choose fabrics with all the same scale of patterns.

➤ Avoid problem fabrics such as corduroy, ginghams, napped fabrics, one-way designs, and striped fabrics.

➤ Line up all your fabric bolts, step back, and squint to make sure the colors blend.

➤ The best source for beginners to purchase fabric is a specialty quilt shop where you will get the most help.

➤ The choice of background fabric of the patch can change the effect from subtle to dramatic.

➤ Buy the best fabric that you can afford.

Part 3
Hands On: It's Time to Start

Washing, organizing, and storing fabrics will keep them in perfect condition. Knowing the characteristics of fabrics—especially the straight-of-fabric grain—makes cutting and sewing your quilt easy.

Templates are used as patterns for quilts. Accuracy is extremely important. You transfer the template shape onto the wrong side of your fabric. Once each fabric has its pieces marked, you add the seam allowances and cut. Then you make your fabric pieces into a block. Be sure to organize all your fabric pieces to avoid losing any.

You may have hundreds of pieces to assemble to make up your quilt top! Where do you start? Simple strategies make hand piecing easy. Pressing gives your quilt a professional look and sometimes irons out your mistakes!

Chapter 8

Knowing and Taking Care of Your Fabric

In This Chapter

➤ Preparing your fabric before you start your quilt

➤ Organizing and storing your fabrics

➤ Understanding the terminology of woven fabrics

We've bought our fabrics and supplies at the store and now we're home. Where do we start? I like to prepare and organize my fabrics first. Fabric has to be preshrunk and tested for colorfastness before you can start working with it. Then you need to have an orderly and systematic approach to storing your collection. As you create more and more quilts, there will be additional fabric to store. Our quilting ancestors saved every scrap—we don't want to squander our fabric!

Fabrics have certain characteristics—I feel that fabrics have a life of their own. Some are stiff, wrinkly, stretchy, or raveled. And the same length of fabric can react in a different way just by holding it differently. Knowing these factors will help you manage your fabric and make your quilt last a lifetime. Let's jump in and get our fabric wet!

Don't Forget to Wash!

Quilting Bee
You can tell if a fabric runs if the water turns color. You can also put a small piece of a white fabric in to see if it discolors. I've had many blues and reds that tend to not be colorfast and bleed onto the white.

Quilting Bee
Small quarter-yard cuts of fabric will get tangled in the dryer, so let them line dry.

Don't Get Stuck!
Sometimes when you take your fabric out of the dryer, the fabric is very stiff and wrinkled. If you use this same fabric in your quilt, after washing your quilt, it will have this same appearance. You may not want to use this fabric. Remember, quilts cannot be ironed once they are completed—the inner puffy batting will compress and become flat.

As soon as you get home from the store, wash your fabrics! This way you don't have to wonder later if you washed them or not. Two qualities of fabrics may give you difficulties: (1) shrinking and (2) fading or running when washed. Both have to be addressed before making your quilt. A friend forgot to wash a red fabric, and after making 15 patches and stitching them together, she started to quilt. Then she wanted to take off a little stain. Unfortunately, as she applied water, the stain got worse—the red fabric started bleeding into the white background fabric. She had to wash the entire quilt and the white background turned a pale shade of pink. You know what happens when a red sock is put in with your white clothes.

Check to see if your fabric is colorfast. Even if the bolt at the store says that it's colorfast, don't trust it. I divide my fabrics into darks and lights, and soak them in a sink of warm water to see if they run.

Keep changing the water until it remains clear. After four times of doing this, if the dye still comes out, then desperate measures need to be taken. I soak the fabric in a sink filled with very hot water that has two cups of white vinegar added to it. Keep the fabric submerged for about 30 minutes. Then try the colorfast test again, soaking your problem fabric with a scrap of white fabric. If after several times of doing this the color is not set, I would advise not using your fabric.

Besides making sure that the colors are set, let's preshrink the fabric. All fabric has some residual shrinkage. To prevent shrinkage, treat your fabrics as you would a finished quilt. I put the fabrics in warm water and even throw them into the dryer.

If one material shrinks and the others don't, then the quilt top will pucker wherever that fabric is used. Actually some people like that puckered look, because they feel that it gives their quilt an antique look. My advice to you is to buy your fabric, come home, and shrink and wash your fabric that same day. Then you'll know the qualities of your fabric and you'll be ready to go.

Keep Your Fabrics Dry!

I always have wistful feelings when I read quilt books with chapters on planning your quilting studio. If you are like me, you can only wish for a separate room for your projects. But no matter how small your working space, organizing your fabrics is a necessity.

To keep your fabrics "healthy," be sure to store them away from light and dampness. There is nothing worse than thinking you have leftover scraps of the perfect fabric only to find that it faded or has that moldy smell. Keep fabrics more than half a yard folded with similar colors. Stack these folds of fabric in full view on shelves, so you can easily see your stash. If you don't have a spare closet or bookcase, store similar colors of fabric in those clear plastic boxes that fit under a bed. Avoid storing fabric in the basement or any place with high humidity. Mildew and a musty odor are almost impossible to remove.

I also keep little scraps smaller than a fourth of a yard in a separate bag. You never know when you need just a few inches of that perfect color for a pillow. Never throw away that last little smidgen of a material. Save it so you can match the color or design if you need to buy more. I also keep a bag of novelty fabrics, like velvets, satins, and laces, for projects like crazy quilts. Whenever I shorten a velvet dress, I save the material I cut off from the hem.

Save your scrap fabrics for a rainy day when you don't want to run out to the store. It's just more economical to reuse your leftovers. So set up your studio!

Quilting Bee
Keep snippets of fabric for a quilt project in progress on a small index card and carry this around with you for reference. You never know when you will find a terrific additional fabric or accessory that will be perfect with your quilt.

The Straight- and Narrow-of-Grain Line

Have you noticed the different ways that fabric feels, drapes, and reacts? There are certain characteristics of fabrics that will determine how you use them. The most important factor is the fabric *grain*. This determines how your fabric reacts and needs to be handled. There are several types of grain. When fabric is pulled in different directions, it reacts differently. Each grain or direction has a specific name and characteristic.

The threads that run the whole length of the fabric are called the lengthwise grain and need to be very strong in order to endure the weaving process. Because of

Quilt Talk
Grain is the direction that the threads are woven into fabric. Fabric is made up of threads that run perpendicular to each other on a loom. There is a *lengthwise grain*, which runs the length of the fabric, and a *crosswise grain*, which is woven at a right angle to the lengthwise thread.

their strength, they have very little stretch. The direction that runs parallel to these threads is called the *lengthwise grain.* The crosswise threads, or *crosswise grain,* are not quite as strong and have some "give."

Where the crosswise threads turn around the outer side of the fabric is known as the *selvage* or selvedge.

Look at the directions of the different lines of grain.

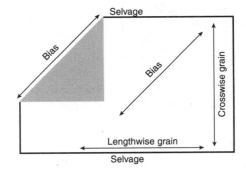

Because the selvage is thicker and has a denser thread count than the rest of the fabric, it reacts differently. The selvage shrinks and puckers and is very difficult to sew through. Many quilters cut the selvage off as soon as they wash the fabric, but I like to keep it on so I can tell the lengthwise grain. The lengthwise grain is also known as the straight of the grain, as it runs parallel to the selvage.

Quilt Talk
The *selvage* is the outer finished edge of your fabric. It is the edge that doesn't ravel and is more closely woven than the rest of the fabric.

The tried-and-true technique has templates (quilt patterns) put in a particular direction so that the fabric is easy to handle. The straight of grain is the strongest direction and each template will have a straight-of-grain arrow that should be placed parallel to the selvage. We'll talk about marking templates on your fabric in Chapter 10, "On Your Mark, Get Set, Cut!"

Illustrated are several templates with the straight-of-grain arrows indicated.

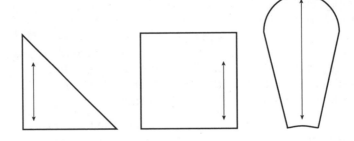

The last type of grain is known as *bias*. Bias is the diagonal direction of fabric. True bias is at a 45-degree angle to the grain lines.

The bias direction has quite a bit of stretch and is more difficult to handle. Some blocks have a bias piece on the outside edge, and if you are not careful when ironing, it will stretch out of shape. Quilters use bias for preparing the outer binding, because the binding needs to conform to the outer curves, and bias strips make it easy.

Now that you have washed and organized your fabrics and learned about certain fabrics' characteristics, we're ready to move to the next level: making templates.

The Least You Need to Know

➤ All fabrics have residual shrinkage.

➤ Wash your fabrics to check for shrinkage and colorfastness.

➤ Lengthwise grain is stronger than crosswise grain, and templates should be put on the straight of grain.

➤ The bias direction is stretchy and more difficult to handle but is useful in making bias tape.

Chapter 9

Words to Live By: Templates Are the Patterns of Success

In This Chapter

➤ Learning about the different materials for making templates

➤ Transferring templates from books

➤ Preparing templates for hand and machine quilting

Look in the color photo section. In a quilt like the Trip Around the World, how do you cut all those squares neatly? Quilters use templates. A template is anything you draw around to mark pattern pieces for your quilt. Templates can be made of many different materials. Appliqué quilts can use heart-shaped cookie cutters for templates. I've even used a quarter to mark a center of a flower.

Now that you've chosen a quilt block to piece, you're ready to start the quilting process. You can draft the templates yourself, but it is very tedious and time-consuming. When I first taught beginners, I had them draft a Double Nine Patch made of two squares: a four-inch square and a $1^1/_3$-inch square. Even using graph paper, it took almost the entire two-hour class. That's why all the patterns in this book are full size and ready to copy.

Machine-sewn quilts use different templates than handmade quilts and both will be discussed. Templates can also be purchased from quilting catalogues or specialty quilt stores. Let's find out how to make our patterns of success.

Materials for Making Templates

A template or pattern must be made for each shape in your quilt block.

These three shapes make up the Eight Point Star block.

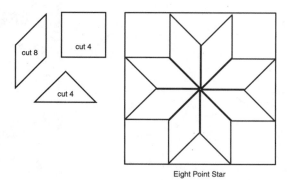

Eight Point Star

Patterns for quilts are totally distinct from patterns with which you sew clothing. If you are used to sewing clothing, quilt patterns or templates may seem very unusual. Commercial clothing patterns are made from printed tissue paper with seam allowances marked on each pattern piece. Quilting patterns have to be extremely accurate in order to have the parts of the block fit together like a jig-saw puzzle, so the templates are made the exact size of the shape in the hand-pieced block. We will add the seam allowances on the fabric later in Chapter 10, "On Your Mark, Get Set, Cut!"

Since many quilts have hundreds of pattern pieces to draw, templates must be durable. Usually templates are made of cardboard or plastic sheeting. You can find cardboard around the house: file cards, gift boxes, even cereal boxes that are cut apart. Optimally, oak tag or poster board are the best weight—easy to cut but durable. As you mark your fabric by drawing around these templates, the points on cardboard templates tend to wear away. If you know that this may be a problem, plastic sheeting may be advantageous. The plastic sheets can be found in craft stores. A student who was a nurse used exposed x-ray sheets for templates. The most durable template I've seen was purchased at a booth at a quilt show and constructed from metal with sand glued onto the bottom.

Don't Get Stuck!
You can photocopy your pattern pieces, but beware: If the page is not flat against the machine, the patterns will be skewed. Many copying machines enlarge the pattern very slightly. Even $1/16$ of an inch makes a difference in a quilt. It's best to trace the patterns.

Accuracy Counts

If one patch is crooked, then your whole quilt is out of alignment. Does that frighten you? It need not. If your templates are precise, then your quilt will be, too. The best type of templates for beginners are made from cardboard and sandpaper. Here are some guidelines to help in the quest for accurate templates.

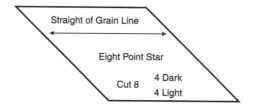

Straight of Grain Line

Eight Point Star

Cut 8   4 Dark
         4 Light

This is the diamond template from the Eight Point Star. It is important to include the name of the block, the number of pattern pieces you need to cut, and the straight-of-grain arrow.

1. Choose a block. (That's easy enough!)

2. Copy each pattern of the block. Either use tracing paper to redraw the patterns or carefully photocopy the page. Be sure to mark the name of the block, the number of blocks you need to cut, and the straight-of-grain arrow.

3. Use rubber cement to affix medium-weight sandpaper to the cardboard. Be sure to apply the rubber cement to the smooth side of the sandpaper.

4. Glue copied patterns onto the cardboard/sandpaper with rubber cement. The template has the copied pattern on top and the rough sandpaper on the bottom.

5. Now it's time to cut very carefully around the outer edges through all three layers—pattern, cardboard, and sandpaper.

6. Test for template accuracy by putting your template over the book's pattern. If it is inaccurate, carefully recut it.

7. Store all your templates for each block together. I like to use zippered plastic bags for each individual block. Be sure to label the block name—you do not want to mix them up!

Remember, accuracy counts. The outside of these templates will mark the sewing lines on your fabric, and when sewn, these pieces must fit together perfectly like a jig-saw puzzle.

That doesn't seem too hard, does it?

Quilting Bee
I know you are asking, "Why glue sandpaper to the template?" The reason is that the sandpaper keeps the template from sliding around while you are marking the fabric.

Don't Get Stuck!
Be sure to use rubber cement and not any other type of glue because only rubber cement dries flat and won't make the cardboard ripple. If your template is not flat, it will not be accurate.

Templates for Machine-Piecing

Quilting Bee
Sometimes when you try to cut small slivers off the templates, you only make it worse by cutting too much. To straighten an uneven edge, file it down with sandpaper or an emery board. You have more control.

Templates for machine-piecing are slightly different from those for hand quilting. The $1/4$-inch seam allowances are included in the template. The cutting line is drawn on your fabric—not the sewing line.

When machine sewing quilts, the cutting edges are aligned and pinned together. The seam line is determined by the sewing machine's $1/4$-inch presser foot, not by a line drawn on the fabric as in hand quilting. Accurate cutting is extremely important for machine piecing. This book will not discuss techniques that use multiple-template, but there are several terrific books listed in Appendix B, "Suggested Reading: Books That I Love to Look at and Read."

A template for machine-piecing has the $1/4$-inch seam allowance incorporated in the template.

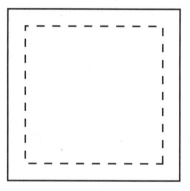

Multiple templates drafted together in a row.

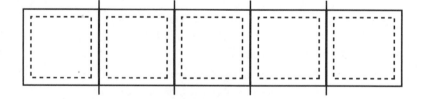

Sometimes machine-sewn quilts have multiple templates (templates that are drawn in a long line). It saves time to mark and sew multiple templates rather than marking and sewing each separate template. The Trip Around the World and Lone Star quilts are examples of quilts with multiple templates. Although I have taught how to make them many times, it still seems like magic when all these templates come together. There are several books that deal specifically with this method.

Many machine-made quilts don't have special templates, for example, the Rail Fence. A fabric strip of the correct width is cut from selvage to selvage and sewn together in the strip-pieced method, then cut apart and resewn to form a block. The blocks are sewn together to form the quilt top.

The Rail Fence and Log Cabin blocks will be discussed in depth in Chapter 16, "Use Your Sewing Machine: Machine-Pieced Blocks."

Remember, no matter whether you are hand or machine quilting, you must be sure your templates are exact. Any deviation will cause your quilt not to line up. Check all templates for accuracy against the patterns in the book, and use a T-square ruler for testing right angles in squares and rectangles.

Be sure to keep templates sorted by blocks. I always have at least one student who tries to put a Double Nine Patch square into an Eight Point Star corner. The templates may look the same, but they are $1/4$ inch different in size, and there is no way they will fit. So keep them separated in envelopes or my favorite— zippered plastic bags.

Quilt Talk

Strip piecing is a method of creating quilts by taking long strips of fabric and sewing them together in a set sequence. This newly combined material is then cut apart and resewn to form a part of a quilt.

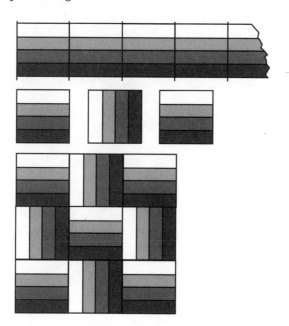

Notice how the strips are sewn together, cut apart, then resewn to form a Rail Fence block.

The Least You Need to Know

➤ Templates for hand-piecing are pattern pieces that are the exact size of each element in a block.

➤ Templates for machine-sewn quilts have the $1/4$-inch seam allowance included so that only the cutting line is drawn on the fabric.

➤ The best templates for beginners are made from cardboard and sandpaper glued together.

➤ All markings must be transferred to the templates—be sure to include the name of the block, cutting directions, and straight-of-grain arrow.

➤ Draw and cut templates accurately; then check them for preciseness.

Chapter 10

On Your Mark, Get Set, Cut!

> **In This Chapter**
>
> ➤ Choosing the correct equipment to mark on fabric
>
> ➤ Tracing around the template carefully
>
> ➤ Economizing on fabric
>
> ➤ Cutting out the pattern pieces
>
> ➤ Organizing and storing fabric pieces

We've spent a long time making perfectly accurate templates, now it's time to transfer those shapes onto the material. Can you believe that we draw right on the wrong side of the fabric? Using the correct equipment will help your "markability."

Templates for hand-sewn quilts have no seam allowances. The traced shape is the exact sewing size. We need to draw them onto the fabric after the template is marked. Proper placement of the patterns will help economize the fabric. With all these marked lines, you should think before you cut. Think twice, but cut once.

In short, templates make fabric pieces, those pieces make up a block, and blocks make up a quilt. If there is only one block repeated throughout your quilt, there may be hundreds of cut pieces of fabric. How do you keep them all together and not lose them? Keep reading and you'll find out.

Equip Yourself

There are several considerations to make before marking your fabric. Choose a tool that is easy to see, marks finely and accurately, and does not run or bleed into the fabric. A #2 pencil is usually best. Because the wrong side of the fabric is a lighter color than the right

Quilting Bee
I really prefer an artist's pencil over the ones made for marking quilts. Some pencils are too waxy, make a line too thick, break easily, and need to be sharpened too often—you know, like eyebrow pencils. Avoid those pencils.

Quilting Bee
It is easy to tell the wrong side of a printed fabric—the design is fuzzier and lighter in color. With solid fabrics, both sides seem to be the same color. There may be a slight difference in values, so make sure you use the same side consistently. I sometimes put a pin or masking tape on the wrong side to remind me of which side I chose.

Your templates should be lined up parallel to the selvage of your fabric. Draw dots in each corner of the template.

side, lead pencils make terrific fine, visible lines. If the fabric is a dark color or has a busy pattern, you may have to use a white, silver, or yellow pencil for the lines to be seen. I usually keep a variety of colors with my supplies to test which color pencil is best.

Some quilters use ballpoint pens for marking. Be very careful to test if the pen markings are permanent. Avoid them if they bleed when wet—the color will stain a light-colored fabric.

Be sure your pencil is sharp! You don't want a thick line. Even that small difference multiplied over hundreds of pieces will change the alignment of your quilt. Keep your sharpener handy.

It's as Easy as Drawing from Dot to Dot

It's time to mark our fabric! Here are some simple steps to follow.

1. Be sure the fabric is preshrunk and colorfast.

2. Choose the template and the fabric. Turn the fabric to the wrong side.

3. Find your selvages—these finished edges are your guidelines to pattern placement. Place the straight-of-grain arrow parallel to the selvage. This makes your quilt more durable and the fabric easier to work with when placing it on the lengthwise grain.

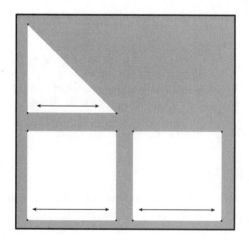

4. Start by placing a template ¹/₂ inch away from the selvage with the straight-of-grain arrow parallel to it.

5. Put a dot in each corner of the geometric shape of the template. You will use the dots to help maintain accuracy. This is very important—so make those dots!

6. Carefully draw around the outside edge of the template, connecting the dots. Take care not to press down too hard with the pencil because it drags the fabric and the markings will be out of shape. Lift the template and check for accuracy. Redraw if necessary.

One template down, how many to go?

Cut Between the Sewing Lines

Now that you have drawn your sewing lines, let's draw the cutting line. Don't forget to add the seam allowances onto the outer edge of the markings. Seam allowances for hand-pieced quilts are ¹/₄ inch (not ⁵/₈ inch as typical in commercial clothing patterns).

Before you cut, you must make some additional marks on your fabric:

> **Don't Get Stuck!**
> Do not use the selvage—it continues to shrink after the rest of the fabric has been preshrunk and will make your quilt pucker. Also, because selvage is thick, it is extremely difficult to sew and quilt through.

> **Quilt Talk**
> The *quilter's quarter* is an eight-inch-long four-sided rod of plastic that is ¹/₄ inch wide. It is very easy for beginners to line up this ruler with the seam line in order to draw the cutting line.

1. Draw a line ¹/₄ inch around the marked seam line. Beginners sometimes use a colored pencil to mark all the cutting lines. This way there is a real visible difference. Use a ruler or *quilter's quarter* to measure the quarter inch.

Look how the cutting line is drawn ¹/₄ inch around the seam lines.

2. Place the next template on the fabric, making sure to leave enough room for the seam allowance.

3. Check that you drew the correct number of pattern pieces, and be sure you drew all the seam allowances.

4. Cut out fabric pieces on the cutting lines. Use sharp scissors to avoid blisters on your hands.

There is a perfectly logical reason for a $1/4$-inch seam allowance. The $1/4$-inch seam allowance is enough to keep the quilt from raveling, but not too large that you would have to quilt through it. Those pioneer women really thought this through.

There are strategies to marking fabrics that help you economize fabric usage. The first approach is to start at the selvage side and mark the patterns side by side, only half an inch apart. If you start marking in the middle of the fabric and then place the other templates in no particular order, you waste much of the fabric. Be methodical, and mark across the fabric from selvage to selvage or up the side of the selvage.

You can utilize all your fabric by thinking ahead.

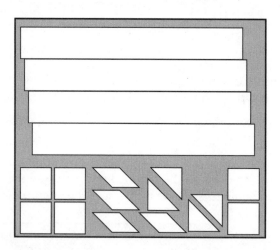

You may want to mark up the side of the selvage if you need the length of the fabric for borders. Another idea is to dovetail pattern pieces. Dovetailing means fitting odd-shaped pieces like triangles or wedges into one another. Remember: Plan ahead.

If you are preparing a quilt with repeated blocks, make one patch before you cut out the rest of the quilt. Sometimes you decide to change the color combination or move their placement in the block. Once the block is perfected, it's time to cut out the rest of your blocks.

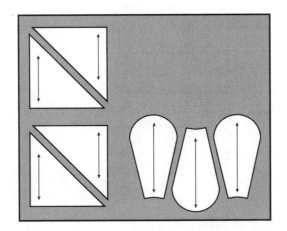

Pattern pieces can be dovetailed to save fabric.

Stack and Store

There are two methods of storing fabric pieces. For example, an Eight Point Star has three pattern shapes—a diamond, a square, and a triangle. Some quilters keep fabric pieces of each template shape in separate plastic bags—one bag for the diamond, a second for the squares, and a third for the triangles. Other quilters like a plastic bag with all the fabric shapes for one block together. If you are making a lap quilt, you may have six plastic bags that contain the diamonds, squares, and triangles that will be pieced together for one block. This is great if you want a portable project. Pick up a bag and take it with you—all the pieces you need are in one bag.

If you don't like the bag method, you can baste your fabric pieces together. Take a long piece of thread with a knot on the end, and stab this through a stack of similar pieces. Don't knot both ends. You can just pull off one piece at a time as you need it. I usually put two threads through a stack just in case one breaks!

If you are making a Sampler quilt, each block will be different and created one at a time, so patches will be cut and sewn as you go along.

Quilting Bee
All patterns for templates in this book do not have the seam allowance included. In other quilting books, sometimes the $1/4$-inch seam allowance is included in the drawn template, and sometimes it has to be added. Templates with included seam allowances usually have a dotted line indicating the $1/4$-inch seam line. If done consistently, it won't matter in the templates or cut pattern pieces.

You can stack and store all pattern pieces by basting them together.

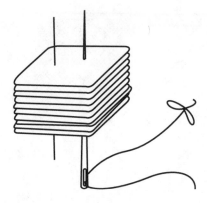

The Least You Need to Know

➤ A #2 pencil is best for transferring templates onto the fabric, but try a different color if the pencil line is hard to see.

➤ Mark on the wrong side of the fabric.

➤ Place templates with the straight-of-grain line parallel to the selvages.

➤ Put a dot in each corner of the template, then connect the dots.

➤ Hand-sewn quilt templates do not have seam allowances; you must add $1/4$ inch all around the outside for the cutting line.

➤ Check twice, then cut on the cutting lines.

Chapter 11

Do Be a Sew and Sew

In This Chapter

➤ Sewing the piecing stitches and appliqué stitch

➤ Understanding how fabric pieces are seamed together

➤ Strategies of piecing blocks

➤ Pressing quilt blocks

Depending on the type of quilt you have chosen, you may have hundreds of fabric pieces to assemble or as few as 13 pieces for one block. If you are a novice, please let me remind you to start small and cut out pieces for one block only.

It's time to sew your pieces of fabric together! There are certain procedures that make piecing logical and easy. We'll start with just two pattern pieces and learn to sew them together effortlessly. Continue sewing until a row is formed, then seam the rows together to form a square block. When you have completed your block, it's time to give your patch the professional look by giving it a real press job. Get your needle and thread—let's start.

Know Your Stitches

We'll examine hand-piecing stitches and the appliqué stitch. When these blocks are sewn, the resultant patches are contrasting in appearance. Compare the angular Ohio Star in Chapter 12 and the rounded Tudor Rose in Chapter 15. The stitches that put these patches together are totally different.

Piecing Stitch: Know the Ins and Outs

Beginners are always amazed that the stitching for hand-pieced blocks is so easy. It's a simple running stitch where the needle goes in and out of the fabric. Start with a quilting needle and quilting thread. Remember to choose the smallest size needle that you can work with confidently. Our quilting ancestors discovered that smaller needles made smaller stitches. Be sure to use quilting thread—it's thicker, more durable, and doesn't tangle.

> **Don't Get Stuck!**
> Don't make the type of knot that I use for making hems (wrapping the thread around my finger and rolling it back and forth till it forms a massive ball of a knot). If you make a knot like that, it may rub against the fabric of your quilt and wear a hole. We want our quilts to be heirlooms.

1. Cut quilting thread about two feet in length. Any longer and it's awkward and tiring to pull the thread through. Any shorter and you have to constantly rethread the needle, and that gets annoying.

2. Put a single knot in the end of the thread. I make a loop with the thread and put the needle through the circle, and pull it through. It should form a little knot with a $\frac{1}{4}$-inch "tail." The tail keeps the knot from unraveling.

Make a loop with the thread and pull the needle through, leaving a small knot with a tail.

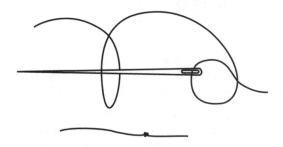

3. Place the two fabric pieces, right sides together, matching the sewing lines. This is it—our first piecing stitch. Poke the needle down through the fabric right on the sewing line and then up through the fabric about $\frac{1}{8}$ inch down along the seam line. It's simply a running stitch using an in-and-out motion that is sewn right on the seam line.

Running stitches used for the piecing stitch are very small.

Draw a pencil line on the wrong side of a scrap of fabric and practice the piecing stitch. In and out—it's easy.

Scraps and Pieces

Quilts have a rich history of superstitions. The most universal bit of folklore confirms that each quilt should have a small mistake in it, either a piecing or appliqué mismatch or a quilting faux pas. My theory is that once a quilt was completed and the quilt maker discovered the mistake, she developed the idiom that "the quilt is supposed to be like that since only God is perfect." Of course I do not recommend making mistakes in your quilt, but this does make a great explanation.

Appliqué Stitch

Beginners also need to learn the appliqué stitch. In appliquéd blocks, a fabric motif is cut out, layered, and stitched invisibly onto the background of another fabric. Several different techniques make these stitches almost invisible to the eye. In true appliqué we want to see only the design, not the stitches.

Scraps and Pieces

There has recently been a revival of folk art. The quilt is the most popular example of traditional American crafts. Quilters used the medium of fabric to make pictures of their world. This was the original folk art. Pioneer women would appliqué stylized people (Sunbonnet Sue), animals, flowers, and farm scenes in a primitive style. In these homespun-style quilts, the appliquéd pieces are embroidered with a decorative blanket stitch. This method will be discussed in Chapter 15, "Traditional Appliqué Block Patterns: Add a Layer to Your Quilt."

This is the appliqué stitch that I was taught and it has worked for me. I'll illustrate how to appliqué a heart motif. The appliqué stitch leaves a small, visible dot of a stitch.

Quilt Talk
Basting is a large, temporary running stitch that is sewn to hold down the raw edges or hold two pieces of fabric together. You should use a contrasting color so it is easy to see and remove after you have finished appliquéing.

1. Start with your quilting needle and knotted quilting thread in a color that blends with the appliqué motif.
2. Prepare the design by *basting* under the raw edges.
3. Baste the fabric motif into position on the background fabric. Now let's appliqué.
4. Start with the needle under the background fabric. Push it up through the background and the edge of the appliqué motif. Pull the thread through.

Only a dot of stitch is seen. The needle goes down through the background fabric and up into the edge of the appliqué piece.

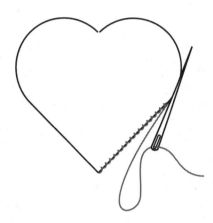

5. Position the needle right next to where the thread came up but on the background only. Take a $1/8$-inch stitch through the background and come up at the edge of the appliqué motif.
6. Continue appliquéing stitches all around the fabric design, ending underneath the background on the wrong side. Knot off.

Don't Get Stuck!
Be sure to mark the dots at each corner of your templates so you know where to start and end your seam lines.

The appliqué stitch does seem more time-consuming. The first appliqué block that a beginner creates is a slow go, but you soon develop a rhythm of stitching that makes your block sing.

How Does It Seam?

"Where do I start?" is a question all beginners ask. The answer is...with just two fabric pieces, three pins, and your needle and thread. We're going to seam the pieces together using the hand-piecing stitch. Let's take two pieces and turn them right sides together so the penciled seam lines can be seen on both sides of the pieces.

The dots marked at each corner of your templates will be the beginning and end of your seam lines. Stab a pin right into the dot of the top piece into the dot of the bottom fabric. Both dots are matched. Match up and pin the dot at the other end. Put another pin in the seam line in the middle of the pencil line.

Get out your quilting needle and thread and make a knot. Put the needle in the seam line $1/8$ inch from the right-hand dot (if you are right handed, the left-hand dot is just the opposite) and take a *backstitch* into the dot. Then sew the piecing stitch along the seam line.

Continue sewing to the end of the seam line, bringing the needle right into the end dot. Take a backstitch $1/8$ inch in reverse and back into the dot. I do not knot this end (knots can rub against and wear out material) but take a 90-degree turn into the seam allowance, make two stitches, and cut off the thread.

Quilt Talk
A *backstitch* is a stitch taken backward from the direction you are sewing to reinforce the seam.

Don't Get Stuck!
Check for accuracy before you sew. Gather several stitches on your needle, but don't pull the thread through. Turn the piece over and check to see if your needle is exactly on the line—if not, take the needle out and shift the seam line.

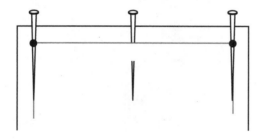

Sew right on the seam line with the hand-piecing stitch.

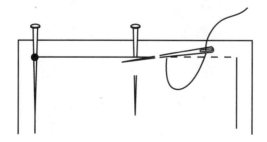

Pin each end dot of the seam line and place one pin in the center of the seam line.

87

Take a backstitch into the dot at the end and then take two stitches into the seam allowance.

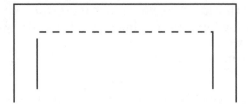

Put Your Blocks Together: Sew Row by Row

Quilting Bee
One student often had to put her work away then set it up again, so she laid out her pieces on a piece of felt or flannel. It was easy to fold up her work, then pull it out again later. The fuzzy nap of the felt kept the pieces in place even when the felt was folded up.

Didn't that "seam" easy? There are certain strategies that make it easier for you to piece your block. First, lay all your block pieces on the table in front of you. Put them in the same position as your finished block. Doesn't it look great? It is easy to decide where to start sewing and then to check if you've pinned correctly.

Each block has specific directions on sewing procedures, but here are some hints. Start by sewing the smallest pieces together to form a larger unit. Those small scraps of fabric are very easy to lose. Stitch pieces together into rows. One student sewed pieces across and then down in an L-shaped angle instead of sewing rows. She came to me and asked, "How do I put in the middle piece?" Don't sew yourself into a "jam." Sew row by row.

It's easy to sew rows together, but difficult to sew a piece into an angle.

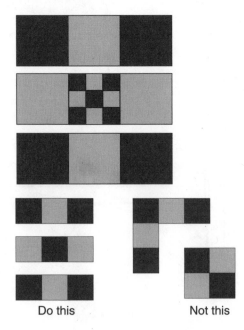

Do this   Not this

Let's learn how to sew rows together. It is important to have the seams match at intersections. Do not start sewing from one end of the row to the other side. Make sure that the seams align, sewing from the middle out. Pin the dots at each end of the row and at each seam intersection.

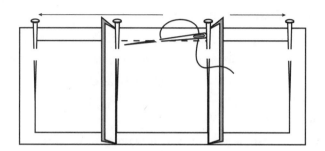

The pins are placed into the dots next to the seam allowances. Check out the direction you should sew.

Don't pin or sew down the seam allowances—you'll need to press them in any direction. Start at one of the center seams, backstitch into the dot and sew to the end of the seam line. If you have to cross a seam line, sew right up to the dot but stand the seam allowance up and pass the needle through it and continue stitching to the end of the row. Backstitch into the dot and take two stitches into the seam. Sew all of the rows in the same manner, and "Hooray," we have a block.

Ironing Out Your Mistakes

When your block has been pieced, it's time to press it to get a professional look. Wait until the patch is completed to see the optimum way to press. I like to use a steam iron set to either cotton or the synthetic setting depending on your fabric's type.

Here are some guidelines to follow for pressing your block.

1. Iron on the wrong side of the block, with all seams pressed to one side—NOT OPEN.

2. Press the seam toward the darker color. If you press in the direction of the lighter color, a dark shadow will appear on the quilt top. Sometimes the weight of a fabric will force you to press the seam in one direction, no matter how you try to press it the other way. Then let the fabric win.

3. If there are any puckers or your block seems out of alignment, use a wet press cloth to smooth it out.

Don't Get Stuck!
Even if only one of your fabrics is a cotton-polyester blend, press your block at the lower synthetic setting to prevent scorching it.

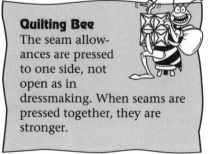

Quilting Bee
The seam allowances are pressed to one side, not open as in dressmaking. When seams are pressed together, they are stronger.

Be careful to move the iron, lifting it up and down. Sometimes pressing back and forth causes the edges of the patch to stretch. Use a light touch. Many times my students come to me with wrinkled patches and are amazed how terrific they appear after pressing. You can definitely iron out your mistakes.

The Least You Need to Know

➤ Thread your needle with quilting thread and make a single knot at the end.

➤ Pin into the dots at each end of the seam line and pin the seam line in the middle.

➤ Use the hand-piecing stitch for pieced patchwork blocks and the appliqué stitch for appliqué blocks.

➤ Sew your blocks together row by row.

➤ Don't sew down intersecting seam allowances; this way you can press them in any direction.

➤ Press seams to one side, not open.

Part 4
Choose a Pattern for Your Quilt

Time to make your first patch! You have gathered your supplies, decided on a project, chosen a color scheme, bought your fabric, and, I hope, practiced the piecing stitch on scraps of fabric.

My first quilt instructor had everyone start with the Double Nine Patch. It has two pattern pieces, both squares—the easiest shape to work with. My practice block was red, white, and blue and, when completed, was much too bright for my taste. Practice blocks are great to see how the colors react with each other. Please start with the Double Nine Patch or a block from Chapter 12, an easy pieced block, and remember, practice makes perfect.

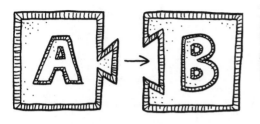

Easy Pieced Patchwork Blocks

In This Chapter

➤ Learning to identify easy blocks

➤ Strategies for piecing nine- and four-patch blocks

➤ Understanding how to make seams match

➤ Practice piecing an easy block

Pieced blocks are designed in different ways: four equal sections called a four patch, nine sections called a nine patch, five rows called a five patch, and some blocks defy rows and are sewn on an angle.

Each section of the block can be divided into smaller squares, triangles, rectangles, or even shapes that are unnameable.

*Four ways blocks
can be designed.*

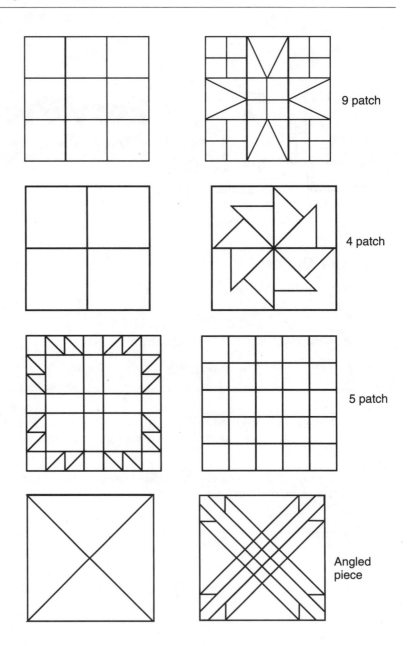

9 patch

4 patch

5 patch

Angled
piece

Double Nine Patch

The Double Nine Patch is a good start for beginners—it has only two pattern pieces and they are both squares, the easiest shape to work with since they are cut on the straight of the grain and there is little stretch. There are only 17 pieces that make up the block.

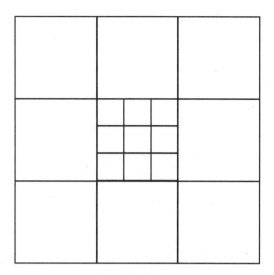

Double Nine Patch block.

Why is it called Double Nine? Look at the picture of the block. It is made up of nine four-inch squares. The middle square is divided into nine $1^1/_3$-inch squares, therefore double nine. See, it does make sense! It's easy to plan the colors. You can use two to four different fabrics. Once the squares are cut out and laid out on the table, you can flip-flop them to have the block look like a plus or a square (see the following figure).

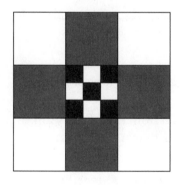

You can vary the color combination of the Double Nine Patch to create different patterns.

Let's start the step-by-step directions and make our first block.

1. Prepare the templates.

2. Decide on your color combination. Traditionally, the large squares are cut from four dark and four light fabrics. The small squares are cut from four light and five medium tones of fabric.

Don't Get Stuck! Remember, if you have hand piecing templates, add on the $^1/_4$-inch seam allowances!

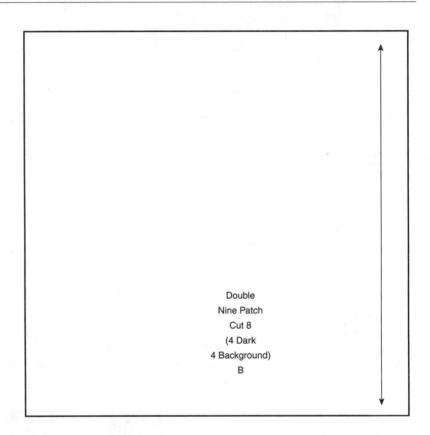

Double Nine Patch templates.

Quilting Bee

Don't rip out and resew seams that do not match exactly. This can make the fabric stretch out of shape, making the block look worse. Turn your block over, step back, and look at the errant seam. If it's not obvious, don't take your block apart. If it makes you crazy, carefully take out the stitches, shift your pins, and resew.

3. Mark around the templates on the wrong side of your fabric.

4. Cut out fabric pieces $1/4$ inch from the traced seam lines. Beginners, please use a drawn cutting line.

5. Lay out the block on the table in front of you.

6. Sew the $1\frac{1}{3}$-inch squares (template A) together in rows in order to form the center four-inch square.

7. Sew the block together starting with the top row of three squares.

8. Sew the middle row of the Double Nine Patch by sewing a B template to each side of the center square (see figure a).

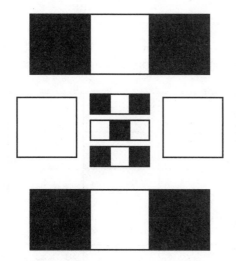

(a) Sew small pieces together to form a larger unit. Sew row by row.

9. Sew the bottom three four-inch squares.

10. Sew the rows of blocks together, stitching from the inside out, and don't sew down seam allowances (see figure b).

11. Press.

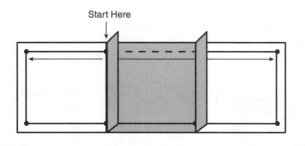

(b) Sew rows from the inside seam to the outside.

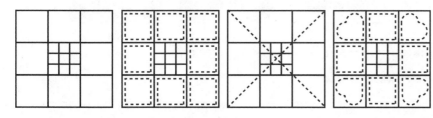

When it's time to quilt your Double Nine Patch, here are some ideas.

Remember, you should have the seams of your block match. If they are out of line, it gives your block an unprofessional or sloppy look. You are the boss of the fabric. Pin right into the dots next to the seam allowances of both pieces of fabric you are sewing together. When you pin and stitch accurately, your seams will match.

Churn Dash

The Churn Dash is a nine patch similar to the Double Nine Patch block. It is also called the Monkey Wrench or Sherman's March, depending on what part of the country you live in.

Churn Dash block.

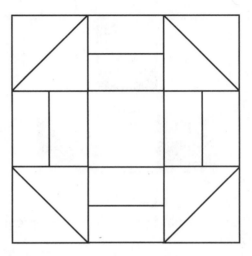

It's a simple patch—great for beginners. There are three major pattern pieces: a four-inch square, a 2×4-inch rectangle, and a large triangle—17 pieces in all. You can use either two, three, or four fabrics. The dark fabric is traditionally the inner rectangles and triangles to form a "churn dash" motif. However, once I made this patch with the dark fabrics on the outside, giving it a totally different look.

Notice how your eye is drawn in different directions when you use a variety of color values.

  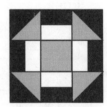

Scraps and Pieces

Legend has it that a pioneer woman who was preparing butter in her churn inspired this patch. It is said that she looked down and saw the shape of the churn blade, known as the dash, and was "stirred" to design this energetic patch.

On your mark, get set, go! Do the Churn Dash and you will win the race by following these directions.

1. Prepare the templates.

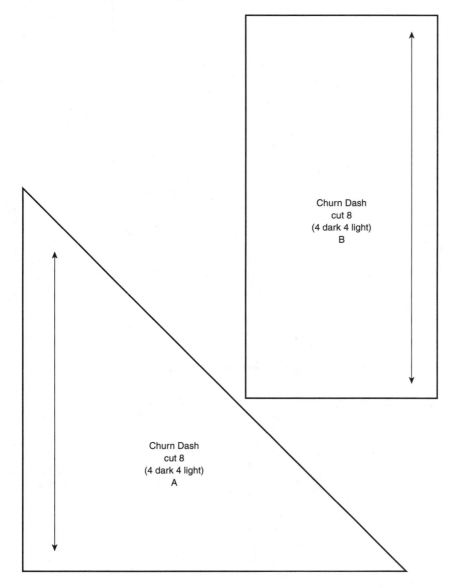

Churn Dash templates.

Churn Dash
cut 8
(4 dark 4 light)
B

Churn Dash
cut 8
(4 dark 4 light)
A

2. Decide on your colors and mark your fabric on the wrong side. Cut eight rectangles—four background and four dark; and cut eight triangles—four background and four dark. The square in the center of the block is usually cut from the background fabric.

3. Cut out the patchwork pieces, adding on seam allowances. Lay out the patches on the table in front of you.

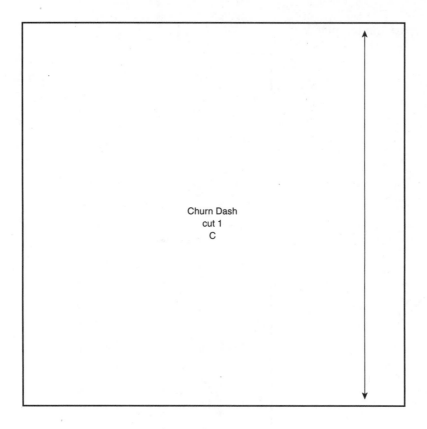

Churn Dash
cut 1
C

4. Pin and sew together the dark and background triangles (template A) to form a four-inch square (see figure a).

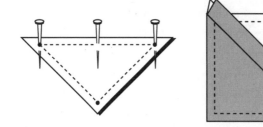

(a) Triangles sewn together to form a square.

5. Sew together the light- and dark-colored rectangles (template B) to form a four-inch square.

6. Sew together the top row, the middle row by using rectangles and template C square, and the bottom row (see figure b).

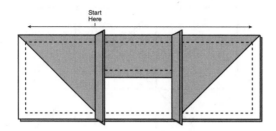

(b) Sewing direction for rows.

7. Sew the rows together starting with the middle square's dot and working across the center square to the outer dot. Then sew from the center square's dot to the end in the opposite direction.

8. Press the finished block.

When it's time to quilt the Churn Dash, here are some ideas.

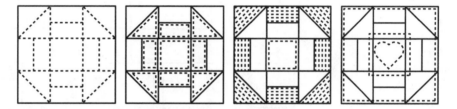

Don't forget to pin carefully, check to see if the piece fits into the block laid out in front, and then sew. Be precise and systematic. Here's to never needing your seam ripper!

Ohio Star

The Ohio Star is a nine-patch design with the star motif built around a central square. This is one of my favorite blocks. It has such a clean look and can be harmonious with either modern or traditional decor. The Ohio Star has two pattern pieces: a four-inch square and a small triangle (the four-inch square is divided into four triangles). There are 21 pieces in the Ohio Star block.

You can use the traditional two colors, giving your patch a very definitive star motif. You can also create it with three colors, making the center square a different fabric. To add another color, change the color of the four inner triangles to make the fabric total four. You can go off the wall and make hourglass shapes by altering the placement of the darkest fabric.

Quilting Bee
Because the nine-patch blocks have similar pattern pieces, you can avoid confusion by making a set of templates for each block and storing them in separate zippered baggies. That way you can find the right triangle as soon as you need it!

Ohio Star block.

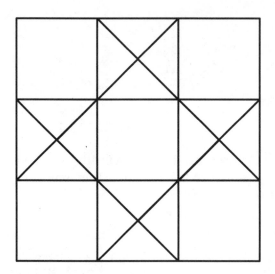

See how different placement of fabrics can change the look of the Ohio Star block.

 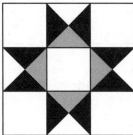 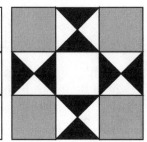

Don't Get Stuck!
Be sure to pin the seam of the small triangles and open the pieces up to check. It is so easy to pin the wrong side of the triangle or, if you've chosen several colors, to pick up the wrong color. I can't tell you how many times I've made a boo-boo.

Let's create an Ohio Star block.

1. Prepare the templates and decide on the colors (two, three, or four fabrics).

2. Mark around the outside of the templates and add the seam allowance onto the wrong side of the fabric.

3. Cut out 21 pieces and lay out the design.

4. Sew together two small triangles (template A) to form a larger triangle (see figure a).

5. Sew two sets of triangles together to form four-inch squares. Make four squares made up of the triangles (see figure b).

Ohio Star templates.

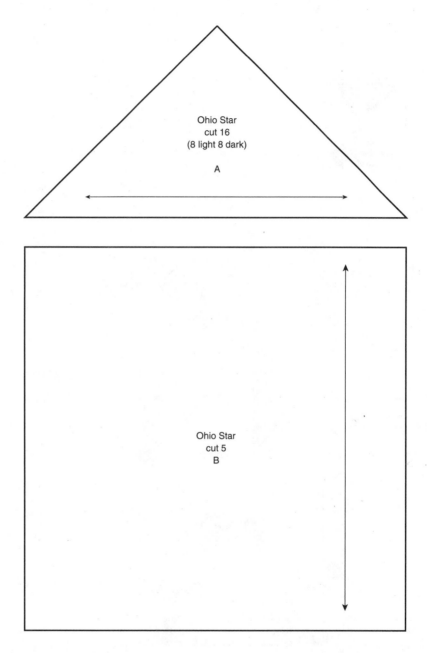

6. Sew together each row of the Ohio Star, making sure that the colors of the triangles are in the correct positions. Stitch the rows together from the inside to the outside dots (see figure c).

7. Press.

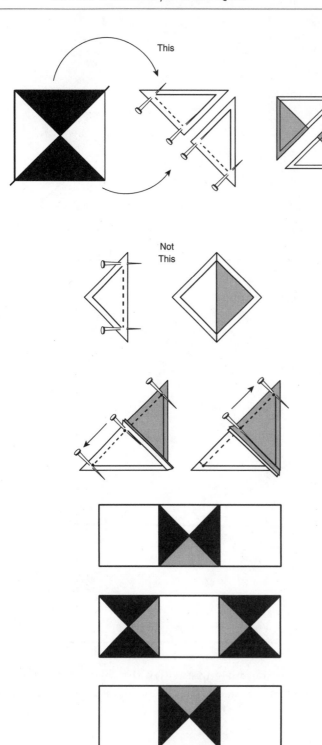

(a) Sewing the Ohio Star triangles together.

(b) Sewing seams of triangles together to form a square.

(c) Rows of the Ohio Star.

Weathervane

I first discovered this nine patch when I was making a quilt for my brother who is a meteorologist. I not only liked the look of the block but also thought the name was appropriate. The blocks are starting to get a little more intricate—this one has 37 pieces.

Weathervane block.

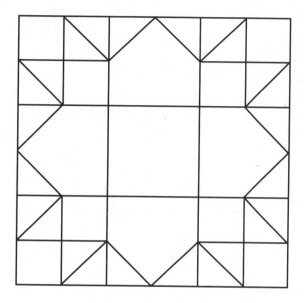

The Weathervane has four pattern templates. There is one central four-inch square, four pentagons, eight two-inch squares (four dark and four background), and 24 triangles (eight dark and 16 background).

This block can look very different if you place the emphasis color in the "arrow" position of the Weathervane or in the angled square.

Notice how different these two Weathervane blocks look.

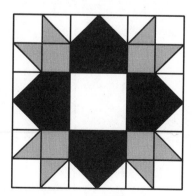

If you use the dark color as the arrows, then your eye is drawn in an X pattern. When the pentagons are a bright accent color, then an angled square is the dominant shape. Decide which is the look you like. Let's let the winds blow us to the directions.

1. Prepare the templates and decide on the colors.

2. Mark, add on the 1/4-inch seam allowances, and cut out the fabric pieces.

3. Lay out the fabric pieces in front of you.

4. Sew the dark triangles to the background triangles (template A) to form a square (see figure a).

Quilting Bee
I sometimes play with scraps of fabric to determine the color placement. Cut fabric the shape of the block's pattern and lay it over the diagram of the block. Change the colors around and decide which design is best for you. I sometimes draw the pattern with colored pencils, but using scraps is better.

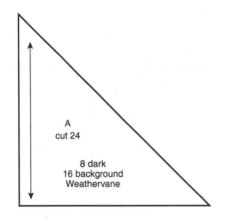

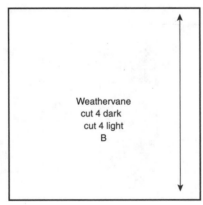

Weathervane templates.

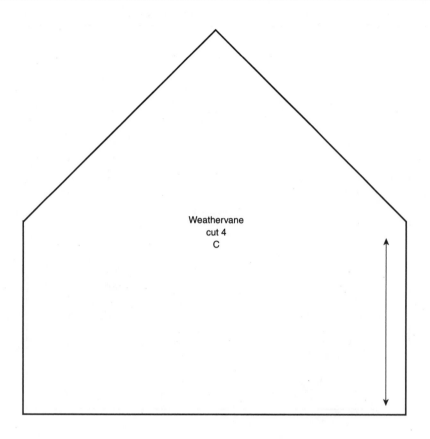

Weathervane
cut 4
C

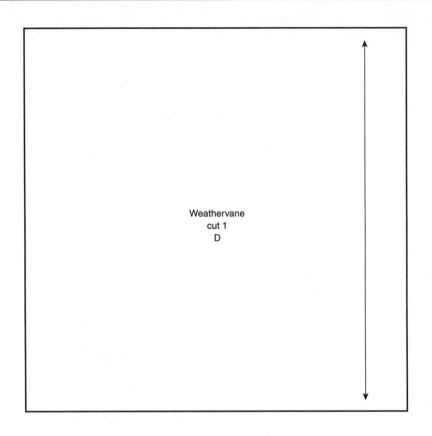

Weathervane
cut 1
D

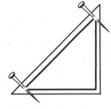

(a) Triangles sewn together.

5. Sew the small square (template B) to the square made up of the triangles. Sew these together in rows, making sure that the position is correct. It really is easy to sew the wrong pieces together (see figure b).

6. Sew the triangles (template A) to the pentagon shapes (template C) making sure to pin into the dots (see figure b).

7. Sew each horizontal row together.

8. Sew rows together from the inside seam to the outer dots (see figure c).

9. Press.

Quilting Bee
Beginners sometimes get nervous because it appears that the seams don't match and the ends of the triangles hang off the sides of the pentagons. Don't fear, only the dots have to match.

(b) Squares sewn together.

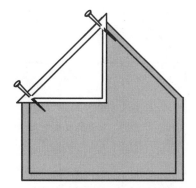
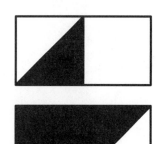

(c) Horizontal rows of the Weathervane.

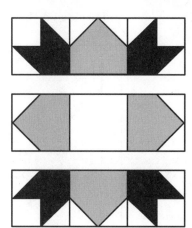

109

Dutchman's Puzzle

I don't know the history behindthe name Dutchman's Puzzle, but I like the spiral pin-wheel effect of the block. It is our first four-patch square; this block is divided into four sections. There are two pattern pieces, a large and a small triangle, and 24 pieces in all.

This block is not a puzzle—it is really fun to create.

Dutchman's Puzzle block.

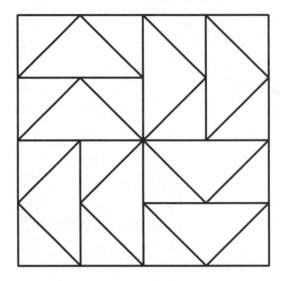

1. Prepare the templates and decide on the color combinations.

Dutchman's Puzzle templates.

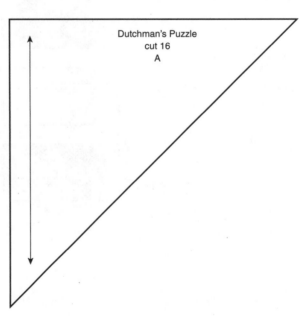

Dutchman's Puzzle
cut 16
A

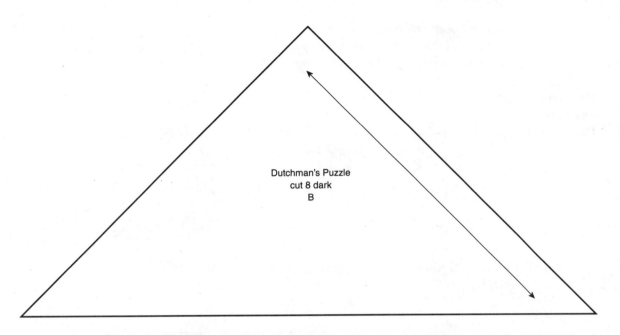

Dutchman's Puzzle
cut 8 dark
B

2. Mark the templates on the fabric, add ¹/₄-inch seam allowances, and cut out fabric pieces.

3. Lay out the pattern pieces in front of you.

4. Pin together the longest side of the small triangle (template A), to the smallest side of the large triangle (template B). Does that sound confusing? I hope not. When the three triangles are combined, they form a 6×3-inch rectangle (see figure a).

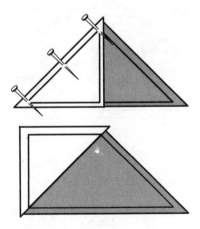

(a) Sewing triangles for Dutchman's Puzzle.

5. Put two sets of the rectangle together to form a six-inch square. Make four of these square units in the same manner. They appear different in the block because you turn each one a one-quarter turn (see figure b).

(b) Sewing rect-angles of Dutchman's Puzzle.

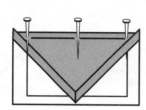
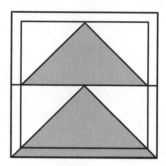

6. Put horizontal rows together, making sure they are in the correct position (see figure c).

7. Press.

(c) Sew from the inside out.

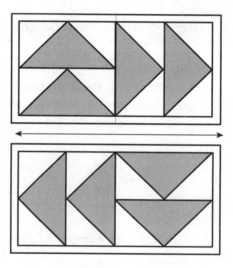

Eight Point Star

This is the first block that is not sewn together in rows!

The Eight Point Star is drafted with eight diamonds sewn together to form a star. Squares and triangles are alternately sewn around the diamonds to square out the block. There are three templates, and you need to cut out 16 pieces in total.

*Eight Point Star
block.*

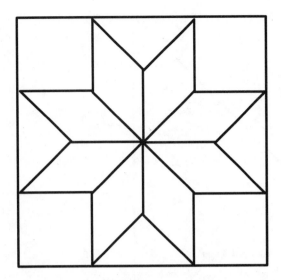

This block can be made with two coordinating fabrics and a background fabric—three altogether. Some students have used five fabrics (one fabric is used for the background, each remaining fabric makes up the star, cutting out two diamonds) to give the star a pinwheel look.

Be a stargazer and make this patch—you'll love it.

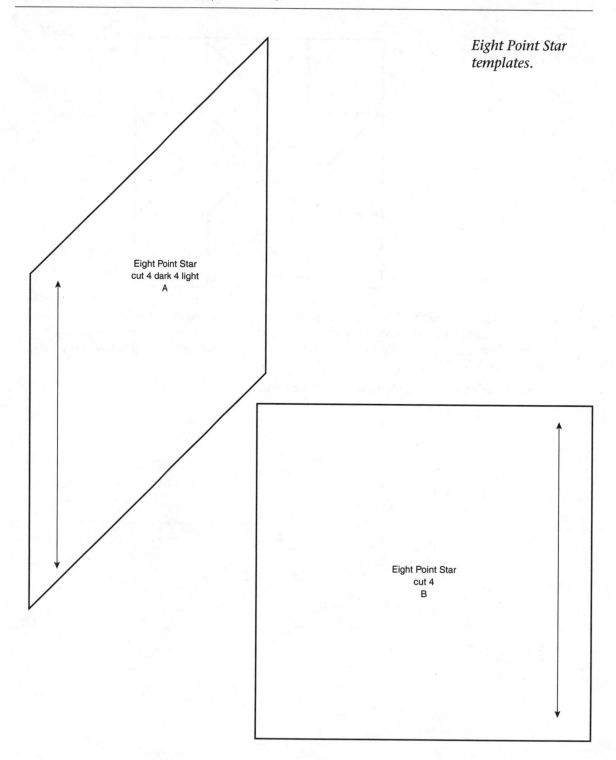

Eight Point Star templates.

Eight Point Star
cut 4 dark 4 light
A

Eight Point Star
cut 4
B

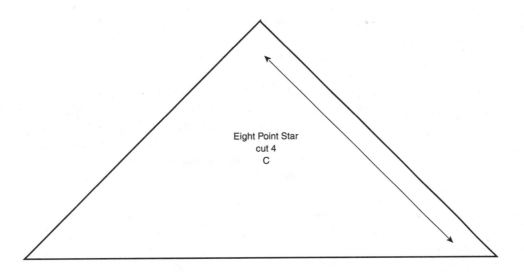

Eight Point Star
cut 4
C

1. Prepare the templates and decide on the colors.

2. Mark and cut out the fabric pieces, and lay out the block in front of you.

3. Start by picking up two diamonds (template A) next to each other. Flip over one diamond so the right sides are together. Pin into the dots of one side of the diamond (one-fourth of the diamond). Sew between these two dots.

4. I like to sew all the diamonds together to form the star. Be extremely careful to match the dots perfectly, and always replace the pinned pieces to check that you pinned it correctly (see figure a). If you pin the diamond to the wrong part of the star, you will end up with a herringbone zigzag. That's not a star.

Don't Get Stuck!
Be sure to sew only between the two dots; I can't tell you how many beginners end up sewing the entire half of the diamonds together forming a nice little pocket.

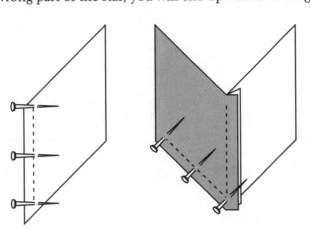

(a) Sewing the diamonds of the Eight Point Star.

Don't Get Stuck!
Be sure to alternate the squares and the triangles, otherwise your patch will be a very weird shape.

5. Alternate sewing squares (template B) and triangles (template C) around the star. While the star pieces are in front of you, flip a square over a diamond so the dots match up with the right sides together. Pin into the two dots. Stitch from the widest part of the diamond to the tip of the star. Replace the block on the table and flip the other side of the square so that it matches the diamond it is next to. Pin and sew from the widest point to the tip of the diamond (see figure b).

(b) Sewing squares and triangles of Eight Point Star.

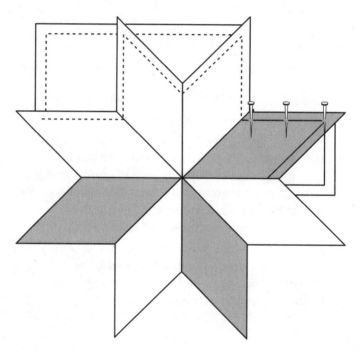

Don't Get Stuck!
Do not use a back-and-forth motion when ironing triangle patches—the triangles are bias and very stretchy. Blocks have been known to change even ¹/₂ inch in size. Use an up-and-down motion and a steam iron.

6. Press all seams of the star in one spiral direction. I like to press the seams of the squares and triangles toward the star, since it makes the star stand out as if it is stuffed. The center of the star may have a small hole, but this will usually press out. To press that mass of seams at the center of the star, put the point of the iron right into the middle and press them flat, spreading them out like petals of a flower (see figure c).

To reduce the bulk you may want to clip off some long ends of the seam allowances but be sure not to trim too close because the fabric may ravel. Turn the block over and press the right side.

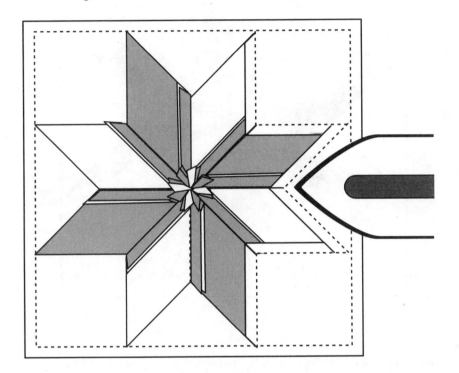

(c) Ironing the Eight Point Star.

Scraps and Pieces

The Eight Point Star block is also known as the LeMoyne Star, after the LeMoyne brothers who explored Louisiana and founded New Orleans. In the North the name was changed to the Lemon Star, probably because Northerners couldn't pronounce the name with a French accent! A variation of this block has each diamond cut in half lengthwise, making a dramatic pinwheel effect (see the following figure).

The LeMoyne Star, a variation of an Eight Point Star.

Rolling Star

If you want to take the Eight Point Star "up a notch," then you should make the Rolling Star. This block has a small central eight-point star, but instead of alternating squares and triangles, there are only squares. Remember how I said your Eight Point Star block wouldn't be squared off if you didn't alternate squares and triangles? This central part of the patch then has an octagonal shape and needs to be squared off with a background fabric to complete the 12-inch square.

There are three basic pattern pieces: a diamond, a square, and a four-sided shape that squares off the block. You will be cutting out 24 fabric pieces in all. This block always coordinates nicely into your quilt project because it combines three fabrics from your color scheme and the background. Be sure to use the darkest or brightest color in the part of the block you want to emphasize, either the diamond or the star or the squares.

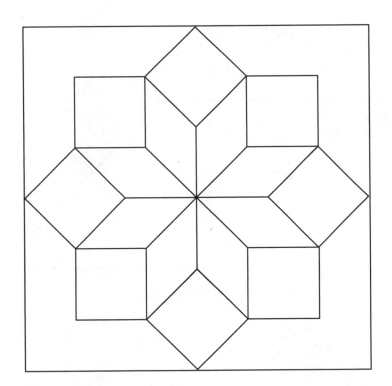

Rolling Star block.

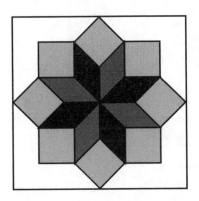
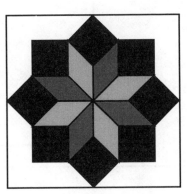

Notice how the placement of the dark color changes the appearance of the block.

If you like the Eight Point Star, go one step further. Check out the instructions and pictures for the Rolling Star. Then let's get rolling on the Rolling Star.

1. Make the templates and decide on the color combinations.

Rolling Star templates.

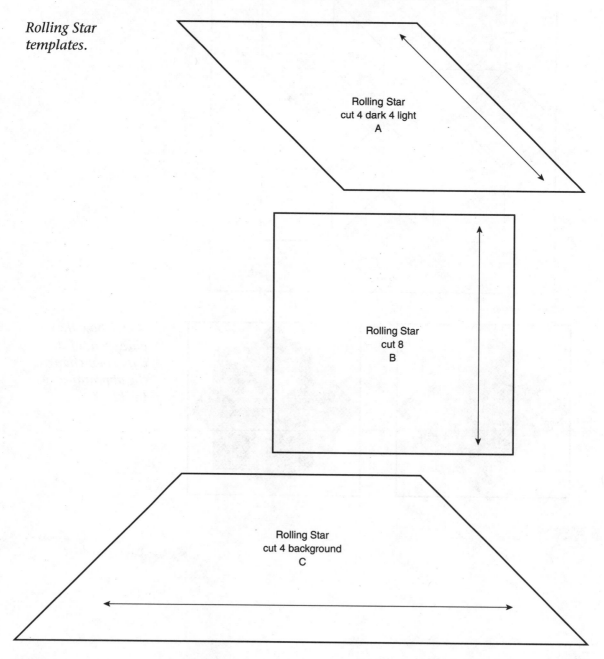

Rolling Star
cut 4 dark 4 light
A

Rolling Star
cut 8
B

Rolling Star
cut 4 background
C

2. Mark, adding on seam allowances, then cut out the fabric pieces and lay out the block in front of you.

3. Start by picking up two adjacent diamonds (template A). Flip over one diamond so their right sides are together, and pin the dots. Sew from dot to dot only (see figure a).

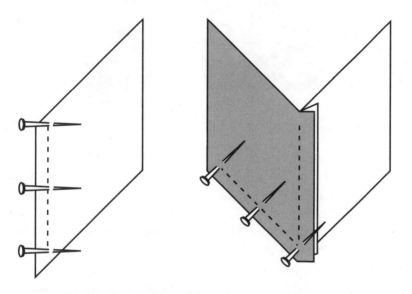

(a) Rolling Star diamonds.

4. Sew all the diamonds together making sure to pick up the correct color diamond and pin it in the right position.

5. Sew the squares (template B) into the diamonds. Turn the square over the diamond with the right sides together. Match the dots. Sew from the widest part of the diamond out to the tip of the star. Sew in all eight squares (see figure b).

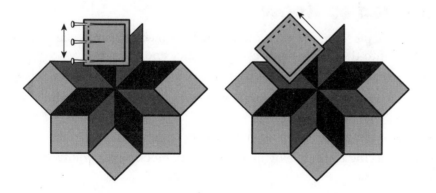

(b) Put squares all around the Rolling Star.

6. Now for those weird-shaped trapezoids. Flip template C so that the "top" of the shape matches one side of the square (see figure c). Pin and sew only between dots. There will be unsewn ends at each side. Don't worry, we'll sew them next.

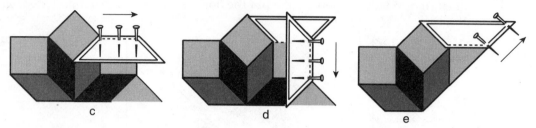

Sewing the background for the Rolling Star.

7. Fold the square in half onto itself, and pin one end of the background to the adjacent square. Sew from the inside dot to the outside of the block (see figure d).

8. Pin and stitch the center of another rectangle to the next square. Now we have to attach the two ends of the background that are hanging loose. Fold the square in half at an angle so that the background ends meet. Pin the dots and sew from the inside to the outer part of the block (see figure e).

9. Sew in all the background pieces.

10. Press the inner star in the same way you would press the Eight Point Star. Iron the star and square seam allowances toward the background pieces to reduce bulk.

I hope you have prepared several blocks from this chapter to give you a good background of hand piecing. The next chapter covers blocks that are more challenging. Are you ready?

The Least You Need to Know

➤ Lay the cut-out fabric pieces in front of you and pin two pieces together; be sure to lay the pieces back into the design to check for accuracy and then sew.

➤ Sew small pieces together to form a larger unit.

➤ Pieces of a block are sewn together horizontally in rows or sewn into units that are pieced on the diagonal.

➤ Be sure rows are sewn from the inside seam line to the outer edge.

➤ Perfect your hand-piecing technique by making an easy block before you tackle a more complicated pattern.

Chapter 13

Challenging Pieced Patchwork Blocks

In This Chapter

➤ Learn what makes a block challenging

➤ Special cutting techniques for mirror-image pieces

➤ How to sew curved seams

➤ How to handle challenging blocks

This chapter covers patchwork blocks that will make you think. You will fine-tune your piecing ability, learn how to mark and cut strange shapes, and sew many, many, little pieces together. Each of these blocks has an unusual peculiarity to it.

Challenging blocks make you think and work hard, and you will love them. But you need to know how to avoid pitfalls, or overcome them. Beware of the number of pattern pieces and templates that have special peculiarities. Blocks with curves are always a threat to beginners. Let's take up the challenge and defy these blocks by knowing what to expect and how to avoid problems.

What Makes a Block Difficult?

There are some blocks you can just look at and know they will be hard to piece. If the pieces are small, you can be sure you will need many of them to fill up your 12-inch square. I feel that more than 40 pieces make a block a challenge—it is more time-consuming to mark, cut, and sew that many pieces, let alone keep track of them all. The Virginia Star has 40 pattern pieces while the Churn Dash has 17 pieces. That's a big difference. But what visual diversity the Virginia Star has!

A block can be obstinate because there are so many seams to match up. Five-patch blocks require you to align 25 seams! Look at the Bear's Paw block in this chapter—when you start sewing the rows together you will appreciate quilts that are a four-patch—like the Dutchman's Puzzle or a nine-patch like the Ohio Star. Patchwork blocks that have many pieces or seams are only time-consuming, not troublesome.

Pieces such as squares, rectangles, equilateral triangles, and diamonds are easy pieces to cut and sew. However, there are some shapes that will cause problems. Any asymmetrical shape could give you a headache if it is cut incorrectly. My class once made appliquéd Santa wall hangings. All of the pieces were nonreversible. One student traced and cut out all her templates backwards. We ended up with 12 Santa wall hangings facing left and one nonconformist Santa wall hanging facing right. The student was lucky—she made all her templates wrong, but at least she was consistent, because they all fit together. Non-reversible pieces are asymmetrical in shape and care must be taken to prepare the template correctly.

Look what happens if one piece is cut wrong! No matter how you move it, it doesn't fit!

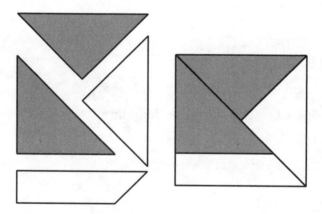

Many times I have cut the outer trapezoid of the Pinwheel block in the wrong direction and all the other pieces in the right direction. In one case, the saving grace was that the piece was muslin, which meant the wrong side was the same color as the right, so it did fit in. There was the pencil marking line showing on the right side! With nonreversible pattern pieces, be sure your patterns are marked and cut out accurately. Backward pieces will not fit into your block. If a template says "This side up," believe it.

Quilting Bee
To cut in the *mirror-image* method, first trace around your template the normal way. Then flip it so that the sandpaper side is facing up, not down toward the fabric. Trace around the template for the remaining pieces.

Mirror Images

Several patchwork blocks have pieces that are called *mirror images*. That means there are left and right sides to the patch. If you look at the 54-40 or Fight block, you will notice a mirror-image template. The long, narrow triangle is asymmetrical, and if you cut the pieces all the same way, half the blocks will not fit. The template will specify if the pieces have to be cut in a mirror-image way (cut four regular and four mirror image, totaling eight fabric pieces from one template).

Slow Down on Curves

The last and probably the most difficult piecing problem is sewing curves. We're used to flipping over our fabric pieces so that right sides are together. When that is done with curves, it looks like there is no way they will match. Take it step by step and it will be easy. When marking curved templates, be sure to make a small mark in the middle of both rounded edges of the seam line. It will be indicated on the template.

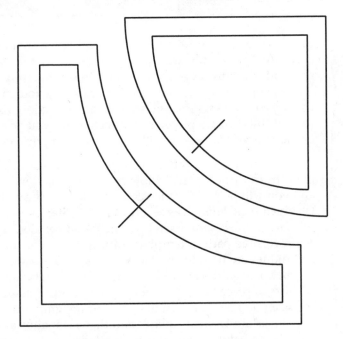

Make a small mark in the middle of the seam line on both pieces.

I start by flipping the pieces right side together. Don't panic. Then pin the curved seams right into that center mark on the seam line. Move the top fabric piece so the dots at one end match up. Pin. Shift the top fabric to match the dots at the other end of the seam line.

How do those pieces fit? Pin the centers and shift the top fabric to pin the ends.

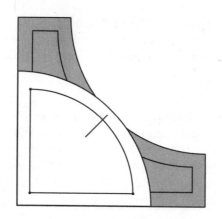 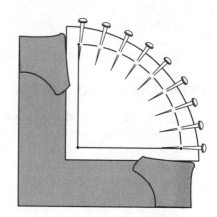

Quilt Talk
A *clip* is a small cut that you make in the seam allowance. A clip or two in a seam allowance enables you to open the seam up and press it flat. Be sure not to clip too far or you will cut into the seam and make a hole.

Don't Get Stuck!
All quilters should mark the templates clearly with their letters, because pieces can look very similar. With the Bear's Paw, make sure you use template B for the corners, template C for the end of the cross, and template F for the center of the block.

I like to use about nine pins in the seam line to hold the curve into place. Start with a backstitch into the dot at one end and stitch using your hand-piecing stitch, removing pins as you sew up to them. Ease the fabric as you go so there are no tucks. Press the seam in one direction, usually toward the concave piece, and in most cases you do not even have to *clip* the seam allowance to void puckers.

We've learned about pitfalls you may encounter with the patterns in this chapter. Follow the directions step by step and you will be making blocks by the dozen. The Bear's Paw, Clay's Choice, Flying Geese, and Virginia Star blocks all have many pieces for assembly. The Pinwheel block has a nonreversible pattern template. Mirror-image cutting techniques are used in the Mexican Star and 54-40 or Fight patches. Lastly, the Drunkard's Path (I love that name) consists of pieced curves. The templates in this chapter are the size you need for each design—but remember that all the blocks are 12-inch squares and that seam allowances must be added on when you are marking.

Bear's Paw

This block looks like a bear's four footprints, even with toe nails. There are 53 separate pieces in this patch and six templates. It is a five-patch, which means there are many intersecting seam allowances that must be matched. It is a real challenge. Take it slow and row by row.

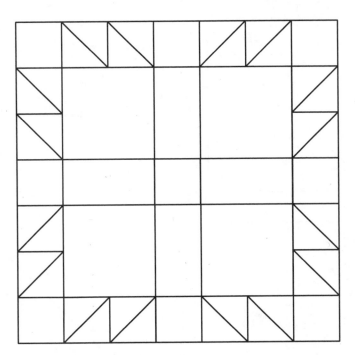

Bear's Paw block. Can you see the four paw prints?

Scraps and Pieces

The Bear's Paw is four dark footprints on a light background, but the name is changed if the colors are shifted. It is called Duck's Foot in the Mud when the colors are reversed, with a light-colored fabric on a dark background. Can't you see the pioneer women being inspired and naming this block? Quakers in Philadelphia did not name this block after animals as the quilters in the wilderness did, but called it the Hands of Friendship.

Bear's Paw templates. Remember to add seam allowances!

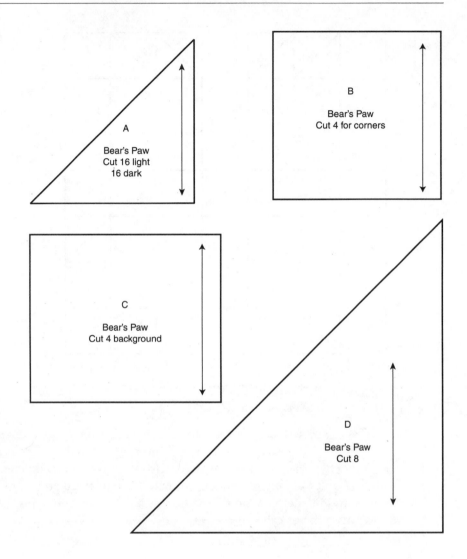

A
Bear's Paw
Cut 16 light
16 dark

B
Bear's Paw
Cut 4 for corners

C
Bear's Paw
Cut 4 background

D
Bear's Paw
Cut 8

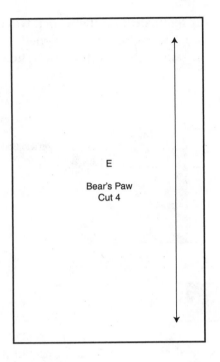

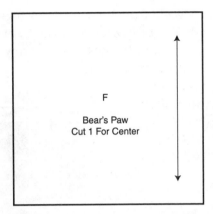

1. Make the templates and decide on the color scheme.

2. Mark and cut out the fabrics, adding on seam allowances.

3. Lay out all the fabric pieces in front of you.

4. Pin the longest side of the triangles (template A) and sew them together. Piece a dark triangle to a background fabric triangle so that it forms a square (see figure a).

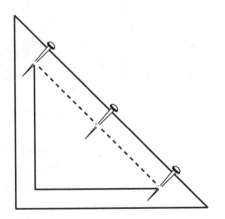

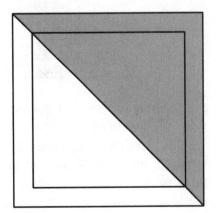

(a) Sew triangles together.

5. Piece the top horizontal row together, using template B for the corner, two combined A triangles, template C, two combined A triangles, and the corner template B (see figure b). Make another row exactly the same for the bottom row. These form the toe nails.

(b) Three rows of Bear's Paw. Just like fitting puzzle pieces together!

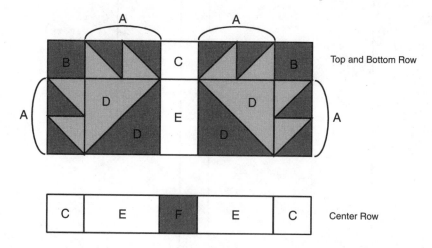

6. Pin and stitch the next row. This row is several pieces thick and forms a unit that combines two triangle A units of the nails, two combined large triangles (template D), rectangle E, then another set of D templates, and the small triangle A nails (see figure b). Make two of this row.

Sewing the rows of the Bear's Paw block.

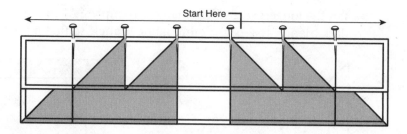

7. Sew together the center row. Piece together rectangle C and rectangle E to center square F, then to piece E, and end with rectangle C.

8. We now have pieced five rows! Wow! Pin and stitch the rows together one at a time, sewing from the inside out. Pin each dot where the seam lines intersect.

9. Press. With so many seam allowances, try to press the rows from the outside to the inside pieces where the pieces are larger.

Clay's Choice

This block was Clay's Choice, and I hope it will be yours. It is a four-patch, with triangles and squares that form 16 squares. These squares are joined into four six-inch-square units.

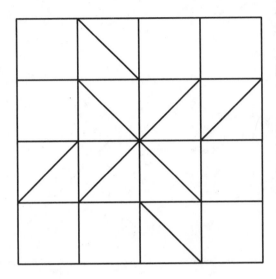

Clay's Choice—a politically inspired block!

There are only two templates, triangle A and square B, but the color placement can make it appear as if there are diamonds. Plan out where you want your colors, because changing the dark color placement will make the patch appear extremely different.

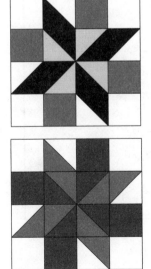

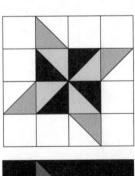

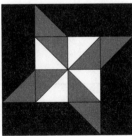

Look how different Clay's Choice can appear by rearranging colors.

I like the spiraling pinwheel effect this block has; so try out different color schemes.

Clay's Choice templates—only two!

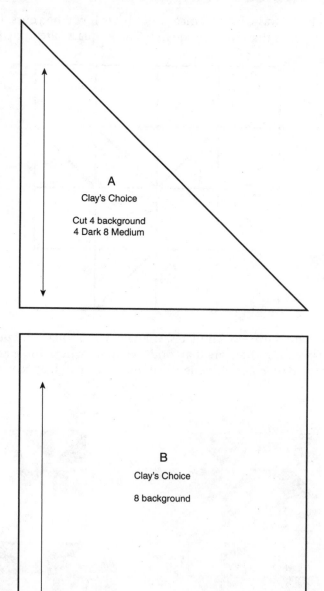

A

Clay's Choice

Cut 4 background
4 Dark 8 Medium

B

Clay's Choice

8 background

1. Make the templates and choose the color combination.
2. Mark and cut out the fabric. Then lay the design out in front of where you are working.

3. Pin and sew two A triangles together to form a square. Be sure to pick up the correct color triangle—it is so easy to sew these incorrectly. Pin and check by fitting them into your laid-out pieces.

4. Make the left top unit by sewing the triangles into squares (see figure a).

5. Stitch two units into the top row, then two units into the bottom row.

6. Sew the rows together (see figure b). Don't forget to sew from the inside of the center seam to the outside.

7. Press.

Quilting Bee
When sewing two rectangular units of triangle pieces together, flip a unit so that the point of the triangle you are going to seam is on top. Hold up that middle seam allowance and put a pin in the dots in each side of it. Sew from the inside out. This will make the point line up perfectly.

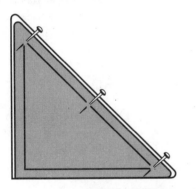

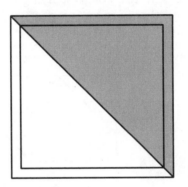

(a) Sew triangles into units.

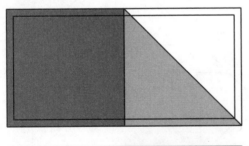

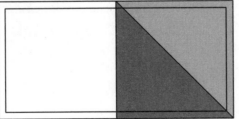

(b) Sew squares into units.

Scraps and Pieces

I'm sure you are asking the question, "Who was Clay and what was his choice?" My husband, the history major, gave me the scoop. Henry Clay was a popular statesman from Kentucky, who actually ran for and lost the presidency three times from 1824 to 1844. He was instrumental in drafting the treaty after the War of 1812 and in attempting to avert the Civil War. His "choice" was probably trying to negotiate between the North and the South. Politics were inspirations for quilters.

Flying Geese

Doesn't this block look like lines of geese flying south? This is a four-patch that has four six-inch units sewn together in rows. It is deceiving because the center appears to be a square, but is really four triangles. There are 52 pieces, and all three templates are triangles.

Flying Geese block. The V shapes mimic wedges of geese flying south in the fall or back home in springtime.

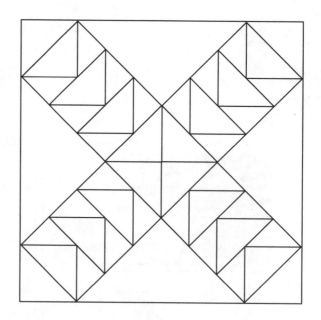

Let's find out how we get all of the geese into a line. Here are the directions.

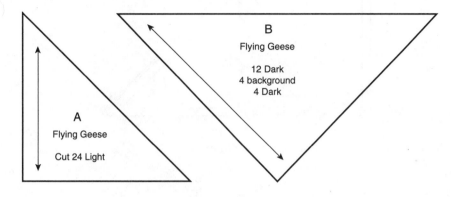

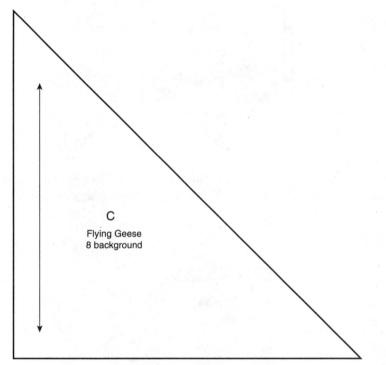

Flying Geese templates. Make templates carefully to keep the geese on their flight path!

1. Prepare the templates and choose the fabric colors.
2. Mark and cut out the fabrics, adding on seam allowances.
3. Lay out the cut-out pieces in front of you.
4. Pin two small A triangles to each side of a medium triangle B. Place the long side of template A to the short sides of template B and stitch to form a rectangular unit (see figure a).

135

(a) Sew two A triangles to triangle B.

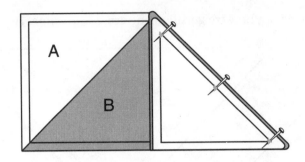

5. Sew three of these rectangular units together (see figure b).

(b) Putting the rectangles together, look at the pins on each side of the middle seam, holding up the seam allowances.

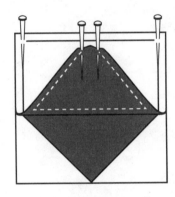

6. Sew a medium triangle (template B) to each end of the "line of geese," and a large triangle (template C) to each side of the line, forming a six-inch square (see figure c).

(c) Putting six-inch squares together.

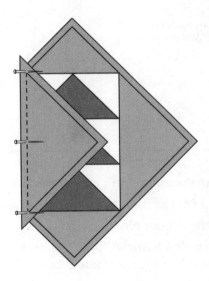

7. Pin and stitch the top two six-inch units together, then the bottom two to make two rows (see figure d).

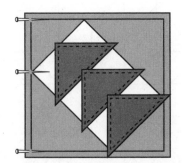

(d) Rows of Flying Geese—they're on their way!

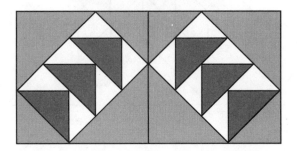

8. Pin and sew these two rows together, starting at the center seam line and stitching to the outside.

9. Press the seam allowances toward the larger piece.

Virginia Star

Now for another version of the Eight Point Star. When you look at the block, notice that each diamond is divided into four smaller diamonds.

There are three templates: a small diamond (template A), a square (template B), and a triangle (template C). In all there are 40 pieces. Once the diamonds are assembled, review the construction of the Eight Point Star in Chapter 12, "Easy Pieced Patchwork Blocks." This patch is also known as the Eastern Star or Blazing Star, but I like the name Virginia Star. I love the way you can select colors that make this block blaze. If you like this block, then you are ready for the largest variation—the Lone Star—but instead of 40 pieces, it may have a thousand! Lone Star quilts are pictured in the color photo section and can range from wall hanging to king-size quilt.

Virginia Star block. The colors can make it look like a sunburst.

Virginia star templates.

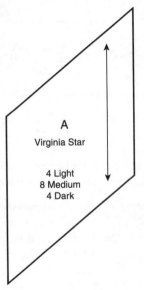

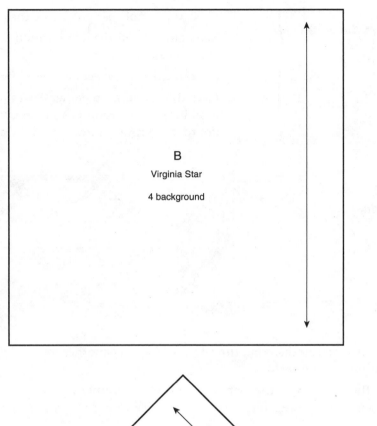

B

Virginia Star

4 background

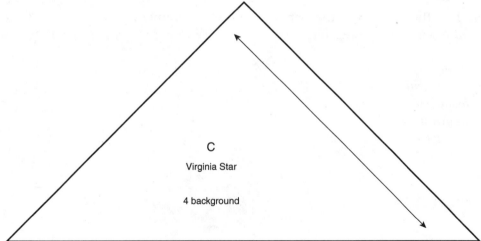

C

Virginia Star

4 background

Don't Get Stuck!
Make sure you pin into the dots. Don't worry that the seam allowances do not match at the end, it's the dots that count.

1. Make the templates and choose the colors.
2. Mark and cut out the fabrics, adding on seam allowances.
3. Lay out the fabric pieces in front of you.
4. Piece the diamonds together. First flip the tip diamond one to the center diamond two. Pin and sew dot to dot forming a row (see figure a).

(a) Sewing the small diamonds together into a large diamond unit.

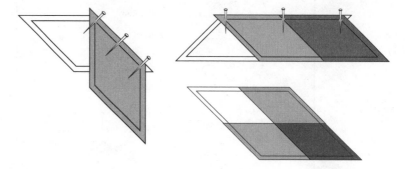

5. Flip, pin, and sew diamond three to four forming another row (diamonds two and three are the same color).
6. Turn the right side of the diamond right sides together with the left side. I know this sounds confusing, but look at figure b. Sew from the inside seam to the outside.

(b) Press seams in one direction. It will be easier to quilt if the seam allowances are pressed consistently.

7. Sew all diamond units together like the Eight Point Star. Pin two diamonds, right sides together, matching seams of smaller diamonds (see figure c).

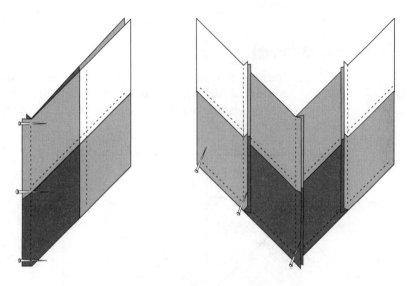

(c) Sewing diamond units together in an Eight Point Star.

8. Sew the square template B around the star alternately with the triangle template C (see figure d).

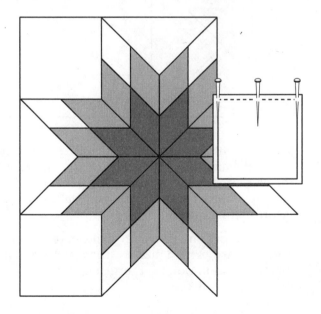

(d) Sewing squares and triangles onto the Virginia Star.

Pinwheel block. These spinning blocks are great for a child's quilt.

9. Press the background seam allowances of the squares and triangles toward the diamonds. Now step back and you can gaze at your star.

Pinwheel

Don't get your head "spinning." This is a great patch but be careful—it's the first block with a *nonreversible template*. If you put a line down the center of the shape, each side of the line is different.

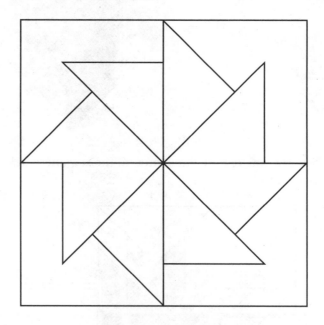

Some students have traced the templates and by mistake drawn the template upside down. When they try to piece the block, they are baffled that the pieces don't fit. I like to cut one of the tricky templates and make sure that it fits before cutting the rest.

This patch has only 16 pieces so it can be assembled quickly. There are two pattern pieces: a triangle A and the nonreversible trapezoid B. Don't get turned upside down—follow the directions for success.

1. Prepare the templates and choose the colors.

2. Mark and cut out your fabrics, adding on seam allowances.

3. Lay out the pieces in front of you, making certain that the trapezoid pieces fit.
4. Sew the colored triangle A to the trapezoid B, matching the dots. Then pin and stitch (see figure a).

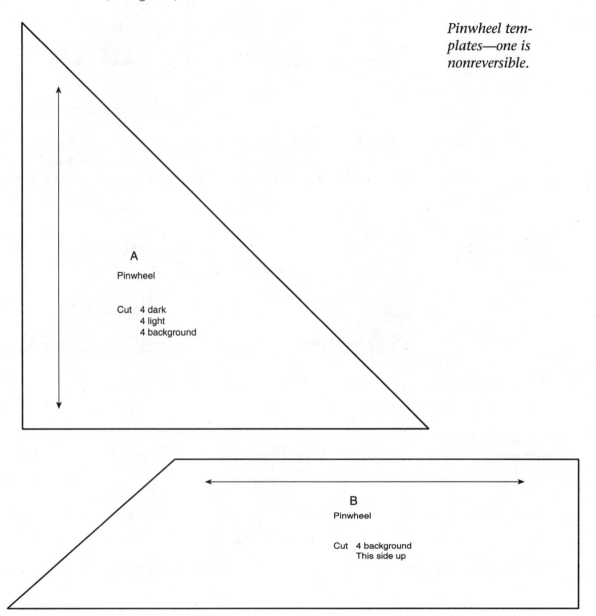

Pinwheel templates—one is nonreversible.

A

Pinwheel

Cut 4 dark
4 light
4 background

B
Pinwheel

Cut 4 background
This side up

(a) Sewing a triangle to a trapezoid (templates A and B).

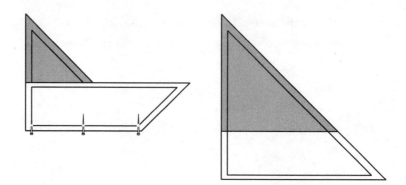

5. Sew a colored triangle A to a background piece A. Match the short sides together, pin into the dots, then fit the pieces into the laid-out pieces on the table. Check that the colored triangle is in the correct place, otherwise your pinwheel won't spin (see figure b).

(b) These triangles (template A) make up the rest of the Pinwheel block.

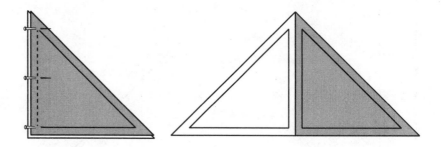

6. Sew these two pieced triangles (from steps a and b) together to form a six-inch square (see figure c).

(c) Making six-inch squares of the Pinwheel.

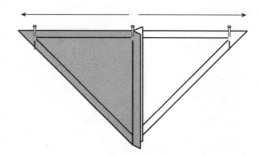

7. Sew top two six-inch squares together, then the bottom two squares to form rows (see figure d).

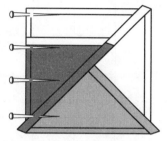

(d) Sew rows together to create the Pinwheel.

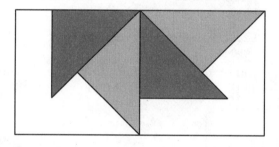

8. Pin the top row to the bottom row matching the center seam. Sew from the center seam to the outside.

9. Press.

54-40 or Fight

I know you are wondering, so I will tell you—this block was named after a political slogan popular during the 1830s and 1840s. It was a rallying call to support the United States in a border dispute with England over the Oregon territory. Obviously the United States won, since Oregon and Washington are both states.

When you examine this block, it is really only a nine-patch, which means there are nine four-inch squares assembled in rows of three.

It is a simple block to piece once the four-inch square units are assembled. The problem comes when marking your fabric. This is the first block that has *mirror-image cutting*, necessary when a block has a fabric piece that needs to be duplicated in a reverse fashion.

Quilt Talk
In *mirror-image cutting*, the template is used to mark a pattern piece, then turned over with the sandpaper side up, and then traced again.

145

54-40 or Fight block, a politically correct block.

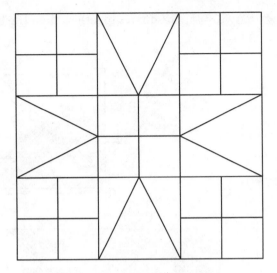

Look at triangular template A. If you try to fold it in half vertically, each side is different, and if you cut out the templates all the same way, half of them will not fit.

54-40 or Fight templates—one is a mirror-image template.

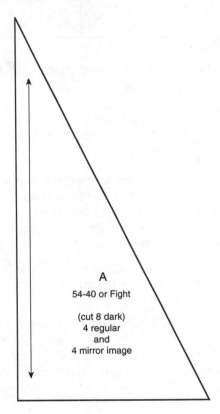

A
54-40 or Fight

(cut 8 dark)
4 regular
and
4 mirror image

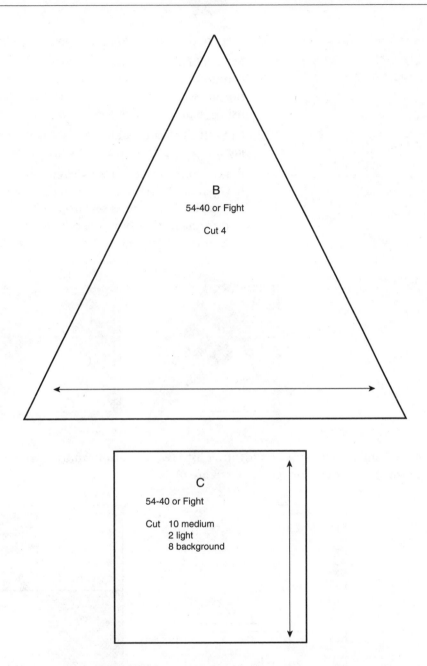

The templates usually indicate if any pieces need to be cut in a mirror image. But not all patterns do, so analyze your block for any abnormal-shaped templates.

This block has three templates, with 32 pieces in all. You can use three or four different colored fabrics. Let's start a rally of our own, but don't fight with this block—it is truly fun to do.

Don't Get Stuck!
When you trace around a template while the sandpaper side is up, it may slide around, making your markings inaccurate. Be careful to hold the template in place, draw the dots first, and then connect them.

1. Prepare the templates and choose the fabrics.

2. Mark all fabrics, adding on seam allowances. Make certain to cut template A with four pieces cut the normal way and four cut with the sandpaper side up using the mirror-image method.

3. Cut out the fabric, adding on seam allowances, and lay out the patch in front of you.

4. Pin the longest side of triangle A to one side of triangle B. Open up the pinned pieces to make sure the correct side is pinned and then sew from dot to dot. Sew the mirror-image piece onto the opposite side of triangle B. This forms a four-inch square (see figure a).

(a) Pin and sew star points for 54-40 or Fight.

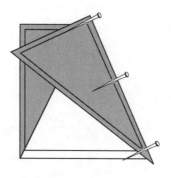
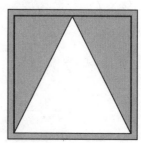

5. Pin and stitch four C squares together into two rows to form the corner and center four-inch squares of the block (see figure b).

(b) Sew the squares together.

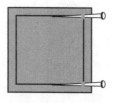
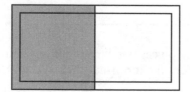
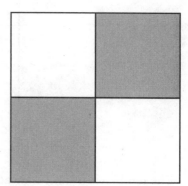

6. Sew the top three four-inch square units together to form a horizontal row. Then repeat for the middle and bottom rows. There should be three rows of three squares (see figure c).

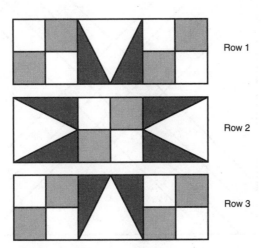

Row 1

Row 2

Row 3

(c) Rows of 54-40 or Fight.

7. Pin and sew the rows together starting from one of the center seams to the outside, insuring that the seams align (see figure d).

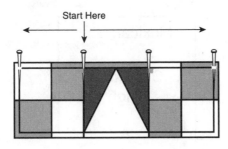

Start Here

(d) Top and middle row sewn together.

8. Press and give a cheer.

Mexican Star

I really like the Mexican Star, but it can be troublesome for beginners. This block has templates that need to be marked and cut in mirror images. Besides that, it also seemingly defies the piecing by rows that we are used to. Instead, the block is pieced on the diagonal.

Mexican Star block—pieced on the diagonal.

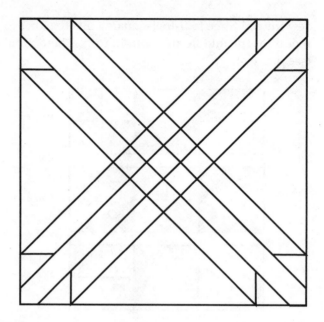

There are five templates ranging from the simple square and triangle to crazy shapes like trapezoids and pentagons. Beware of the trapezoid B, it has to be cut in the mirror-image method.

Mexican Star templates.

Mexican Star

Cut 5 dark
4 light

A

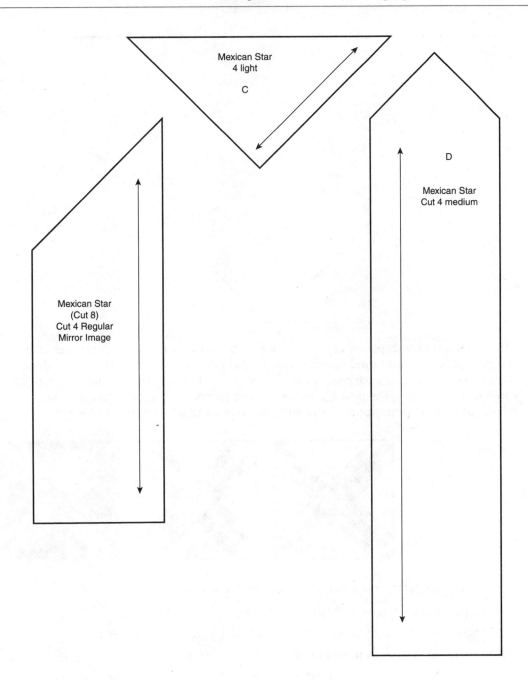

Mexican Star
4 light

C

D

Mexican Star
Cut 4 medium

Mexican Star
(Cut 8)
Cut 4 Regular
Mirror Image

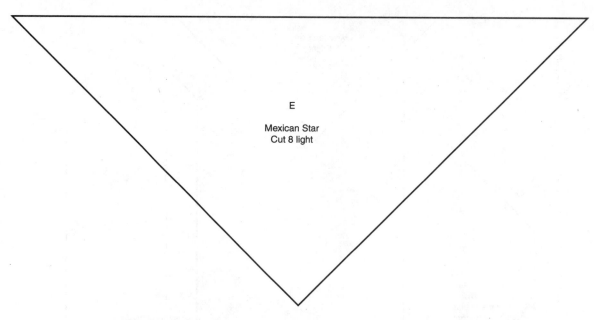

E

Mexican Star
Cut 8 light

This block gives the appearance of an X superimposed over the star. The center of the star is a nine-patch made of nine squares creating a checkerboard effect. The strong diagonal lines make this patch a nice contrast to the other star blocks. See how different this patch can look by changing the position of the darkest colors. A Mexican Star quilt takes on a whole different appearance with diagonal lines crossing through the whole quilt.

Mexican Star color variations.

So let's turn our patch on its side and learn how to angle our piecing.

1. Prepare the templates and choose the colors.
2. Mark and cut out the pieces, adding on $^1/_4$-inch seam allowances.
3. Lay out the pieces in front of you.
4. Piece template A squares together in rows to form the central nine-patch checkerboard (see figure a).

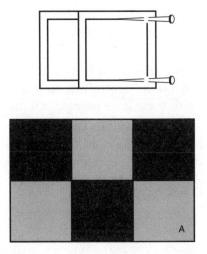

(a) Sewing the rows together.

5. Pin small triangle C to the end of trapezoid B. Pin and sew the mirror image of the template to another triangle. Make four of these sets of pointed shapes (see figure b).

(b) Sew triangles to trapezoids.

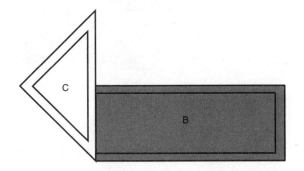

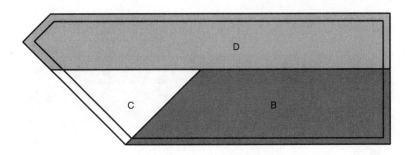

Don't Get Stuck!
When blocks need to be pieced on an angle, don't get confused with the way the unit looks. We are piecing the corners, not rows of the block. Everything is slightly askew and pieced on the diagonal.

6. Pin and sew these units to each side of the pentagon D forming a point (see figure b). Make four corner units.

7. Pin two large E triangles to the sides of the above corner unit forming one large triangle. Make only two of these large triangular units (see figure c).

8. Pin and sew the remaining two point corner units to each side of the center checkerboard forming a row with a point at each end (see figure d).

(c) Add triangles to make corner triangles.

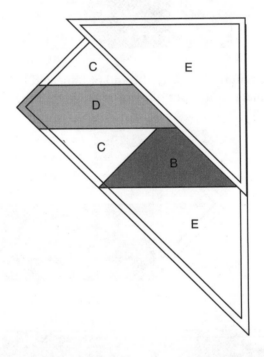

(d) Center row.

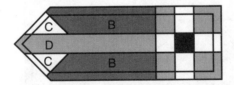
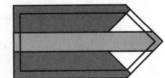

9. Pin carefully and sew the three sections together. Be sure to pin so that the seams of the center nine-patch square match with the point's seams. It's a matter of pinning accurately and sewing the center nine-patch square first. Then sew to the outside edges (see figure e).

10. Press.

(e) Three rows to sew together—the Mexican Star is formed!

Drunkard's Path

This block is not for beginners! Stitching curves is probably the most challenging of piecework. But I know that you have been marking, cutting, and piecing blocks as you read through this book. If you are comfortable with hand piecing, maybe now is the time to break away from the straight and narrow.

Drunkard's Path block—impossible to walk a straight line.

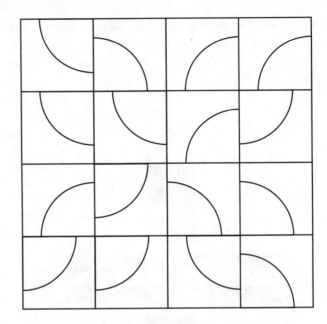

The Drunkard's Path is a very versatile patch. It is created from two templates, an L-shaped template A and an arced wedge B.

Drunkard's Path templates.

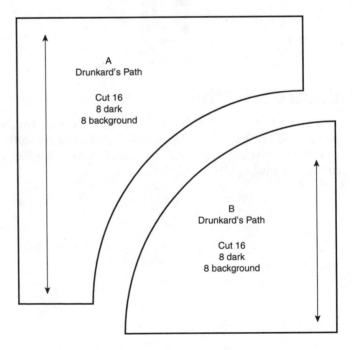

A
Drunkard's Path

Cut 16
8 dark
8 background

B
Drunkard's Path

Cut 16
8 dark
8 background

These two templates fit together to form a three-inch square. Four of these square units are put together into four rows, making it a four patch. It is really amazing how many variations these templates can create. There are books written just about the Drunkard's Path and its mutations. Pictured are two of my favorite variations, Baby Bunting and Fool's Puzzle.

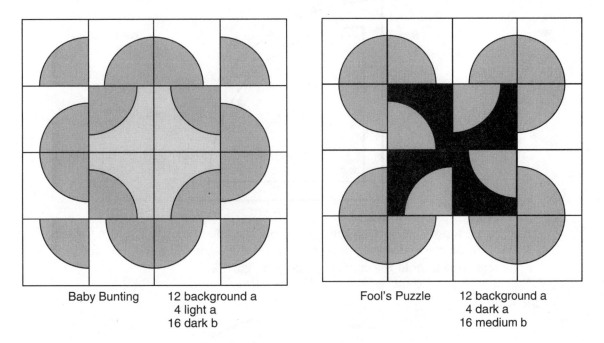

| Baby Bunting | 12 background a
4 light a
16 dark b | Fool's Puzzle | 12 background a
4 dark a
16 medium b |

Baby Bunting and Fool's Puzzle variations.

Fabric choices are usually limited to two colors for the Drunkard's Path, and possibly three fabrics for the Baby Bunting and Fool's Puzzle. Let's read the directions carefully, I don't want this block to drive you to drink.

1. Make the templates and choose your fabrics.
2. Mark templates onto the fabric, marking the center of each seam line with a dot. Add on the 1/4-inch seam allowances and cut out.
3. Place the L-shaped piece A and the wedge-shaped piece B right sides together. Match the center dots and pin (see figure a). It doesn't look like it will fit, but don't worry.

(a) Match the center dots.

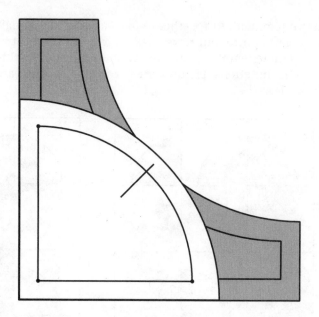

4. Move the top wedge, forcing the end dot on one side to match. Pin into the dot. Readjust the pieces until the dots at the other end align and pin. I put nine pins into the seam line to hold the curve in place (see figure b).

(b) Pin the seam line.

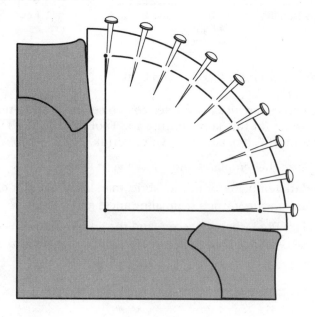

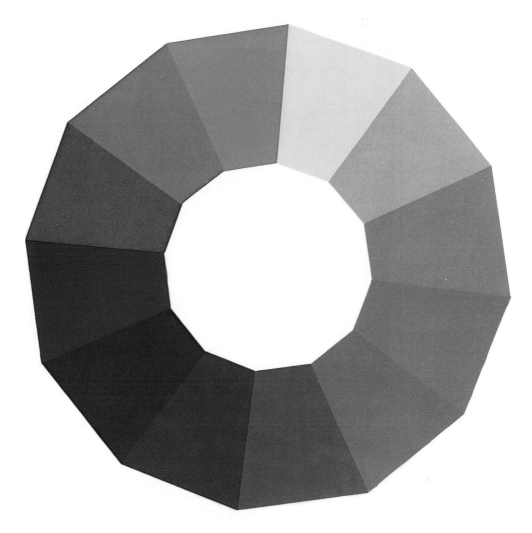

Color wheel.

This traditional Amish Square design wall hanging was made by Laura Ehrlich. The fabrics exemplify the solid, bright colors and black accents of the Amish quilts.

Look at the intricate quilting designs in the Amish Square close-up.

A quilt doesn't have to be square! This Lone Star octagonal wall hanging, made by Laura Ehrlich, uses three sleeves attached to the back of the quilt to invisibly hang the quilt.

Look at the detail of this 72" × 72" quilt. It is a Virginia Star, taken to the extreme!

Detail of a Log Cabin quilt purchased in Lancaster, PA. This quilt owned by Nita Munson has the Log Cabin blocks positioned in the Barn Raising design.

Another Log Cabin variation is the Christmas Tree Log Cabin wall hanging made by Laura Ehrlich.

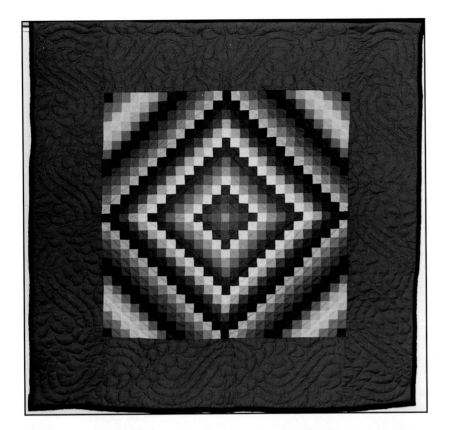

Here's an Amish Trip Around the World wall hanging (30" × 30") in vibrant jewel-tone colors, owned by Nita Munson.

Compare the muted tones of this queen-size Trip Around the World quilt made my Edith Bihler.

The rounded edges adds a softness to the Double Wedding Ring lap quilt (36" × 48") made by Laura Ehrlich.

The white background spaces traditionally are filled with a quilted motif, as in this detail of a Double Wedding Ring quilt.

Here's a Sampler Medallion quilt assembled by the New Milford Quilters and quilted by Eileen Esposito. See if you can find the Ohio Star, two styles of Dresden Plate, Hearts All Around, Mexican Star, Pinwheel, and Virginia Star blocks.

The pieced and appliquéd center medallion is a Carolina Lily block.

The first quilt (75" × 103") made by the author using only Dresden Plate, Churn Dash, Eight Point Star, and Ohio Star blocks. Each block is repeated using different color placement and framed with muslin lattices.

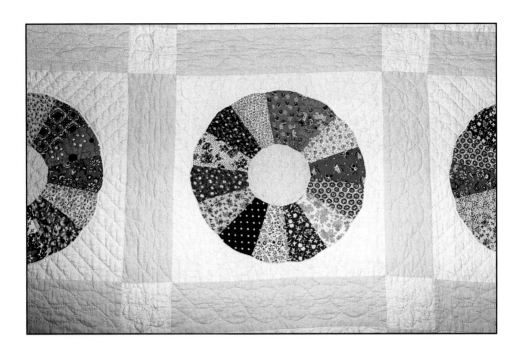

Detail of antique quilts owned by Nita Munson. The Dresden Plate and Basket quilts, circa 1930s, are made from feed-sack fabrics.

With the Variable Star quilt, Pearl Roth used up many of her scraps of peach and green fabrics. Because of the scraps of fabrics in the blocks, a swirling peach lattice frames each star. Look at the close-up picture and notice the range of scale in the size of the fabric pieces.

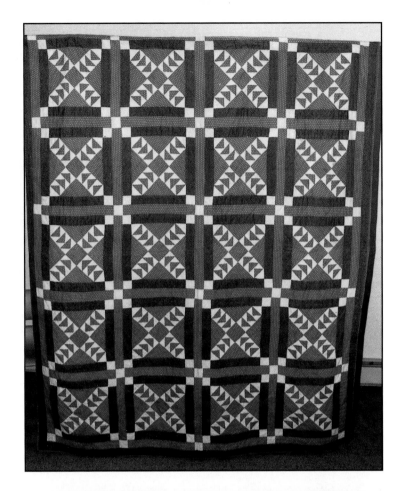

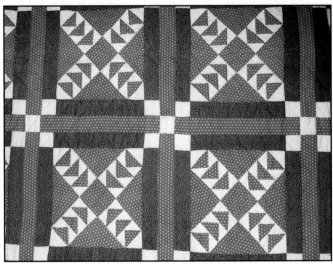

This Flying Geese quilt is owned by Nita Munson. Notice how the three strip lattices and checkerboard corner blocks make diagonal lines.

The Hearts All Around wall hanging is made by Yvonne Gaudier in memory of her husband. Most of the fabric has been cut from his favorite shirts.

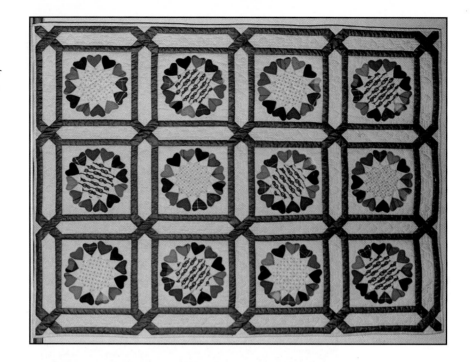

Note the intricate latticework.

This is the appliqué Storybook quilt made by the New Milford Quilters for the children's room of the town library. See if you can find Madeline, Charlotte's Web, Little Toot, Curious George, and Winnie the Pooh. Just enlarge a picture from a children's book and use as a pattern for a Storybook quilt like this.

Labels can be creative—this one is an open book!

This Christmas quilt won the People's Choice Award of the Brownstone Quilters Quilt Show, 1997. It was made by Lucille Riccio and was inspired by a design in the Great American Quilt Book 1992.

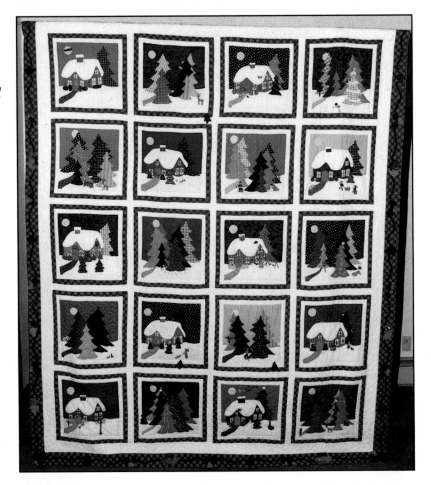

Lucille may have started with a pattern, but she has embellished this quilt with her own whimsical embroidering.

This patriotic Lone Star wall hanging used tab loops to give it a banner-like appearance.

This full-size Sampler quilt (80" × 104") made by Laura Ehrlich, consists of many beginner and challenging blocks found in this book. Find the Rolling Star, Log Cabin, two variations of Drunkard's Path, Clay's Choice, Pinwheel, Weathervane, Ohio Star, Flying Geese, Virginia Star, Rail Fence, and Eight Point Star.

5. Start sewing about $\frac{1}{8}$ inch away from the dot on one side, first stitching a backstitch into the dot. Using the hand-piecing stitch, sew on the seam line, removing pins as you sew. Be careful to ease the fabric so there are no folds in the seam (see figure c). Make all 16 square units.

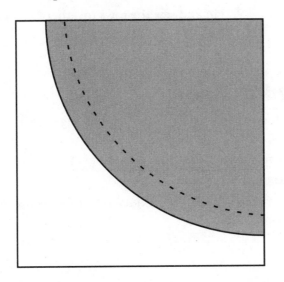

(c) Curve sewn and pressed toward the concave curve.

6. Press the curved seam allowances of the wedge toward the L-shaped square (see figure d).

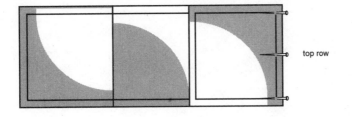

top row

(d) Rows of Drunkard's Path.

Quilting Bee
Some people like to start sewing in the middle of a curved seam where the dot is, and stitch to the end of the seam.

7. Lay out all the squares on a table to form the pattern of the block.

8. Sew all squares in the top horizontal row together then sew each of the other remaining three rows.

9. Pin and sew the rows together to make the block.

10. Press.

The Least You Need to Know

➤ Asymmetrical-shaped templates need extra care in marking since they are non-reversible.

➤ Some patches have mirror-image pieces that are similar but exactly reversed.

➤ Some blocks are pieced on the diagonal.

➤ Curved piecework is difficult—match up the dots, pin, and sew the seam line to prevent tucks and folds.

Chapter 14

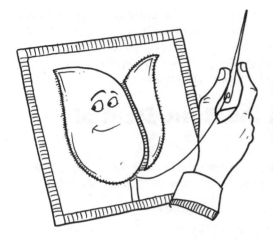

Combination Pieced and Appliqué Blocks

In This Chapter

➤ Understanding combined pieced and appliquéd blocks

➤ Steps for applying fabric motifs to your blocks

➤ Learning to make some of the most popular combination appliqué and pieced patterns

In this chapter we are easing into appliqué with blocks that start with piecing the pattern, and finish with some appliqué. You'll learn tricks and tips for handling appliqué and get directions for tackling some of the most popular combined pieced and appliqué patterns. I'll show you the traditional steps to prepare appliqué pieces and also easier ways to finish the design's fabric edges. You'll also learn when these tips are appropriate to use.

Appli-What?

Appliqué is a French term that means to apply or lay on. In appliqué quilting, small pieces of fabric or a pieced unit are cut into a specific design that is then stitched by hand or machine onto a background fabric. Appliquéd quilts can be either graceful and sophisticated or cute and folksy. The patterns can range from elegant flowers to stylized designs of animals, birds, houses, or almost anything else. There are several different methods of tackling appliqué. You can appliqué individual motifs (the teardrop shape in the Honey Bee), pieced units (the plate of the Dresden Plate), or use the totally different method called *reverse appliqué*, where small amounts of a fabric show through your patchwork.

Quilt Talk
In *reverse appliqué*, you layer one or more fabrics under your block and cut designs away from the top of the block to show the bottom color. The fabric is then held in place by the appliqué stitch.

The range of shapes you can make is almost limitless. You are using your fabric as paint and your quilt is a painting. Heart designs have appeared in almost every period of quilt designs. Some of the best crib quilts are appliqué designs borrowed from children's coloring books.

Let's Learn the Basic Steps of Appliqué

There are several steps involved in making an appliqué block. You may want to skip some of these steps, but please don't.

1. Cut out the fabric pieces, mark, and sew together if necessary.

2. Sew a line of *stay stitching*, a small basting stitch, on the sewing line using a contrasting color.

3. Pin under the raw edges and for beginners, baste these outer seam allowances down. This will prevent the edges from raveling.

4. Press using an up-and-down motion. Because fabric is so pliable, be sure not to use a side-to-side motion because it might stretch your motif out of shape.

5. Pin your appliqué piece into position.

6. Baste your appliqué piece onto your background fabric.

7. It's time to use the appliqué stitch discussed in Chapter 9. Try to invisibly stitch your motif securely into place.

8. Take out all basting stitches so that the beauty of your block will show.

9. Press.

Quilt Talk
Stay stitching is a line of small basting stitches that hold the fabric in its proper shape and make it easier to turn the raw edges under. Be sure to use a contrasting color thread so it is easy to see and remove later.

Beginners sometimes avoid appliqué because they think it is difficult. Don't let yourself be scared off. We have already learned the appliqué stitch in Chapter 11, "Do Be a Sew and Sew." Now you can start practicing it. Two of the basic beginner patches are the Dresden Plate and Grandmother's Fan. All of the blocks in this chapter have a great deal of patchwork piecing. Then the pieced unit is appliquéd onto a background (Dresden Plate and Grandmother's Fan) or the background is pieced with shapes appliquéd on top (like the Honey Bee or Peony Patch). Choose one of the patterns to hone your skills and let's begin.

Dresden Plate

The Dresden Plate is one of the most popular appliqué blocks. It is believed that this patch was named for a china plate made from a Dresden, Germany, factory. This patch became popular in the l850s. You can almost see a pioneer woman, needing a quilt pattern, take one of her dishes, trace around it, and then cut it into wedges. Instant quilt templates!

Dresden Plate with 15 wedges. Does this look like your china?

The Dresden Plate can be made in many different sizes and styles. I've seen as few as 12 wedges and as many as 20. The patches can be 10 inches to 24 inches in size. The colors can range from two, so that the plate looks like spokes of a wheel, all the way up to 20, with each wedge in a different fabric. Wedges can be rounded or pointed. If you have more than one type of Dresden Plate in your template collection, be sure to keep them separate. You don't want to confuse them and try to fit a 20-wedge plate for a 24-inch square onto a 12-inch block.

Our pattern for the Dresden Plate is 12 inches square and the plate has 15 wedges of either three or five different fabrics. There are two templates: a wedge A and center circle B.

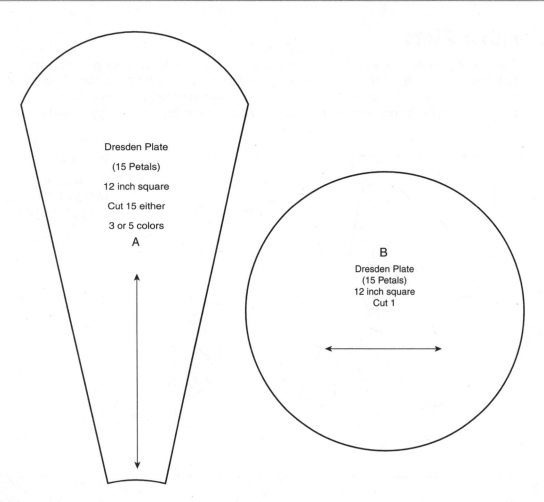

Dresden Plate
(15 Petals)
12 inch square
Cut 15 either
3 or 5 colors
A

B
Dresden Plate
(15 Petals)
12 inch square
Cut 1

Dresden Plate templates. Cut your fabric carefully.

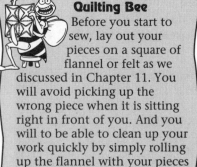

Quilting Bee

Before you start to sew, lay out your pieces on a square of flannel or felt as we discussed in Chapter 11. You will avoid picking up the wrong piece when it is sitting right in front of you. And you will to be able to clean up your work quickly by simply rolling up the flannel with your pieces safely clinging to it.

1. Prepare your templates made out of poster board and sandpaper as discussed in Chapter 9.

2. Cut a generous $12\frac{1}{2}$-inch square out of your background fabric.

3. Mark and cut the wedges, adding on the seam allowances. If you are using three fabrics, cut five of each fabric; if you are using five fabrics, cut three of each one.

4. Lay the plate out on the table in front of you. Decide on the correct placement of your fabrics. There should be a set sequence in the progression of

fabrics; for example, a yellow, green, and blue wedge, then repeating yellow, green, and blue wedges in the same order all around the plate.

5. Pick up two wedges that are next to each other and put their right sides together. Pin into the dots you marked at each end. Put the pins right into the dots perpendicular to the seam line (see figure a).

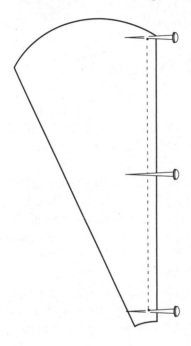

(a) Pinning the wedges together.

6. Sew from dot to dot, backstitching at each end. Do not sew the right-hand turn that goes through the seam allowance. This is one of the few times when the seams are pressed open.

7. Put the wedges back down onto your plate pattern and pick up the next wedge, pin, and sew. It is so easy to pick up the wrong wedge or pin it on the wrong side.

8. Sew the wedges all around, like spokes of a wheel, to form the plate.

9. Press the seams open. You should press these seams open because the square background fabric adds stability (see figure b).

Don't Get Stuck!
Remember, before you sew your Dresden Plate, check that you pinned correctly. Put the wedges back into the plate to make sure. If the color pattern is not correct, repin the wedge.

(b) Press the seams open and baste on the outer seam line.

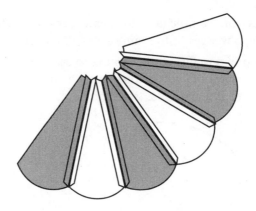

10. With a contrasting thread, baste along the outside rounded seam line. Your basting will show where to turn the raw edges under. Turn the edges under to prevent raveling, then baste.

Don't Get Stuck!
Be sure to use a contrasting thread when basting. It will be easy to see when you have to take the basting stitch out. There is nothing worse than ripping out your appliqué stitch by mistake!

Quilting Bee
Try to take away any points on your rounded edge by pushing them in with your needle as you sew.

11. Center the plate on the background block. You can easily find the middle by folding the block diagonally in both directions and finger pressing. If you hold or pinch the fabric, it will temporarily press it and an X should appear at the center of the open part of the plate.

12. Baste with a large stitch through the middle of each wedge up to within an inch of the outer edge. This will hold the plate securely in place to the background.

13. Now it's time to appliqué. Use lots of pins to hold down the rounded outer edge. I usually use at least five pins for each wedge. Turn under the seam allowance of one wedge and pin under each end where the dots are. Be sure to turn under right on the basting line. Then pin the center of the wedge at the top of the arc, and put one or two more pins on each side. Pin only two wedges at a time (see figure c).

14. Appliqué around the entire block. Refer to Chapter 11 to review the appliqué stitch.

15. Cut the center circle B. Be sure to add the seam allowances. The center circle can be any of the colors of the plate or the background fabric.

16. Baste on the sewing line with a contrasting color thread, then turn the seam under and baste again. Pin into position, and baste the circle onto the plate so it will not move. Appliqué around the center.

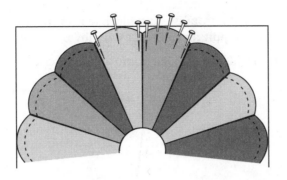

(c) Pin your plate to the background.

17. Remove all the basting threads.
18. Press.

The Dresden Plate is a wonderful block that uses both piecing and appliqué techniques. Many antique Dresden Plate quilts use the wedge shape pieces side by side around the border, giving the appearance of cones surrounding the quilt, hence the name Ice Cream border. Can you imagine piecing hundreds of the wedges for a border? When you see the scalloped-edge results, you will appreciate the workmanship even more.

Grandmother's Fan

The Grandmother's Fan is an easy appliqué pattern that has six wedges positioned in the corner of a 12-inch block. The fan was very popular during the Victorian era when it was made with velvets, satins, and brocade fabrics. It was decorated with lace and elegant embroidery. It can also be successfully made with pastel fabrics for a crib quilt.

Quilting Bee
Grandmother's Fan is a great pattern for using up all your scraps, because it is made with a variety of colors and fabrics.

Grandmother's Fan block. Do you have a fan like this in your attic?

I've even created a fan quilt using red, turquoise, and black fabrics that made a very Oriental-looking Grandmother's Fan quilt for my niece who loves Far Eastern cultures.

There are two pattern pieces in this block: a wedge A and a quarter circle for the corner piece, template B.

Grandmother's Fan templates.

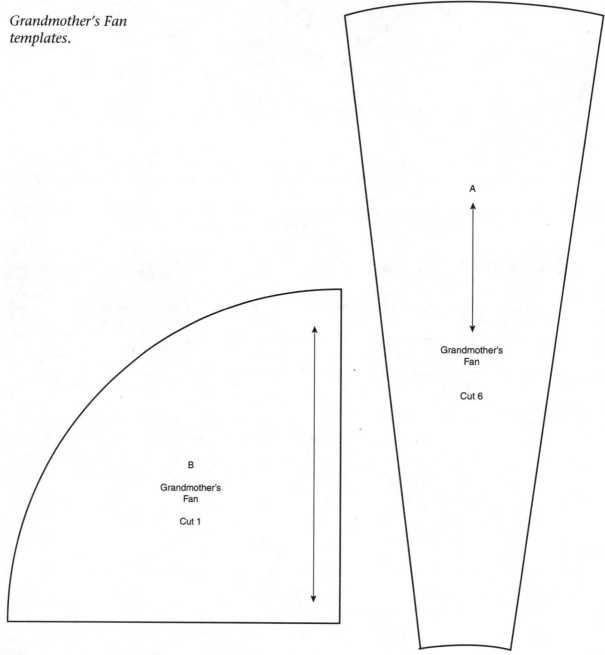

A

Grandmother's
Fan

Cut 6

B

Grandmother's
Fan

Cut 1

Following are step-by-step directions.

1. Prepare the templates.
2. Cut a generous 12^1/$_2$-inch square out of your background fabric.
3. Mark and cut out six A wedges from your fabrics and one corner piece, adding on the seam allowances.
4. Lay out wedges in a pleasing progression of colors.
5. Sew together the pieces of the fan.
6. Press the seams open; the background fabric will add stability.
7. Turn the ^{1}/$_4$-inch seam allowance under on the wide part of the fan. Baste with a contrasting color thread, turning under the seam allowance as you sew (see figure a). This will prevent fraying edges.

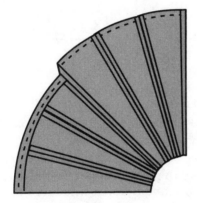

(a) Press the seams open.

8. If you want to put lace or piping on your Grandmother's Fan, this is the time. Baste the lace or piping to the edge as you baste the seam allowances under.
9. Pin the fan into the corner of the square and baste down the center of each wedge.
10. Appliqué the fan onto the background.
11. Now for the corner piece template B: Turn the ^{1}/$_4$-inch seam allowance of the curved edge under and baste it down. Pin it in the corner and appliqué it to the fan.
12. Press.

If you are making a quilt out of only Grandmother's Fans, there are many interesting ways to arrange the blocks. You can attach the blocks with or without lattices.

Look how different a quilt would look just by rearranging your Grandmother's Fans.

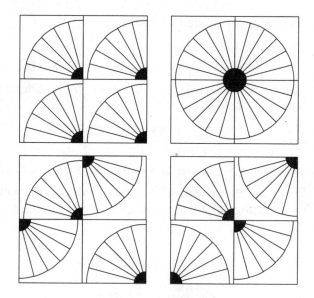

Honey Bee Patch

The Honey Bee block is a nine patch within a nine patch with bee bodies and bee wings appliquéd on top. It is different from the previous appliqué blocks because the base of the patch has to be completely pieced before you appliqué the teardrop bee pieces.

There is a checkerboard in the center of the pieced patch with the outer square forming the head of the bees. This patch has four pattern pieces and can be made with either two, three, or four different fabrics. I once had a beginner student who loved this pattern and made a whole quilt with 30 Honey Bee blocks. The first few blocks were fun, but by number 30, she dreaded those bee wings. We figured there were 30 blocks and 12 teardrops on each block, so that added up to 360 teardrops appliquéd onto her patches!

Honey Bee block: Look at the four "bees."

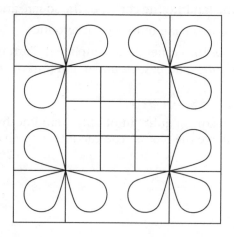

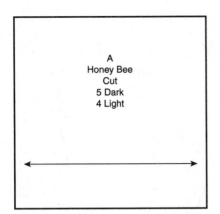

A
Honey Bee
Cut
5 Dark
4 Light

*Honey Bee
templates.*

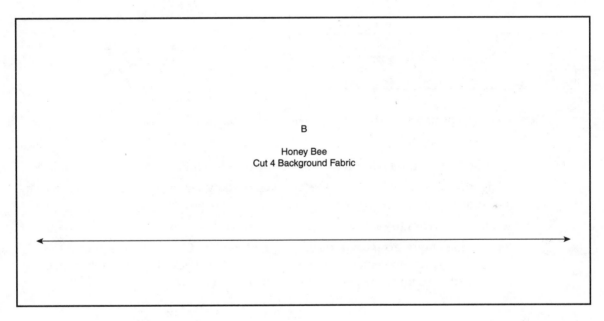

B

Honey Bee
Cut 4 Background Fabric

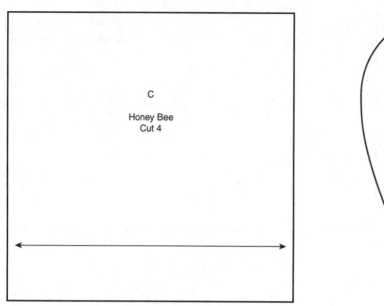

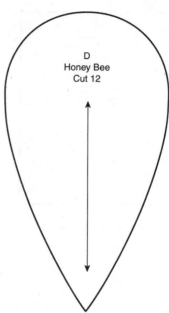

Here are the steps to follow for making a Honey Bee block.

1. Make the templates.

2. Mark and cut out the pattern pieces, adding on seam allowances.

3. Using piece A, assemble the middle checkerboard by sewing squares together row by row as discussed in Chapter 11.

4. Sew the rectangles to each side of the checkerboard.

5. Sew the top and bottom rows together using template C, (two large squares) to template B. Then sew rectangle B to each side of the checkerboard center. Sew three rows together to form the pieced base of the block (see figure a).

(a) Sew rows of Honey Bee together.

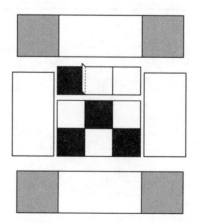

6. Sew the rows together forming the 12-inch square base. Pin into the dots at each end of the row and pin at each intersecting seam.

7. Now it's time to sew on the bees. Baste on the seam line of the teardrops to make a line of stay stitching. First turn under the tip of the teardrop, then turn under the raw edges on your basting line and baste this seam down.

8. Position bee pieces. Pin and appliqué.

9. Press.

Quilting Bee
Remember to start sewing the middle sections of a row first, and then sew out to the ends of the patch. We want to make sure that the seams that form the corners match. Always sew from one of the middle seams to the outside edge.

Look at how different the Honey Bee can appear by varying the positions of the colors.

Peony Patch

What does this block remind you of? If you study the Peony block you will notice that it is very similar to the Eight Point Star discussed in Chapter 12. We even use the same diamond, triangle, and square templates.

Peony patch. This was probably created in the spring when the pioneer women grew these beautiful flowers..

The background of this block is pieced, then the stem and leaves are appliquéd on top. Let's get started.

1. Make the templates.

2. Cut a $12^1/_2$-by-$3^1/_2$-inch rectangle of background fabric.

3. Mark and cut out the fabric pieces, adding on the $^1/_4$-inch seam allowances, and lay out the block in front of you.

Don't Get Stuck!
Remember to always sew from the inside of the patch to the outer seam allowance. We want to make sure the squares and triangles will lay flat and all the dots line up.

4. Start by picking up two diamonds and sewing them from dot to dot with the right sides together. Sew all six diamonds together to form the petals (see figure a).

5. Sew on the triangles and squares in the correct positions. Be sure to sew from the widest part of the diamond to the tip of the points.

6. Sew the background rectangle onto the bottom of the block.

7. Prepare the appliqué stem and leaves. Baste along the seam allowances. Turn the tip of the leaves down then baste all around, turning under the raw edges. Use a contrasting color thread to baste (see figure b).

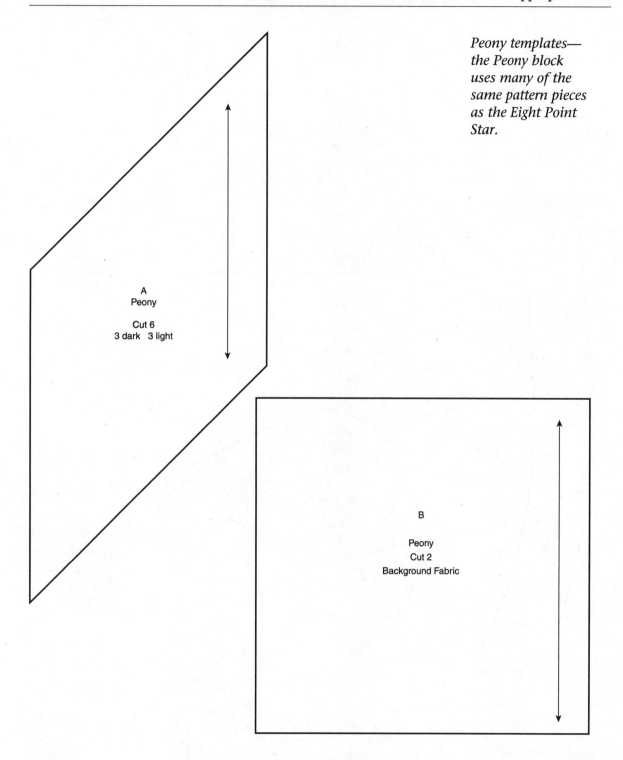

*Peony templates—
the Peony block
uses many of the
same pattern pieces
as the Eight Point
Star.*

A
Peony

Cut 6
3 dark   3 light

B

Peony
Cut 2
Background Fabric

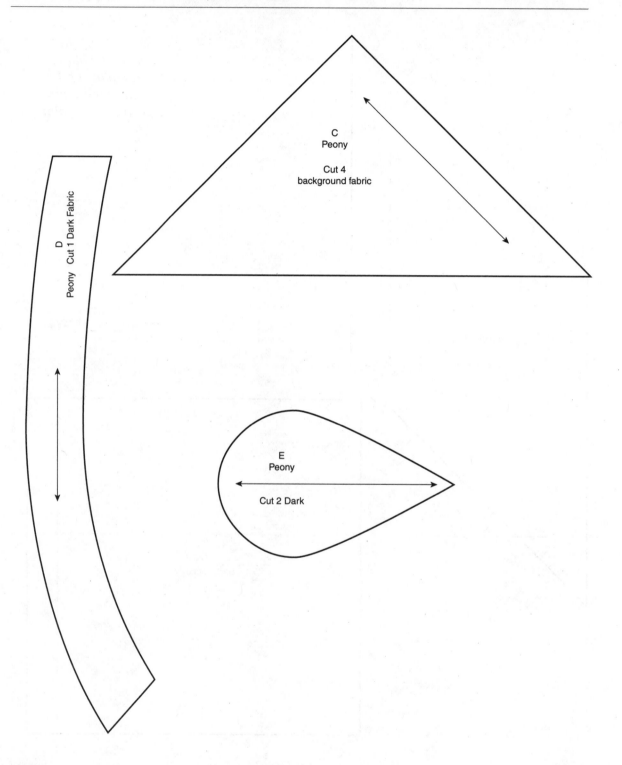

C
Peony

Cut 4
background fabric

D
Peony Cut 1 Dark Fabric

E
Peony

Cut 2 Dark

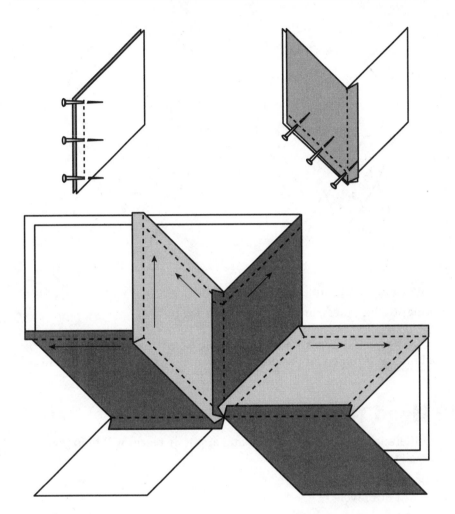

(a) Sew the dia-monds together.

(b) Baste the leaves in place before stitching.

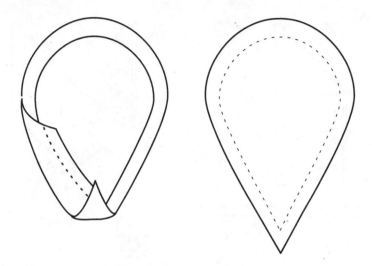

8. Appliqué the leaves and stems into place.

9. Remove all basting stitches, press, and you have your Peony.

These quilt blocks are getting us ready for traditional appliqué, where shaping is so important for a visual picture. I hope you've enjoyed appliqué. It opens a whole world of quilting design.

The Least You Need to Know

➤ Identifying the difference between patchwork and appliqué pieces will help you choose blocks equal to your ability.

➤ When you decide to appliqué, make sure you complete all the necessary steps to ensure the edges will not ravel.

➤ Baste on the seam line to stay stitch your appliqué design.

➤ Look at the fabric motif—if it has a point (the teardrop in the Honey Bee or leaves in the Peony or a heart) make sure you turn it under first, then baste.

➤ Press using an up-and-down motion so your appliqué fabric will not stretch.

Chapter 15

Traditional Appliqué Block Patterns: Add a Layer to Your Quilt

In This Chapter

➤ Reviewing techniques of traditional appliqué

➤ Alternative methods of preparing fabric for appliqué

➤ Specialty stitches for decorating appliqué pieces

➤ Preparing traditional appliqué blocks

Many of my students are reluctant to attempt traditional *appliqué*, probably because the appliquéd shape has to look like something, whether flowers, hearts, or animals.

Traditional appliqué motifs are separate pieces of fabric that form pictorial designs when positioned in a set pattern. The cut-out shapes of fabric need to have the edges turned under then sewn to the background or base fabric. The traditional appliqué differs from the combined pieced and appliqué blocks in that there is very little or no hand piecing in these patches.

In this chapter we'll review handy hints for creating appliqué, and you'll get directions for tackling some of the most popular traditional appliqué blocks. I'll show you some interesting and unusual methods to prepare appliqué pieces and also easier ways to finish fabric edges. Soon you will be "painting" your quilts with fabric designs and loving it.

Strange Ways to Check Your Frays

It's time for your traditional appliqué to take shape. Each fabric piece, cut from the templates, needs to get "finished off" to remove all the edges that may ravel or fray. Turning under the edges may be done as described in Chapter 14, "Combination Pieced and Appliqué Blocks."

Don't Get Stuck!
Be sure to clip the seam allowance to within a few threads from the dot. Do not cut all the way to the dot because the fabric may ravel and cause a hole in your quilt. Spray starching may alleviate stretching or use a product called Fray Check to prevent raveling.

The fabric shapes must be exact so they will look like the design. As you are working with fabric pictures, you will be using your iron to press these pieces into shapes. As you press, you may have to manipulate the edges to get them to lay flat. Small indentations around the outside need to be turned under and pressed. But deep "Vs" (such as those on the outer edge of the center of the Hearts All Around) need to be clipped. Clipping means making one small cut into the seam allowance allowing that fabric to lie flat when turned under. Make a clip toward the dot at the bottom of the V.

Press the seam allowance down by putting the tip of the iron right by the dot, spreading the seam. On concave curves, if the seams do not lie flat, clip the allowance a few times throughout the curve, then press down. Don't let these patterns throw you a "curve."

Pressing indentations and curves.

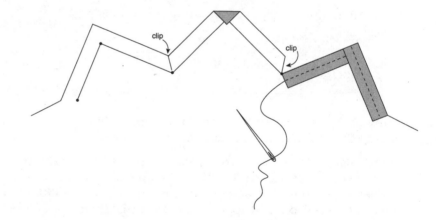

I've already described the traditional steps to prepare your fabric designs for appliqué in Chapter 14. There are several unique methods that quilters have created that are slightly different and you may want to try. You may need some strange materials like spray starch, freezer paper, or even used dryer sheets in your quest to make your appliqué pictures. Check out each method and see which one you prefer.

Spray Starch Your Templates

In this method you are going to iron the template itself.

Prepare the template, then mark and cut out your fabric design. Cut out a second template made only of cardboard—you should not put sandpaper on the back because we don't want any glue on this pattern. Put your fabric wrong side up so you can see the markings. Spray a fine mist of starch over the seam allowances around the edge of the fabric. Match the cardboard template with the markings. Don't use steam, but a dry, hot iron. Carefully iron the seam allowances over the template, making a firm crease on the sewing line. Remove the cardboard template and you should have a perfect shape. Turn the fabric piece to the right side and press again. This forms the sharpest motif of all the following methods, but some quilters still prefer the other techniques.

Don't Get Stuck!
Be sure your template is made of rigid cardboard and not a plastic that may melt. Wouldn't that be a mess!

Plastic Templates Only

This method of appliqué needs a plastic template, water-soluble glue, and masking tape. Sheets of plastic can be purchased in craft and art stores in squares the size of poster board.

Mark and cut out your fabric motif adding on $1/4$-inch seam allowances. Position the plastic template on the wrong side of the fabric motif. Using a water-soluble glue stick, spread glue around the outer edges of the plastic pattern. Turn the seam allowances onto the glued edge. Press with your fingers to hold the seam allowances down.

Apply glue along the outside edge of plastic template.

Quilt Talk

A *whipstitch* is similar to the appliqué stitch. It holds two finished edges together with tiny straight stitches. The fabrics are folded back on each other and the needle is inserted at a right angle to the edge from the back fabric to the front.

Turn the fabric motif with the template right side up and position it onto the block's background. Use masking tape on the right side of the block to hold the motif into place. You don't need pins! Turn to the wrong side of the block, and carefully fold the background under the motif. The plastic template will hold this fold rigid. Using the appliqué stitch or a *whipstitch*, sew the piece into place, stitching from the wrong side of the background. The stitches should catch the end of the background and the motif, hitting the plastic template so the stitches should not go through to the front of the block.

Turn to the wrong side of the block, fold the fabric over the template, and take small stitches around the pattern through the fabric motif and background.

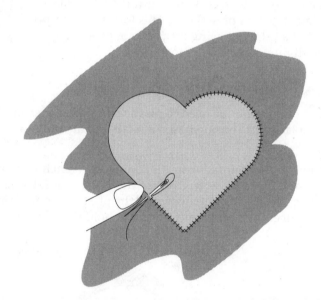

Now I know you're are thinking that the template is still inside, and you are right. We have to remove the plastic pattern. Turn the block over so the wrong side of the background fabric is facing up. With sharp small scissors, make a cut into the background fabric and trim it away to ¼ inch from the stitches. Pull out the template.

This technique makes a stabilized, perfectly shaped motif but is not for the faint of heart. Beginners are hesitant to cut and trim out that background, and you do have to be careful not to clip into the right side of the block. Beginners beware, this technique may not be for you.

Trim away the background to take out the plastic template.

Freezer Paper

You may think this is crazy, but you can use freezer paper from the supermarket to make appliquéing easier. This method is similar to the template method but the background of the block is not trimmed out. Trace the templates onto the dull side of the freezer paper; do not add on any seam allowances. Cut the freezer paper out on the traced lines. Pin all the shapes shiny side down on the wrong side of your fabric. Press these onto the fabric using an iron set at a low temperature. The freezer paper will stick to the fabric. Now add on the ¼-inch seam allowances around the outside edge and cut around the shapes. Press, turning under the seam allowances, so that when folded the fabric sticks to the freezer paper. Pin the piece into position on the background of the block and start stitching the appliqué into place. When you are almost finished sewing the design, pull the freezer paper out through the small opening, and then complete appliquéing on the motif.

Iron freezer paper onto fabric, cut out around shapes, and press under seam allowance.

Dryer Sheet Method

This is the technique that I like to use when preparing hearts, flowers, or any freestanding shape for appliqué, because the appliqué will turn out the perfect shape as long as you can sew accurately. It does require using the sewing machine. It's great for recycling all those dryer sheets once they have been used and used and used so all the scented finish has been removed. That's when we are ready to use them in our quilts. Here's how.

Quilting Bee
The dryer sheet method needs to be sewn by machine because the stitches have to be extremely small and stable to allow the piece to be turned inside out.

Mark the wrong side of the fabric with the templates. Cut out, adding ¼-inch seam allowances. Pin the right side of the fabric to a dryer sheet (see figure a). Sew by machine on the marked seam line.

Clip and trim the seam allowances (see figure b). Carefully pull the dryer sheet away from the fabric and put a small cut into the sheet.

Be careful when cutting the dryer sheet not to cut into fabric.

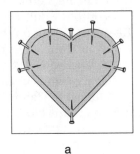

a

b

c

Pull the right side of the fabric through the dryer sheet cut, turning it inside-out to form the fabric motif. Press out the design so that it is the correct shape. I sometimes use a pointer, a sewing tool, or an orange stick, which is a pointed stick used to push back your cuticles when manicuring your nails. Press.

Quilt Talk
Bias strips are cut on the diagonal of the fabric. Find the finished selvage and fold it up on a perpendicular angle. The diagonal that is formed is the true bias.

Pin and baste the fabric motif into the correct position. Then appliqué. This gives a good stabilized base so that appliquéing is easy, and there is no chance of the edges raveling. The dryer sheet remains attached and is thin enough that quilting through it is a breeze.

Appliqué on the Bias

In Chapter 8, "Knowing and Taking Care of Your Fabric," we discussed the bias grain line. Now it's time to use that bias. Small strips of fabric, cut on the bias, are used for stems of flowers. It is easier to appliqué *bias strips*, or fabric that is cut on the bias, because they curve and bend without puckering.

Measure and cut on the bias the amount designated for the stem. For most, cut the length of the stem one inch wide.

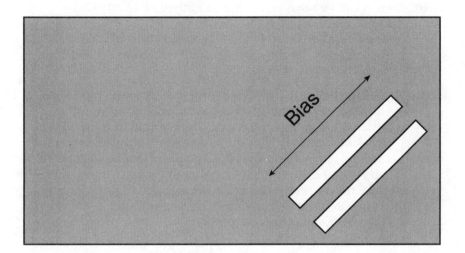

Cutting bias stems.

Fold the fabric in half all the way down the length, wrong sides together, forming a long tube, matching the raw edges. Sew by hand or machine 1/4 inch down the long side with the raw edges. Shift the seam line so it is in the middle of the tube. Press flat so the seam doesn't show.

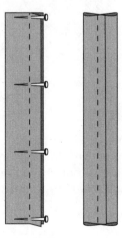

Sew down the long edge to make a tube and press.

Position the stem so the seam does not show, then pin and appliqué. This way makes appliquéing easy because the tube that is formed will not change size or ravel. Now you can draw your stem lines with bias and they will stretch whichever way you want.

Decorative Stitching for Appliqué

Sometimes when you appliqué, there are decorative stitches that you can use to embellish your designs for a country look. I like the blanket stitch or the buttonhole stitch. They are similar, but the buttonhole stitches are closer together. When you use these stitches to hold the fabric design, the piece to be sewn on should be pinned and basted into position. It can also be held in place with a *fusible fabric* webbing inserted in between the fabric design and the background of the block. When the design is secure, use a decorative stitch to embellish the edge.

Quilt Talk
A *fusible fabric* is a webbing made of a fiber that turns into a gluey substance when ironed and holds your fabric design in place. Two brands of fusible fabric are Wonder Under and Stitch-wichery.

The blanket stitch is worked from the left to the right with the edge of the fabric facing toward you. Bring your first stitch up from under the block background into the edge of the fabric design. Point the needle toward you and insert it about 1/4 inch above the edge and over from the first stitch and into the fabric design. Be sure to keep the thread under your needle. Push the needle through the edge of the fabric design and the thread loop. Then take another stitch 1/4 inch over, repeating the process.

The blanket stitch gives your appliqué a country look.

Put Your Techniques to Work

We've examined the different ways to prepare your fabric for application to the background fabric. Now it's time for you to practice what I've preached. The blocks in this chapter exemplify pure traditional appliqué. Look through each block's directions and decide which finishing methods you want to use to turn under the edges of your fabric designs.

Hearts All Around

This patch has 12 hearts surrounding a "pointed" circle. The base of the hearts touch the points of the center. When preparing this patch for a Sampler quilt, it is a good foil for the rounded look of the Dresden Plate. By the time the block is completed, you will be an expert on folding under the points of the seam allowances and making hearts.

Hearts All Around: This block will steal your heart.

There are two templates, a pointed, circular center (template A), and a heart (template B). The 12 hearts can be cut in two, three, or four colors—whatever your heart's desire.

Several years ago one of my overachiever students made an entire quilt of Hearts All Around blocks within a month! Her husband had just passed away and this quilt helped her work through her grief. My class was admiring her workmanship and I mentioned that her fabric looked unusual. She said that she used fabrics cut up from her husband's shirts. I said that it still looked like strange shirt fabrics. She finally admitted that she did make several hearts by cutting up boxer shorts! Recycling started with the pioneer women's frugality. You can see this Heart All Around quilt in the color photo section.

Quilting Bee
When choosing a fabric for a Hearts All Around quilt, pick a well-woven fabric that doesn't ravel or stretch for the center of the block. Manipulating all those points and "Vs" in the center would be a disaster with a flimsy fabric.

1. Prepare the templates and choose the fabrics.

2. Mark your fabrics and add on the ¹/₄-inch seam allowances; then cut.

187

*Hearts All Around
templates.*

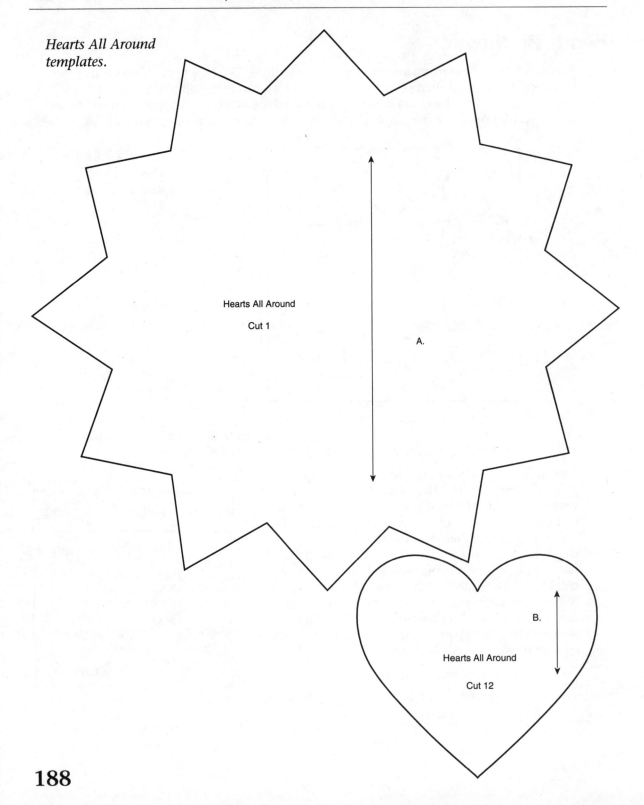

Hearts All Around

Cut 1

A.

B.

Hearts All Around

Cut 12

3. Cut out the background patch by marking a 12-inch square, and then adding on ¹/₂ inch all the way around. I like to make seam allowances slightly larger to accommodate all the handling and raveling that may occur. Be sure to mark the normal seam line so that you don't position the design so it is too spread out.

4. Prepare the center template A. Turn under the tip of the point; then fold under the seam allowances. Mark the dots accurately and clip the seam allowances almost to the point of the V as illustrated. Baste the seam allowances down as you go around the center.

Don't Get Stuck!
Clipping opens up the seam allowance so the fabric lays down flat. Don't cut too close to the dots or the seams will ravel forming a hole in your quilt.

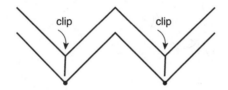

clip   clip

Clip your Vs.

5. Position the center piece in the middle of the background fabric. Pin and baste around the outside edge.

6. Appliqué around the outer edge of the center piece.

7. Prepare the hearts for appliqué in your favorite method explained in the beginning of this chapter.

8. Position the hearts so their tips just about touch the points of the center piece. Pin and baste down; then appliqué.

9. Remove the basting and press.

Scraps and Pieces

During the days of quilting bees, there were many strange beliefs relating to quilts and their preparation. One of my quilting teachers taught me some of the strange ones. The heart motif was used only for engagement or wedding quilts. It was bad luck for a normal quilt to have hearts on it. There was also a superstition that if an engaged girl quilted or even touched a heart on the quilt she would have bad luck.

189

Tulip Block

Let's try to draw a picture with our fabrics. Tulips are a Pennsylvania Dutch or Amish motif. This block has four tulips with intersecting stems that make an X pattern on the background fabric.

Tulip block. Tulips symbolize love in quilts.

There are three templates: tulip base (template A), tulip petal (template B), and leaves (template C). We'll use bias strips to make the stems.

Each tulip can be made with two different colors, or you can have distinctive color combinations for each tulip. Don't worry if you don't have any green fabric in your color scheme. You may choose a fabric with a dark value for the stems and leaves. Get a green thumb, and grow tulips.

Quilting Bee
As you are appliquéing a block, the background fabric can ravel and stretch. It is always better to have more seam allowance and cut off the excess when the patch is complete, because you can't add on.

1. Prepare the templates, and choose the fabrics.

2. Mark, then add on $1/4$-inch seam allowances for traditional appliqué. Cut out the fabric designs.

3. Cut out the background fabric by marking a 12-inch square. Cut the seam allowances $1/2$ inch larger all the way around.

4. Fold the background square in half on the diagonals. Then fold it on the horizontal and vertical fold. Baste on these lines to help the placement of the stems.

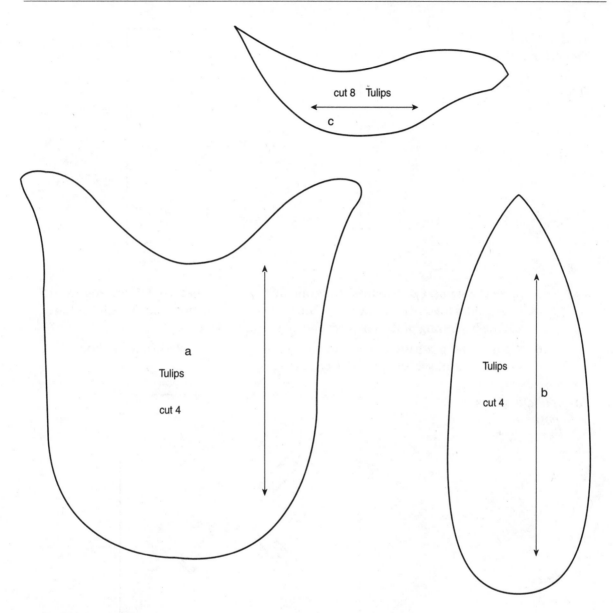

cut 8   Tulips

c

a

Tulips

cut 4

Tulips

cut 4

b

Tulip block templates.

Fold the background in half and baste on those lines.

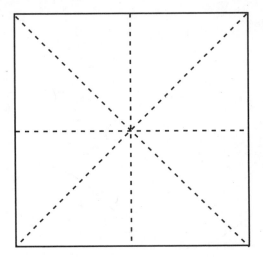

5. Make the stems. Cut two bias strips one inch by six inches. Fold them lengthwise, wrong sides together, and sew a $1/4$-inch seam down the long side forming a tube. See the beginning of the chapter for more details on stems.

6. Position and pin-baste the bias stems on the X diagonals. Baste and appliqué the stems to the block background (see figure a).

(a) Appliqué stems into position.

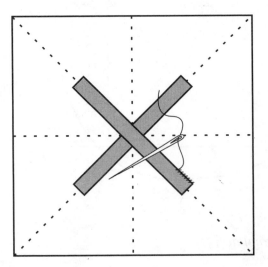

7. Prepare the tulip base (template A). Turn under the tips and baste under the seam allowances. Clip the curved edge and baste (see figure b).

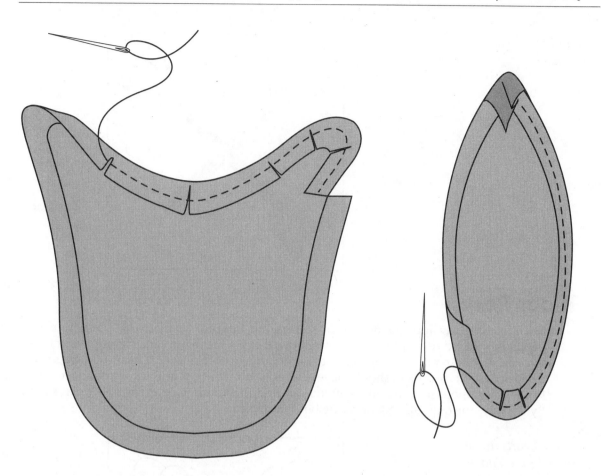

(b) Clip curves and turn under tips.

8. Place the tulip piece A into position at the end of the stems.

9. Prepare the leaves, template C, turning under tips first, then basting around the outside edge.

10. Put the leaves in position with their ends touching the stems. Pin and baste into place.

11. Appliqué around all the leaves and tulips.

12. Prepare the tulip petal B, turning under the seam allowances and basting around. Apply on top of the tulip base. Baste and appliqué to the tulip base A (see figure c).

13. Remove all basting—and there is a lot of it!

14. Press.

(c) Place tulips on stems.

Tudor Rose

There are so many appliqué designs of flowers, but this one is easy to do. The flower petals are stylized hearts. I first discovered this block when my quilting group volunteered to make a quilt to raise money for a little boy in town who needed a heart transplant. We decided that all the blocks should have a heart motif, whether quilted or appliquéd. Look in the color photo section and see if you can find the Tudor Rose in Baby Nicholas's quilt. By the way, the quilt and Nicholas are both doing fine.

These hearts make roses in the Tudor Rose block.

This patch has four templates: a small oval bud (template A), a small heart (template B), a large heart (template C), and a circle for the center of the flower (template D). Check out this patch—you will lose your heart to the Tudor Rose (but hopefully not your fabric pieces!).

194

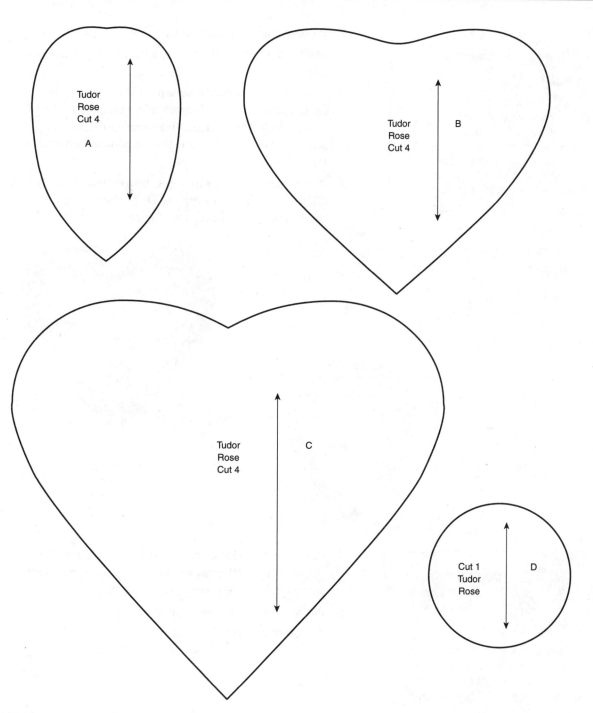

Tudor Rose templates.

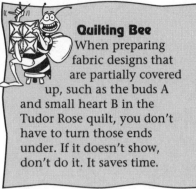

Quilting Bee
When preparing fabric designs that are partially covered up, such as the buds A and small heart B in the Tudor Rose quilt, you don't have to turn those ends under. If it doesn't show, don't do it. It saves time.

1. Prepare the templates and choose the fabrics.

2. Mark the fabric and cut out, adding on ¼-inch seam allowances.

3. Measure out a 12-inch square of the background fabric. Add on ½-inch seam allowance all around the square. Fold the background square in half, and stitch a line of basting on the diagonals, perpendicular and horizontal.

4. Prepare the buds, template A, hearts (templates B and C), and the center (template D) in the appliqué method of your choice (see figure a).

(a) Turn under the edges.

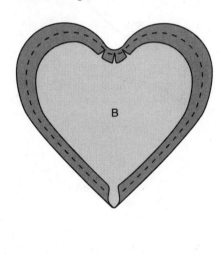

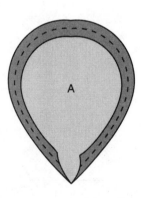

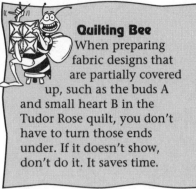

Don't Get Stuck!
When positioning your pieces, use the basting guidelines and continually check that the motifs do not shift as you are working. Fold the background in half to see if the pieces line up.

5. Position each fabric motif onto the background. Use the basting on the background to guide the proper placement of the pieces (see figure b).

6. Pin and baste the pieces securely.

7. Appliqué around all fabric designs.

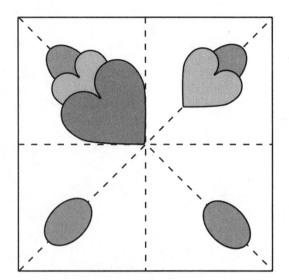

(b) Use your basting stitches as a guide.

The Least You Need to Know

➤ Clipping the seam allowance close to a dot or seam line allows the seam to be pressed flat.

➤ Spray starch the appliqué designs and press the seam allowances under to make crisp creases.

➤ Press the seam allowance of an appliqué motif around the design's cardboard template or freezer paper.

➤ Strips made out of bias fabric can stretch and curve easily and are great for stems.

➤ Use basting lines to mark the diagonal, horizontal, and vertical lines of the background to aid in appliqué placement.

➤ If a portion of an appliqué motif is hidden under another piece, you don't have to finish that edge.

Chapter 16

Use Your Sewing Machine: Machine-Pieced Blocks

In This Chapter

➤ Getting your sewing machine ready for quilting

➤ Choosing and modifying patchwork patterns for the machine

➤ Hints on machine piecing

➤ Directions for machine piecing Log Cabin and Rail Fence blocks

As I grew to love quilting, I envisioned hundreds of quilts, and I wanted to make them all. Unfortunately, most of us can't devote 10 hours a day to quilting. When I started a project I seemed to forget my housework, cooking meals, my family, and so on. The sewing machine seemed to be the answer. I was able to produce quilts at a quicker pace and keep the rest of my life together, which made my family happy.

To create machine-made quilts you first have to really be proficient, and second enjoy, using the sewing machine. It is more difficult to handle piecing the blocks—you will need sound eye-hand, and even eye-foot, coordination. To make your life easier, choose a patch that lends itself to machine sewing, and modify the templates by including the $1/4$-inch seam allowances. There are special techniques, like strip piecing and chaining, that make machine piecing even faster. If you know how to sew and enjoy it, this chapter is for you.

Pressure But No Pain—Your Machine Tension

Knowing your sewing machine and its proper use is utmost in the piecing and quilting process. Be sure your machine is in good working order. Let's learn about parts of the sewing machine so we know the proper terminology. I hate to be talking about the feed dogs and have you think this book is about animals! Get out your owner's manual and compare the diagram of my machine to yours.

Compare this sewing machine to yours.

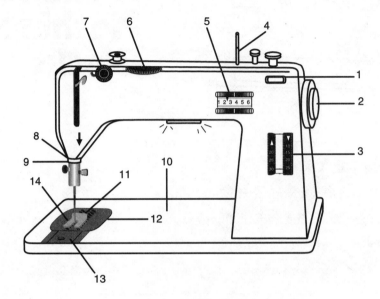

1. Power Switch
2. Hand Wheel
3. Stitch Length Regulator
4. Spool Pin
5. Needle Position
6. Stitch Width Regulator
7. Tension Dial
8. Thread Cutter
9. Pressor Foot Lifter
10. Bed
11. Presser Foot
12. Throat Plate
13. Slide Plate
14. Feed Dogs

Let's Start at the Top

Here are some important parts of the machine that you can easily see. I'll be talking about them in this chapter so make sure you can identify them.

➤ Power on-off switch.

➤ Hand wheel: Raises or lowers the needle.

➤ Stitch length regulator: Changes the length of the stitch.

➤ Stitch width regulator: Determines the width of zigzag stitches.

➤ Spool pin: Holds the spool of thread on top of the machine.

➤ Needle position: Most new machines have this selection. Check to see if your needle is set on the left, center, or right. It can affect the size of your seam.

➤ Tension dial and disc: Control the top thread tension. Tension is the balance of the tightness of the top thread to the bottom bobbin thread. If the tension is unbalanced, the seam will pucker.

➤ Thread cutter: Cuts threads at the ends of the seams.

➤ Presser foot lifter: Lets you raise and lower the presser foot and is found at the back of the machine.

➤ Presser foot: Holds the fabric against the bed as the fabric is fed through the machine.

> **Quilting Bee**
> The width of the stitch will make the stitch zig and zag. A zero stitch width is a straight stitch; usually the larger the number, the bigger the zigzag.

Under the Bed

The following important parts of your sewing machine are not easily seen but are just as important in accomplishing your sewing projects.

➤ Bed: Now is not the time to take a nap, the bed is the work surface at the base of the machine.

➤ Throat plate: Supports the fabric during sewing and has seam line guides for different widths.

➤ Slide plate: Opens for easy removal and replacement of the bobbin.

➤ Feed dogs (or feed system—I just liked the term because it helped jog my home economics students' memory): These teeth move the fabric under the presser foot.

➤ Bobbin case: Under the slide plate, it holds the bobbin, which contains the bottom thread of the stitch.

The lists of sewing machine parts are not intended to teach a novice to sew, but just to acquaint you with common terminology.

Now it's time to start sewing. When you sew the seam, put the right sides together and line up the side of the presser foot with the raw edge. Measure the width of the seam—usually the presser foot when lined up in this manner makes a $1/4$-inch seam—perfect for quilting. If aligning the presser foot along the raw edge does not produce a $1/4$-inch seam, then measure $1/4$ inch from the needle and place a narrow piece of masking tape on the throat plate for your guideline.

Guide your seam with the presser foot or masking tape.

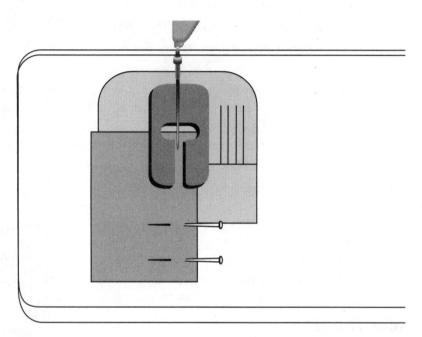

Now your seam should be perfect; let's look at the stitches.

Practice stitching two pieces of scrap fabric together to guarantee that the seam line is not *puckered* and has no *skipped stitches*.

Look in your sewing machine instruction manual to fix your stitches. When there is a problem, always check out whether you have threaded the machine correctly, and then remove and replace the bobbin to see if it is inserted properly. If there is still a problem, here are some hints to troubleshoot when your machine isn't up to the quilt experience.

If you have skipped stitches, check to see if your needle is dull, or if you are using the right thread.

Quilt Talk
A *puckered* seam looks almost gathered, with wrinkles under the stitches even when pressed. A seam with *skipped stitches* has missing stitches, giving the seam large stitches and low durability.

When your seam line is puckered, you may have to change the tension by turning the tension regulator slightly, but read your manual. The tension is very important. You may even need a tune-up for your machine if you can't correct it.

 The top tension is too loose.

The top tension is too tight.

The tension is in balance.

When your stitches are in balance, it's time to sew!

Hints for Machine Piecing

My students complain that I make machine sewing look too easy. I always apologize to them, but it is easy if you pin accurately and work slowly and carefully. I don't think you should try machine piecing until you have done hand piecing. Once you are familiar with the order of piecing and techniques, you can attempt it on the machine.

The first modification can be in changing your templates. As with hand piecing, you can use the typical template and add on the 1/4-inch seam allowance when marking the fabric. Or to save time, you can make the template with the 1/4-inch seam allowance already included. Since the presser foot measures the 1/4 inch, you don't have to mark the seam line. There is a problem, however, because there are no dots to match up—so this method is not as accurate as hand piecing.

To sew basic seams by machine, put the right sides of the fabric together, pin at each end and at every few inches on the seam line. Insert your pin perpendicular to the seam line. For regular piecing, there is no need for backstitching. In most cases, the seam is strong enough. Start at one end, and with the presser foot aligned with the raw edges, sew to the other end. Machine piecing diamonds is a little tricky. When you align the pieces without dots, there is a tendency to pin them incorrectly. You must have 1/4 inch of the tip of the diamond or triangle sticking out for the seams to line up.

Quilting Bee
Choose a thread that is 100 percent cotton or an all-purpose, cotton-wrapped polyester. Do not use 100 percent polyester (the type that is usually in the sale bins at craft stores) because it knots and breaks too easily.

Quilting Bee
Sometimes as you are pinning, you can have trouble getting seams to match. You may have been inaccurate in marking, so take out your template, redraw the seam lines, and mark the dots. Then repin and sew.

Look how the diamonds for the Virginia Star are aligned for sewing.

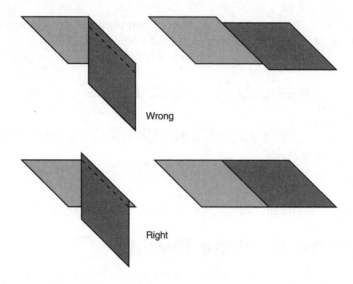

Wrong

Right

Another piecing problem for the sewing machine is inserting right-angled pieces. With this type of piecing, start sewing $1/4$ inch away from the end of the seam allowance, as if there was a dot. Move the hand wheel so that you can position the needle right into the seam, then release the presser foot. Sew from the inside of the angle to the outside. Look at the Eight Point Star. The diamonds are sewn together and it is time to put in the squares and triangles. Position the block on the bed of the sewing machine, and make sure that the fabric is flat with no folds underneath. Sew slowly and carefully, pulling out pins as you sew.

In the Eight Point Star, for inserting right-angled pieces, pin and sew from the inside out.

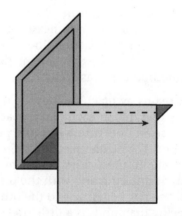

When machine sewing intersecting seams together, it is best to press as you go. This is different from hand piecing where you press when the patch is done. Think before you press. It is smart to butt the seams so that as the machine sews over them, the fabric of the top seam is pushed against the bottom seam and is held in place.

Pin into the seam of the intersecting seam lines. The seam allowance of the top should be ironed in one direction and the bottom pressed the opposite way. When you seam over these lines of stitching, the seam allowances will lay in opposite directions. Look how intersecting seams should be pressed for easy sewing.

The secret to accurate machine piecing is to pin and press carefully. Sew slowly and make sure that the pieces seamed together have no tucks or puckers. Take out your pins as you go.

Quilting Bee
When butting intersecting seams of two rows, the seams of the top and bottom rows are pressed in opposite directions. This yields less bulkiness than having both seams on top of one another.

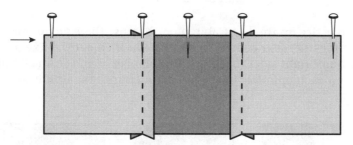

Press the seams that meet in opposite directions.

Quick Methods for Joining Blocks

Now for some quick method strategies. There are so many creative, smart quilters who have developed these methods. Obviously they were in a hurry and needed to finish their quilt by a deadline, like most of us. Check out how to sew in chains and strips and try them out on the blocks in this chapter.

Chain Piecing

I'm for anything that saves time, and sewing fabric pieces in a production line makes sense. Chain piecing makes sewing several blocks at a time easy. I hate cutting threads and restarting seam lines, especially when half of the time when I start the seam, the needle unthreads because I didn't have the needle at the highest point. It's so annoying to have to rethread the needle. With chain piecing, you sew the first two fabric pieces together, but do not cut the threads at the end of the seam line. Instead, you sew two or three stitches more, and then put the next set of fabric pieces by the presser foot and continue the same seam line. Do this for all the fabric pieces, forming a long string of pieces.

Chaining together a long string of fabric pieces.

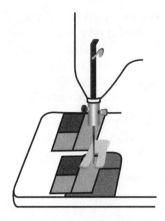

This technique is perfect to practice on the Log Cabin block because there are four units in one patch. You can string together four centers to template A, then cut the line of units apart. Position the first unit right sides together with template B and seam all four units. Cut them apart, and sew each template in a spiral manner until the unit is totally complete.

Chaining together the Log Cabin.

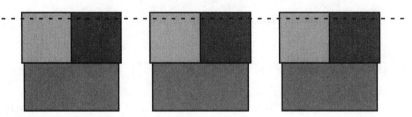

It may sound confusing, but when you take the templates one at a time it really does make sense to chain yourself to this method.

Strip Piecing

My favorite quick sewing method is strip piecing. I have made many different types of quilts with this procedure— sewing squares of the Trip Around the World, Boston Commons, Double Irish Chain, and even the diamonds of the Lone Star. When I teach this technique, I tell my students, "Trust me, it's like magic, it just works!" Blocks are analyzed and long strips of fabrics are sewn together in set patterns. There may be one, two, or three different units of strips. These units are then sliced apart and combined to make a row. Then different row units are pressed and sewn

Quilting Bee
When strip piecing, cut the strips from selvage to selvage, making them approximately 42 inches in length. The strips of fabric can be cut with a rotary cutter in one quick roll, or carefully layer several fabrics, marking only the top fabric. Several strips can be cut at one time. You must have good scissors to give an accurate cut.

together to form the block. There are many great books that give specific instructions on this technique. You can find some of my favorites in Appendix B, "Suggested Reading: Books That I Love to Look At and Read."

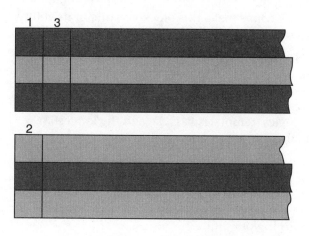

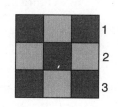

See how easy the center of the Double Nine Patch can be made if you strip piece?

There are many great blocks that use the strip-quilting method. You can practice on the Rail Fence with the patterns and directions in this chapter, and then you'll be ready to strip your quilts.

Scraps and Pieces

The Seminole Indians in Florida first developed the technique of strip quilting. The Indians were given sewing machines on their reservation at the beginning of the 1900s. They perfected the strip method and made long narrow rows of small, intricately pieced squares and triangles. These strips were not used in bed coverings but to adorn colorful clothing. Solid, bright-colored fabric is used. Quilters now use their procedure to make blocks.

Machine-Pieced Blocks

The patches in this chapter, Log Cabin and Rail Fence, can be sewn either by hand or machine. If you stitch by hand, cut and prepare the templates as discussed in Chapter 9, "Words to Live By: Templates Are the Patterns of Success." Mark and cut out the fabrics, then hand stitch the pieces together following the block's directions.

Using the sewing machine for these blocks will be good practice for chain piecing or strip quilting. The patches will whet your appetite for these techniques without overwhelming you. But whether sewn by hand or machine, these blocks are great!

Quilting Bee
If you have a lot of scraps, each template for the Log Cabin block can be cut from a different fabric.

Don't Get Stuck!
In order to make the light and dark colors go on the diagonal, careful planning is important. My first attempt at the Log Cabin was a disaster. I didn't follow the cutting directions for the colors. The darkest and lightest colors are cut from template A. Then each spiraling-out template is cut from both a light and a dark color. Careful placement of the light and dark colors is essential to get the diagonal effect.

Log Cabin Block

The Log Cabin is one of the most popular patchwork quilts, and although it looks complicated, it's not. The combination of light and dark colors make this block versatile in its ability to look either sophisticated, modern, or country.

This patch is formed by strips (logs) that are built around a center square. The strips get longer as they spiral around the center. There are 36 pieces to the 12-inch square Log Cabin block. Five templates, a square for the middle (template A) and four rectangles (templates B, C, D, and the longest E), are used to make a six-inch square unit.

Four of these units are put together as in a four-patch block. The choice of fabrics is extremely important so that the darks and lights will create dramatic diagonal contrast. This half-light–half-dark combination can be turned to make many variations in your quilt.

My first machine quilt was a Quilt-As-You-Go Log Cabin. I made it for my parents' house in the Pocono Mountains of Pennsylvania. The house is now sold but I have the quilt; it's more than a quarter of a century old and I still cherish it. Make your memories, start with a block and follow the directions step by step, and then just keep going for a full quilt.

*Log Cabin block—
do you see the
hearth and logs?*

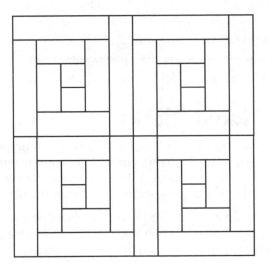

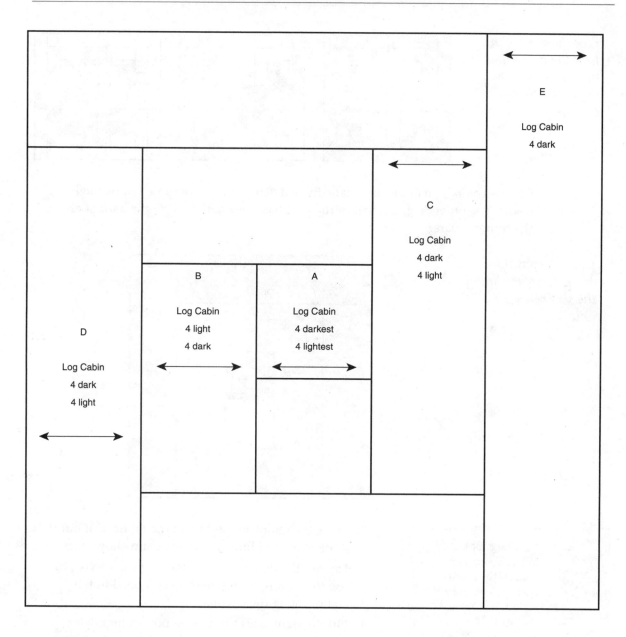

Log Cabin templates.

Look how you can turn the individual unit to change the design of the Log Cabin.

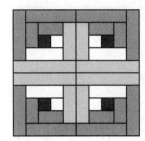 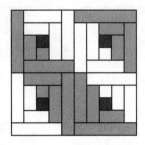 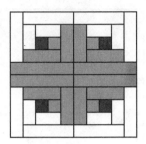

1. Choose colors so half of the square divided diagonally is composed of two light colors. The other diagonal half of the unit has three dark fabrics; the darkest one is the center square.

Study the position of the templates in the six-inch square unit.

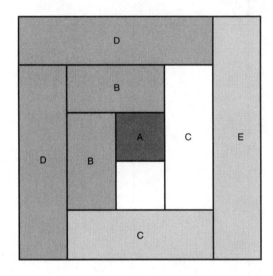

2. Make the templates and mark the fabric. Cut out the fabric pieces adding on ¹/₄-inch seam allowances.

3. Lay out the design on the table in front of you, or use the chain-piecing method described in the beginning of the chapter.

4. Pin the right sides together of both A templates (darkest and lightest color fabrics).

5. Pin the right side of the lightest color of template B to the combined A's unit. Sew the seam down the left side. Sew all other three units in the block (see figure a).

6. Pin the dark piece B to the top of the AB unit. Then sew and open the piece flat (see figure b).

7. Pin the dark piece C to the side of the AB unit and sew (see figure c).

8. Pin the light piece C to the bottom of the ABC unit. Sew and open (see figure d).

9. Pin the light piece D to the left side of the unit and sew (see figure e).

Don't Get Stuck!
Before you sew the Log Cabin block, make sure you open up the pieces to see if they fit into the layout. The darkest A should be on the top, otherwise the colors will spiral in the wrong direction.

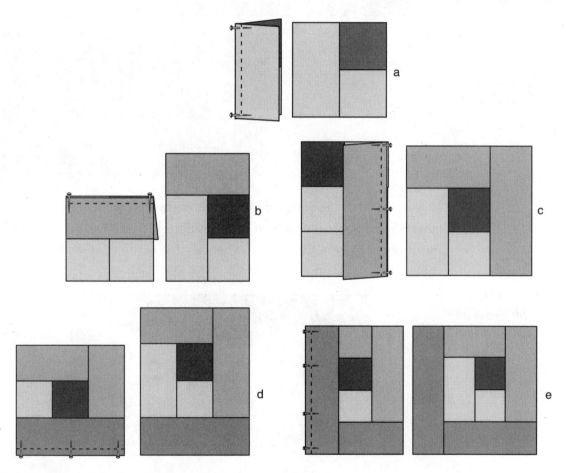

Sewing order of the Log Cabin: Follow figures a through e.

10. Sew the dark piece D to the top of the unit (see figure f).

11. Finally, pin and sew the dark piece E to the right side of the unit (see figure g).

Sewing order of the Log Cabin: Follow figures f and g.

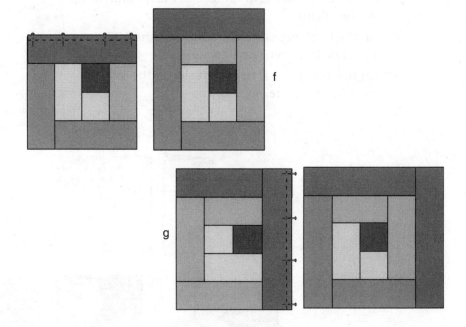

12. Open the last log and press the seams to the outside of the unit.

13. Make the other three units, and decide on their position.

14. Sew two units together to form the top row. Then sew the bottom two units together.

The Log Cabin is assembled as a four patch, sewing the top to the bottom row.

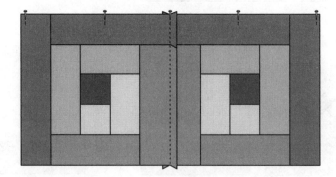

15. Pin the ends and the center seam together. Then stitch from the inside seam line out.

Scraps and Pieces

It is believed that the Log Cabin design started in the 1860s as a tribute to Abraham Lincoln, who was born in a log cabin. Traditionally, the center square was a red square that represented the home fires or the hearth of the cabin. It is not surprising that this patch was unpopular in the South during the period of the Civil War.

Rail Fence

The Rail Fence is a terrific and easy quilt block that uses the strip-piecing method. It is a nine patch in which each four-inch square is divided into four one-inch rectangles. There are 36 fabric pieces in all, but if you are using the strip-piecing method, you need to cut only long strips. No separate cutting or marking is needed. There are four shades of fabric that make up each four-inch square.

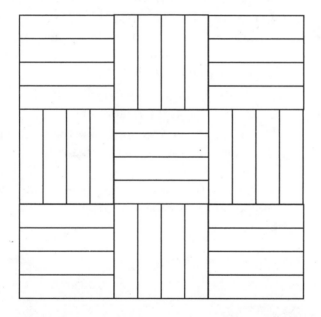

Rail Fence block. Don't the lines of this block remind you of the fences that line a farmer's field?

If you are assembling this by hand, then there is only one template. Cut out the one-by-four-inch rectangle and make the template of cardboard and sandpaper.

Rail Fence templates.

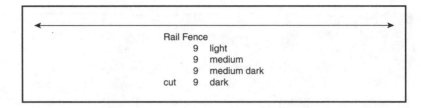

Rail Fence
9   light
9   medium
9   medium dark
cut   9   dark

Don't Get Stuck!
When strip piecing, use a see-through ruler with grids so that the line you are marking is perpendicular to the sewn lines. You do not want the strips to be running on an angle.

Quilting Bee
Cutting the Rail Fence strips into squares is the perfect use for your rotary cutter and clear-lipped ruler. You won't even have to mark—just line up your ruler at $4^1/4$ inches and slice "a la pizza cutter."

Then mark and cut, adding on the $1/4$-inch seam allowances. Put four rectangles together to form a four-inch square. Assemble as in a nine patch. For those that want to attempt the strip-piecing technique, here are the directions; but don't let your anxiety "fence you in."

1. Cut $1^1/2$-inch strips from selvage to selvage from four different fabrics.

2. Sew the four strips together lengthwise, with the lightest on top and the darkest on the bottom.

3. Press all the seams toward the darkest strip.

4. Cut off the left end to form a right angle. Then measure $4^1/2$ inches from the left and mark the sewn strip to form a square. Mark every $4^1/2$ inches. There should be nine $4^1/2$-inch squares.

5. Cut the strips into nine $4^1/2$-inch squares.

6. Lay out the blocks, rotating the colors.

7. Sew the blocks into rows. Press the seams of the top and bottom rows to the right, and the seams of the middle row to the left.

8. Pin the rows right sides together at each seam allowance. Sew the rows together.

9. Press.

Strips of Rail Fence sewn together with darkest strip on the bottom.

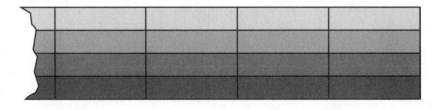

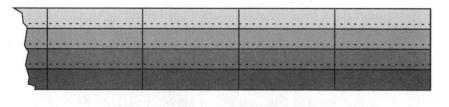

Strips of Rail Fence marked for cutting into squares.

Squares of Rail Fence sewn into rows.

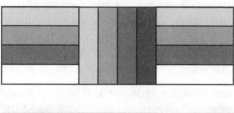

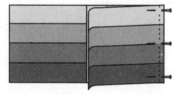

Let's Zig and Zag Your Appliqué Blocks

It is very durable and fast if you appliqué by sewing machine. The look is folksy and homemade, if this is the look you prefer. If you choose to machine appliqué, there are several modifications to consider before starting your appliqué patch.

I think one of the most important things to remember is to be sure to use a fabric that is sturdy and will not ravel. Use a material that is 50 to 100 percent cotton and is densely woven.

The thread for your machine should be a cotton-wrapped polyester or 100 percent mercerized cotton. You can use a thread color that blends into the appliqué motif to give it a softer, more polished look.

Quilting Bee
Fabric always stretches on the bias; but if it stretches along the straight of grain, you will have trouble sewing with the zigzag stitch. On the other hand, do not use a fabric that is too thick, like broadcloth or poplin, because it will be too thick to quilt.

215

Or, if you choose a contrasting thread, your eye will be drawn to the zigzag stitch, which will give it a real country look. Be sure to have your bobbin thread the same color as your top thread.

Don't Get Stuck!
Be sure to choose a fusible webbing like Wonder Under or Stitchwitchery and not a fusible interfacing. The webbing totally dissolves and glues your appliqué design to your background fabric. I've used these several times; but be careful, it is really difficult to quilt through this glue if you are planning to hand quilt.

It's time to cut out your fabric designs and place them on your patch. There are two ways to do this. If you choose a fabric, such as felt, that doesn't ravel, you don't even have to add on the seam allowances or turn them under. This is a real time-saver. The second way is similar to the traditional appliqué method, in which you mark and cut out your appliqué designs, adding on the seam allowances. Baste the seam allowances under and pin them into position.

Keeping these designs flat and in the correct place is really a challenge. I baste, baste, and more baste the designs onto the background. Your machine has a tendency to drag the fabric out of place very easily. You can even use a fusible webbing or a glue stick to hold these designs down.

Cut the sheet of webbing the same size as your template.

Cut the fusible webbing and press it into place under the appliqué designs.

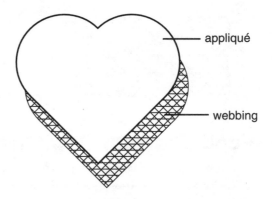

Place the fusible webbing between your appliqué design and the background fabric. Then it's as easy as pressing to fuse these pieces into place. Now for the zig and the zag.

I've talked about the sewing machine and how to use the straight stitch to piece your blocks. Now it's time to learn how to use the other optional stitches on your machine. Experiment with your sewing machine, changing the stitch width regulator and the stitch length. Choose a zigzag satin stitch that is so densely sewn that you will not see the fabric through it. The width of the stitch is your preference, but I find that a more narrow stitch width is easier to maneuver around your design. Allow the machine feed dog to push your fabric through—be sure not to pull the fabric or your stitches will be uneven. Make sure the stitches land exactly on the edge. If the stitches pucker, change the tension on your machine.

Position the zigzag stitching to land on the edge of the appliqué.

The Least You Need to Know

➤ Properly using and caring for your machine is important for perfect stitches.

➤ Use your presser foot or place a piece of masking tape on the throat plate of the sewing machine to mark the $1/4$ inch for seam allowances.

➤ When chain piecing a quilt with one block, you can sew all the patches together at the same time in a production line.

➤ Strip piecing means sewing long strips of fabrics together into several patterns that, when cut apart and resewn, form blocks.

➤ Position the zigzag stitches so that the stitches land on the edge of the appliqué design.

Part 5
Let's Put It All Together and Quilt

I hope you have a stack of finished blocks ready to assemble into a quilt top. There are many ways to set together your quilt, and your decisions will change the look of the quilt and how you attack its construction.

Consider the quilt top as a large patch. By now you can probably figure out how to sew it together, row by row by row. Once the blocks are assembled into the quilt face, you frame it with borders that compliment or accentuate your work of art.

Then we'll breathe life into your quilt by adding the puffy inside to give your quilt warmth and dimension. You are going to build a quilt sandwich consisting of the quilt top, batting, and backing. Basting methods to hold all these layers together will be discussed. Quilt designs do not just serve the utilitarian purpose of holding your quilt together; the quilt design adds a new level of beauty. Let's give your quilt life!

Chapter 17

Setting It All Together

In This Chapter

➤ Positioning and balancing colors and designs

➤ How placement of blocks can change a quilt's look

➤ Piecing blocks into a quilt top

➤ Framing out the quilt top with borders

➤ Mitering corners

You've made all your blocks and probably think you're almost finished. I'm sorry to say that you are only halfway there! You still have work to do—it's time to *set* together your blocks.

Consider the face of the quilt as a large block that you have to sew together. There is no set pattern to place the blocks in a design, so you have many choices on block positioning. You can move the blocks many different ways: place them side by side, frame each block with lattice, alternate a pieced block with a plain block, or even turn them on the diagonal.

In this chapter we will discuss the proper technique in sewing together the quilt top and I will give hints on pressing. Just like a painting, the quilt top needs the correct frame. Borders and how to assemble them will be discussed. I'll also reveal the secret of mitering corners for the long sashing borders. Get ready to be demystified.

Solving the Quilt Puzzle

Before starting to lay out your blocks in the quilt top, you want to make sure the size of all the blocks is the same. All the blocks in this book should measure 12 inches square from seam line to seam line.

Quilt Talk
Setting the top means joining the blocks together to make a complete quilt top.

Don't Get Stuck!
To check the size of your block, remember to measure from seam line to seam line, not from the raw edges of the block. People cut seam allowances inconsistently. Do not cut off any excess. You can cut away the large seam allowances after the blocks are sewn together.

Quilting Bee
If your block does not measure 12 inches from seam to seam, here is an easy way to make it right: Cut a 12-inch square out of cardboard; then turn the block to the wrong side, place the square on top, and redraw the lines as necessary.

You would be surprised how uneven the blocks can get. How can this happen? I've found that fabrics with different qualities may stretch whenhandled or pressed during piecing. This is especially true of patches that have bias edges around their borders—for example, the triangles in the Eight Point Star. I have found that pieces of fabric can grow almost half an inch just by mishandling them. It also could be that you have not stitched exactly on the seam line. Being just $1/16$ of an inch off can grow to a half-inch mistake. So check your blocks and be sure to leave at least $1/4$-inch seam allowances all around.

When the size of your blocks is uniform, it's time to find their correct placement on the quilt top. As a beginner, you may have chosen to do a Sampler quilt to hone your skills. Sampler quilts are more of a challenge when it comes to getting your blocks to balance in color and pattern. This is one of my favorite times in quilt class because everyone has their say. We all stand around a table where the blocks are laid out and call out suggestions where to move them. It is really fun to mix and match block placement in your quilt. At the end, when everyone is satisfied, the quilt will be in perfect balance. Here are some hints on block placement, since you don't have my class with their boisterous suggestions to decide on your quilt face.

➤ Try not to have blocks with the same basic design next to each other. For example, don't put an Ohio Star next to a Churn Dash—there is too much similarity in the nine patches.

➤ Spread accent or bright colors throughout the quilt. Do not have too many dark colors in one area or your eyes will look only at the dark part and not appreciate the whole quilt.

➤ If you have a problem block, one that may have a different background fabric or has a unique design, you may have to move it to the center or make a block that complements it. Unfortunately, your last choice is not to use the block.

➤ Blocks that are similar (like Hearts All Around and Dresden Plate) should be placed opposite each other in a quilt so they will balance.

If you choose not to use a patch, you can always use it later in a pillow project!

Quilting Bee

I use the "squint method" to test balance. I put all the blocks in the designated order on my bed, step out of the room, then come in with my eyes squinted. First impressions make any unbalance obvious, and I can make changes.

Look how you can balance your quilt with different designs.

Side-by-Side Blocks

In this type of layout, the patches are sewn to each other rather than framed with *lattices*, or *sashing*.

The interplay of shapes and colors of the blocks forms new designs and looks very contemporary. Appliqué blocks are perfect for this method, since there is one large uniform background that basically frames out each appliqué motif.

Quilt Talk

Lattices are strips of fabric that separate and frame out each individual block. These are also known as *sashing*.

I have seen Sampler quilts with the blocks pieced next to each other, but I think they appear too busy and confusing with the variety of shapes. In the case of the Sampler quilt, you may want to choose a different method of setting together. Let's look at some other ways.

See how new patterns are formed by the side-by-side design.

Alternate with Solid Blocks

This is an easy way to separate your quilt blocks, alternating a pieced block with a solid 12-inch square of fabric. Your patches are really emphasized by the simplicity that surrounds them.

One nice thing about this method is that you have to piece fewer blocks to complete a whole quilt. Instead of piecing 15 blocks for a twin-size quilt, you need to piece only eight—the other blocks are solid fabric. The solid blocks, however, do need to have an intricate design quilted on them, so it really isn't a time-saver in the long run.

Don't Get Stuck!
If you want to alternate pieced blocks with solid blocks, use this method on quilts with an odd number of blocks only, otherwise the overall pattern will look off-center. It's perfect for the quilt with three blocks across and five blocks in length, but not four blocks across and six blocks in length.

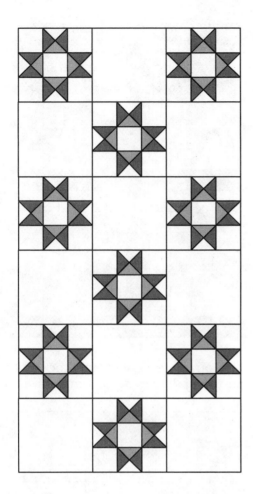

See how the patches are set apart and are more dramatic when separated by solid blocks.

Lattice Alone

Sashing or lattice strips separate and frame the blocks in your quilt. Lattices can vary in size and complexity. Fabrics for the frame are chosen to compliment your blocks, with a color taken from the color scheme, or you can use a neutral, solid-color muslin, or black. Proportionately, the lattices should be no larger than one-third the size of the block, in this case, four inches.

You can insert a solid lattice by cutting a rectangle the length of the block plus seam allowances ($12^1/_2$ inches) by the width decided upon plus seam allowances ($3^1/_2$ inches).

The lattices are sewn to the sides of the patches as you sew the rows together. Then measure the finished width of the quilt row and add $^1/_2$ inch for the seam allowances. The patches seem to be floating on the lattice fabric.

Notice how the solid lattice frames out the blocks.

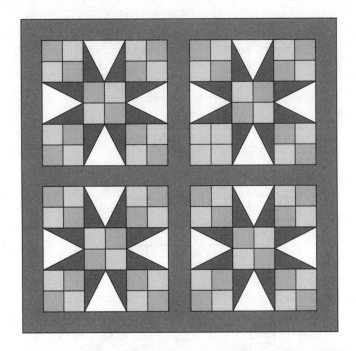

If you want to add a little more interest, you can sew squares into the corner of each block. Many quilters use this technique to add the accent color from their blocks.

Lattice with corner squares.

The lattices will all measure 12$^1/_2$ inches in length by the chosen width (three inches) plus seam allowances—3$^1/_2$ inches. To measure the corner squares, take the width of the lattice and add on the seam allowances (3$^1/_2$-inch square). Be sure to measure and count correctly.

When you become more experienced, you can try a complex lattice. The rectangle can be divided into three different color fabrics or have intricate piecing in each. Look at the following illustration of an advanced lattice.

Intricate lattices can be almost as time-consuming as making your block, but look at the results!

Use a Different Slant

For a slightly different twist, you can use any of the above methods of setting the blocks but turn the blocks on the diagonal. Look at the following figure to see how the blocks can change just by rotating them.

This design can be confusing to a beginner. Notice the sides of the quilt—there are side triangles that square out the quilt. I have used either solid triangles of the background fabric or even cut quilt blocks in half on the diagonal—yes I did say cut quilt blocks—to fill in the open side areas. The plan of alternating blocks is probably the best approach since the solid blocks are easier to insert for a beginner.

Put all your patches in a pleasing order and let's sew them together.

Quilt blocks set on the diagonal.

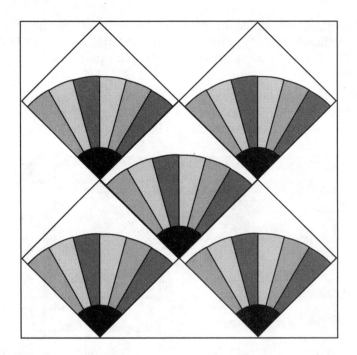

Joining It All Together

Consider your quilt top as one very large block. Once you have decided the block placement you need to analyze how to tackle sewing this together. Don't get overwhelmed—just divide the quilt face into rows, either horizontal or on the diagonal. You now have a plan of attack.

> **Quilting Bee**
> If you press all seam allowances toward the lattices, the seam allowances will butt against each other going in different directions, reducing bulkage.

Each quilt is unique so there are no set rules or instructions from now on. I can just tell you what to consider as you complete your quilt. Calculate how many, and measure the size of framing lattices needed for your quilt. Mark and cut out lattices or blocks making certain to add on the seam allowances. The blocks are alternated with the lattices, then sewn together in a horizontal row. If you have chosen the solid lattice, then one length of fabric is added above and below the row (see the following figure). Then the next row of the quilt is pinned and sewn to the first row unit.

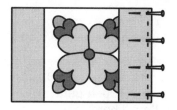

Sewing horizontal rows of a quilt and then adding either a solid lattice or a lattice with corner squares.

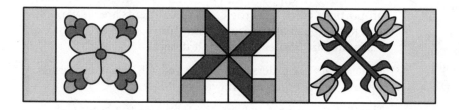

In this stage of quilt making, even if I have hand-pieced my quilt, I usually resort to using the sewing machine. With all those long seam lines, the machine is such a time-saver. However, you must be confident in using the sewing machine because there are so many seam lines to match up. Otherwise slow and steady hand-stitching is more accurate.

When you want to create a lattice with corner squares, you use the same technique of alternating lattice and blocks across the rows. The difference comes in sewing the horizontal framing rows. You need to start with a square, sew it to the short end of a lattice, a square, and lattice all the way across the quilt.

Now it's time to sew these rows together. Sew the lattice row to the top of the block row. Do this for all block rows. Sew the lattices to the top of the blocks only.

Then sew all the row units together, pinning and sewing carefully, aligning all the intersecting seams. Soon you have sewn all these rows together, and before you know it, the quilt top is completed. Press all the horizontal seam allowances toward the lattices. Finally, turn the quilt top so the finished side is facing up and press the right side; then cut off all the threads—that in itself is an afternoon project! Are you ready for the last piecing step?

Don't Get Stuck!
It is tricky pinning and sewing so the squares and lattices align properly. Each intersecting seam is pinned and stitched to assure they match. It helps to sew from one of the seams in the middle of the row to the outside edge.

Sewing the lattices and corner squares. Before sewing, press all seam allowances in opposite directions.

229

It's Time to Cross the Borders

Can you imagine the *Mona Lisa* without a frame? Neither should your quilted work of art be without a *border*.

Quilt Talk
Borders are long continuous pieces of fabric that frame out the perimeter of your quilt.

Quilt Talk
To *miter* is to join together the corner of two perpendicular edges with a 45-degree angle seam.

Borders can be as simple as a solid fabric, or a series of bands of colors chosen from your color scheme. Expert quilters even create intricately pieced or appliquéd borders to surround their quilts. It's all a matter of aesthetics. Balance, proportion, color, and the corner treatments are all variables you have to consider. You should think of borders as an essential part of the overall quilt design.

The corners of borders can be squared off, can have corner squares at the ends, or can even be *mitered*.

The first step is to decide on the fabric for the borders. I usually lay out my quilt top on a bed and fold pieces of fabrics from the quilt next to it. Then I use the "squint method" to see which fabric or combination of fabrics looks best.

Next, measure the finished edges of your quilt and be sure each parallel side is the same size. If they are accurate in length, then it's time to cut out your borders. For the side borders, measure from edge to edge, which is the length you need to cut.

If possible, avoid sewing seams—cut the border from a full length of fabric that runs down the straight-of-grain. If you don't have enough fabric, it is totally acceptable to use the crosswise grain and cut the border from selvage to selvage, creating one seam. Sew the side borders onto the quilt, open them out, and press the seam allowances toward the border.

Simple, mitered, and expert borders.

Now it's time to work on the top and bottom borders. Measure from the edge of the left border across the quilt to the edge of the right border. This is the measurement for both the top and bottom borders. Sew on these borders (see figure a). If you decide on attaching more than one band of color, repeat the process, measuring and adding on the side borders, then the top and bottom borders.

If your corner design includes squares, measure only the top and bottom of the quilt top; do not include the borders. Then cut four squares the size of the width of the side border and add one square to each end of the top and bottom borders (see figure b). Make sure to add seam allowances for the border and square pieces.

There are endless possibilities for border designs, so be creative and go into the borderline.

Don't Get Stuck!
When measuring your quilt, start your measurement two or three inches in from the outer edge. The outer edge tends to stretch, causing your measurement to be incorrect.

Measuring and sewing borders.

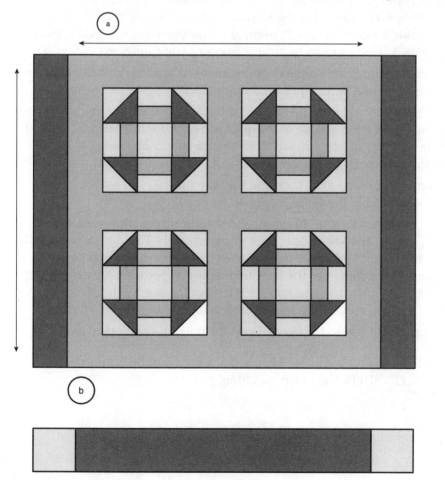

231

To Miter or Not to Miter

Mitering the corners of the border gives your quilt a smooth, professional look. This type of finish requires more fabric than the other borders, so if you are low on fabric, choose another method. When your border design calls for several bands of colors, cut all the fabrics the same size and sew them together into one unit, then proceed with the following directions. When making a mitered border it is essential to measure and sew accurately. These instructions will make mitering effortless.

1. **Measure and cut.** All border measurements are calculated by measuring the length of the quilt top then adding the width of both borders on each side of the quilt. If a quilt is 80 inches by 50 inches and the borders are five inches wide all around the perimeter, let's determine the measurements for the mitered border. The calculations would look like this:

    For the two side borders, add: 80" (quilt length) + 5" (top border width) + 5" (bottom border width) + 1" (fudge factor) = 91" by $5^1/_2$" wide (remember to add on the seam allowance for the border width). For the top and bottom borders, add: 50" (quilt width) + 5" (left-side border width) + 5" (right-side border width) + 1" (fudge factor) = 61" by $5^1/_2$" wide. I always add an inch "just in case"; you can always cut it off.

2. **Pin.** Pin the center point of the borders right sides together to the middle point of the quilt top. There should be an equal amount of fabric hanging off the ends. This really looks strange!

3. **Sew.** Start $^1/_4$ inch from the top edge of the quilt and backstitch. Then sew along the side edge of the quilt top on the marked $^1/_4$-inch seam line. Stop sewing $^1/_4$ inch from the end and backstitch (see figure a).

    Sew all four borders, stopping at $^1/_4$ inch and backstitching. Try to get the stitches from both seams to meet at the same point (see figure b).

4. **Miter.** Most of my students get to this point and then bring me their quilt, with these ends hanging off, and say "Help!" Here's how to finish. Turn to the wrong side of your quilt. Cut off excess fabrics. Take a gridded plastic ruler, one that has a 45-degree angle, and draw a line from the backstitch point diagonally to the corner of the border (see figure c). Pin and check to see if the border lays flat. If so, then sew on the drawn lines. Cut the excess from the border leaving a $^1/_4$-inch seam allowance.

5. **Press.** Press seam allowances to the borders and the mitered seam open.

Whatever border method you have chosen, I know that your quilt top is beautiful but, more importantly, IT'S FINISHED! Next stop—quilting!

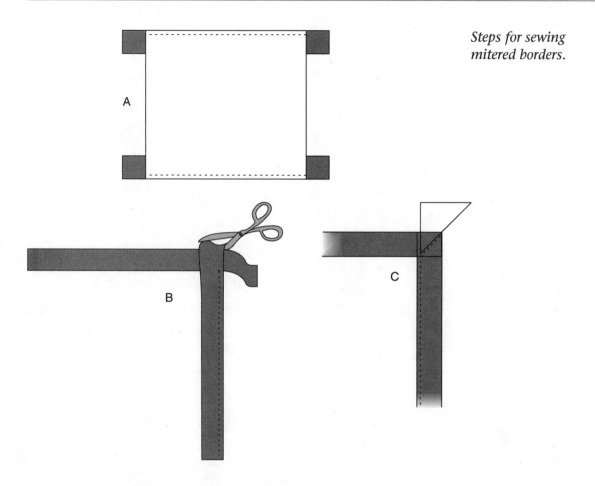

Steps for sewing mitered borders.

The Least You Need to Know

➤ If not all your patches are all 12 inches square redraw the seam lines.

➤ Arrange your blocks so the colors and designs are evenly distributed around the quilt top.

➤ Set your quilt together by sewing horizontal rows of blocks and lattices.

➤ Borders frame your quilt and should compliment its color and proportion.

➤ Mitered border corners are sewn together at a 45-degree angle.

The Three Bs: Batting, Backing, and Basting

In This Chapter

- ➤ Pros and cons of different kinds of batting
- ➤ Choosing backing for quiltability
- ➤ How to assemble the quilt top
- ➤ Various methods of basting for a wrinkle-free quilt

Now is the time for all good quilters to unite your quilt! Your quilt top demonstrates your artistry and creativity—now let's add dimension. When I first started quilting, I assumed that my quilt would turn out to be like a big puffy comforter. I quickly found out that the thicker the inside material, the harder it was to sew. The type of batting you choose will affect your ability to execute the quilting stitches. Most of the quilts with delicate quilting stitches use a very thin batting. I have since revised my thoughts about quilts and discovered that thinner is better for beginners.

The back of your quilt isn't always the back. Some quilters like to make their quilts reversible, so don't think that your fabric choice is insignificant. Besides looks, the "quiltability," or the ease of putting the needle through the fabric, is extremely important. Purchasing the wrong backing will make your quilting life difficult.

Your quilt is ready to be assembled and it is very important to hold the three layers securely together. Basting is essential. There will be weeks, months, or sometimes years of handling your quilt while you stitch and put on the finish touches. There are several methods of basting that can be used to secure a stable unit. You can choose which method best suits your needs. But get ready to baste, baste, baste.

Don't Go Batty—Know All the Types of Batting

A quilt has three layers: the quilt top, batting (or filling), and backing. The middle layer is usually a soft, puffy batting, which adds dimension to your quilt. The type of batting you choose will dramatically change the quilt's appearance and your ability to quilt. Let's consider different types of batting and find out their good and bad characteristics.

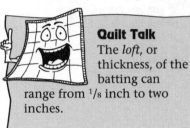

Quilt Talk
The *loft*, or thickness, of the batting can range from ⅛ inch to two inches.

Polyester Batting

This is the most popular and easy to use of all the fillers. It comes already cut in a variety of sizes and packed in plastic bags. All you have to do is open the bag and unroll the batting. These manufactured battings come in different *lofts*, or thicknesses, and are bonded to prevent shifting when quilted.

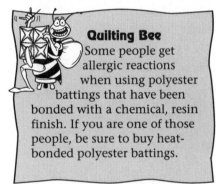

Quilting Bee
Some people get allergic reactions when using polyester battings that have been bonded with a chemical, resin finish. If you are one of those people, be sure to buy heat-bonded polyester battings.

The thicker the loft, the warmer the quilt. Each manufacturer has its own description of thickness: low loft, Fatt Batt, or Ultra-Loft. Ask to see samples to determine which thickness you prefer. Polyester battings are bonded by heat setting or a resin finish. Did you ever have a comforter that after you washed it, all the stuffing had moved around and formed uneven lumps? It would be really discouraging to have that happen after all the work you have done. So it is important to have battings that are bonded.

Polyester Batting on a Roll or Bolt

This type of batting is found in many fabric or craft stores. It is the same quality as the batting found in bags, but the advantage is you can feel the weight and loft. Then the sales person can unroll and cut off the exact amount you need. It is sometimes more expensive than the bagged batting though.

Cotton Batting

This type of batting works well in clothing and thin quilts. It is not as puffy as polyester batting, but is a more traditional thickness. Students who have used cotton batting have said cotton is very easy to quilt through, and your stitches can be very small. One disadvantage is that cotton shrinks—many brands of cotton batting need to be shrunk and some also need to have residual cotton oil washed out before use. Check to see if the cotton batting you are considering needs to be washed. (It is messy a project to wash this in a bathtub.) Some of the newer cotton battings are already washed, but please make sure. You do have to stitch your quilting lines closer together than with the polyester batting because it will shift in the quilt.

Other Fillings

The fillings discussed earlier are the most popular battings for quilts. Here are some unusual items that can be used for the inside layer. Cotton flannel sheets or wool blankets add warmth but not fluffiness. I've used a flannel sheet in a quilted tablecloth where I wanted a thin batting. It would be horrible to put down a wine glass on a puffy tablecloth and have the glass not sit right—dry cleaner, here we come. A flannel sheet, which feels cooler than polyester, can be used in quilts meant for summer use. Many times old quilts were used as a batting. Open up one quilt and find another!

Scraps and Pieces

Quilters, being very resourceful, have filled their quilts with many unusual items. I've heard of women who, during the pioneer days, used cotton right from the harvested boles or carded wool. Antique dealers can authenticate a quilt by holding it up to a light and seeing if any seeds are visible in the cotton filling. Many times frugal quilters who had nothing else for batting pieced together sacks that held cottonseed, flour, or fertilizer products. During the Depression, women also used newspapers, rags, old clothes, or even feathers—anything to add warmth to the quilt.

Backing: It's Not Always the Wrong Side

Is the backing the wrong side of the quilt? Not always. Many times quilters use an attractive fabric for the quilt back so they can use the quilt on its reverse side. Traditionally a single length of fabric, the backing can be solid, printed, or pieced. It was expensive for pioneer women to purchase a solid length, so many times they pieced together feed or flour sacks that were opened and cleaned.

One trait that a backing should have is "quiltability," or ease of quilting. A backing fabric should have a low thread count and should be loosely woven. Traditionally muslin was used because it was the easiest to sew and inexpensive. You may be tempted to use a bedsheet because of its size. Don't do it! One time I made an octagonal wall hanging and I thought that a

Don't Get Stuck!
Don't use a percale bedsheet for backing—the thread count is much too dense for a needle to pierce it. You should not use a muslin sheet either. There may be a finish that makes them unquiltable.

bedsheet would eliminate the necessity of seaming it together. What a mistake! I suffered with blisters through the whole quilting process.

Since quilting has become so popular, manufacturers have started marketing muslin that is 80 to 90 inches wide, perfect for quilt backing. Muslin and all fabrics for the backing must be shrunk before use, as were your fabrics for the quilt top.

What Size Should the Backing and Batting Be?

Quilting Bee
Open up your bag of batting, unroll the batting carefully, and let it sit out for a few hours to relax the folds it accumulated from being in the bag.

The batting and backing should be slightly larger than your finished quilt top. For the batting, it is easy to get the correct size—just measure the finished top and purchase a bag with the size that corresponds to your measurements.

Don't worry if your batting is too small or if you want to use up leftover pieces—there is a way of joining them together. Make sure that all the battings are the same loft or thickness. Then cut out as many pieces as you need to form the correct size, one inch larger than your quilt top. But do not overlap the battings that need to be united (see figure a).

(a) Join batting pieces with a basting stitch.

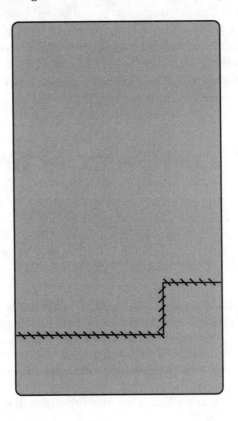

Using a needle threaded and knotted with quilting thread, baste the battings together. I use what I call a Z stitch. Take a horizontal stitch on the right batting to the left batting, then move your needle down ½ inch, taking another stitch in the right to left batting (see figure b).

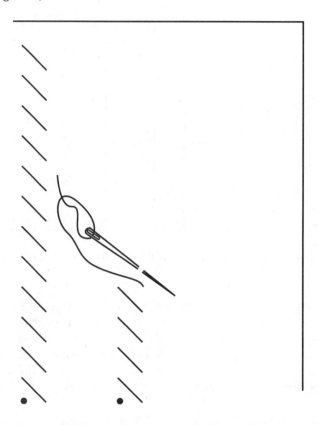

(b) Don't let these Zs put you to sleep—your quilt will be finished soon.

If you are making a bed quilt, it is probably necessary to seam the backing. You can do this in several ways, and the method you choose depends on your preferences and the size of the quilt. Look at the following figure to see three ways you can seam together the backing.

Determine how much fabric you need to buy. If you are making a small quilt, like a wall hanging or a crib quilt, measure the dimensions of the quilt top and add two inches all around the perimeter. If the quilt is large, a bed size for example, you will need to piece the backing. There are several ways to seam the backing together. Traditionally, the most acceptable way is to seam three lengths of fabric, of equal widths, vertically down the backing. This is used especially

Don't Get Stuck!
When basting battings together, don't overlap them or pull the stitches too tight because a lump will develop.

when the quilt is wider than two lengths of fabric sewed together. I am more practical and don't mind piecing together fabric of unequal widths as long as the seams run parallel to the sides and are not crooked. Depending on the size of your quilt and the amount of fabric you have, you may even seam the backing horizontally.

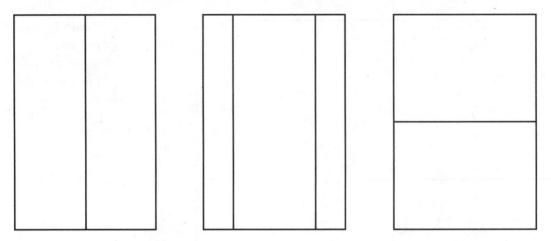

You can seam your backing vertically down the middle, vertically into three sections, or horizontally across the middle.

Whichever method you decide to use, measure the quilt top and compute how many lengths you need to purchase. Shrink the backing fabric and cut off the selvages. Remember that the selvage shrinks and puckers when washed, so remove it first. Sew together the seams and press. If you are sewing by machine, press the seams open. Press the whole backing. Now you are ready to layer your quilt. Some quilters want a traditional hand-made quilt. Besides hand-piecing, they will even hand-stitch the backing.

Wrinkle-Free Basting for Your Quilt Layers

When each of the three layers is pieced, prepared, and cut to the correct size, you are ready to assemble your quilt. Remember, this is the last time you will be able to press the quilt top and the backing, so make them look perfect.

I use two different approaches to basting, depending on the size of the project. Find a large, flat working space (a dining room table, Ping-Pong table, or a hard floor) and, if possible, a friend to help you—an extra set of hands is a great time-saver.

Basting a Small Project

Follow these steps to baste a small project.

1. Put the backing fabric on the floor, wrong-side-up. It should be two inches larger all around the circumference of the quilt top.

2. Lift the batting carefully and put it over the backing fabric. (The batting is cut about one inch smaller than the backing and one inch larger than the quilt top.) Spread with your hands to smooth out the lumps.

3. Center the quilt face on top of the batting, right-side-up.

4. As you spread these layers, the fabric shifts. Cut off any excess of batting and backing: backing that is more than two inches all around quilt top; and batting one inch all the way around quilt top.

5. Pin through all three layers using extra-long quilting pins with very large heads.

6. Using a contrasting thread with a large knot, start stitching the Z stitch at the center of the quilt and baste parallel to the side of the quilt until you reach the bottom edge. Then start in the center and baste up. Each time start in the center of the quilt and baste vertically, horizontally, and then diagonally. The basting lines should look like a sunburst. If there is any slippage, it may be necessary to baste more lines parallel to the sides.

Don't Get Stuck!
This literally is a don't-get-stuck! When pinning together your quilt layers, be sure you can see all of the pins so you can remove them after you stitch up your quilt. I made a quilt for my niece and her husband, and a pin must have gotten lost in the batting. They soon learned pins and waterbeds do not get along. Use pins with large heads or safety pins that won't wander into the quilt.

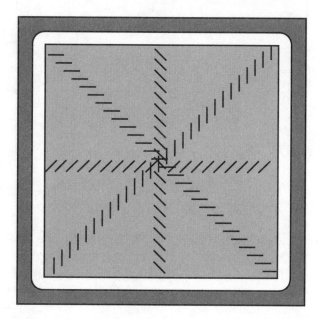

Baste a small project in a sunburst pattern.

Basting Large Projects

Don't Get Stuck!
There are some problems to watch out for if you are laying out your backing on a rug. First, the masking tape will not stick to a rug, so the backing may be wrinkled. Secondly, you might baste through your quilt to the rug. I've done this and had to cut some of the basting stitches. You can purchase a six-foot folding cardboard cutting board if there is no table or floor to use.

Follow these steps to baste large projects.

1. Lay the backing on the floor, wrong-side-up. Hold the edges down with masking tape so the backing is stretched taut against the floor with no wrinkles.

2. Place the batting on top of the backing and then spread it smooth with your hands.

3. Center the quilt face, right-side-up, on top of backing and batting. Measure to see that the backing's seams are parallel to the sides of the quilt top.

4. Pin the layers together with extra-long quilting pins with large heads. Be sure to pin through all three layers.

5. Starting at the center of the quilt, run a line of basting stitches (Z stitches or running stitches) vertically and horizontally. On large projects, run the basting stitches every four to six inches parallel to the sides, forming a grid of basting.

Baste large projects in a grid. Sew from the middle to the outsides.

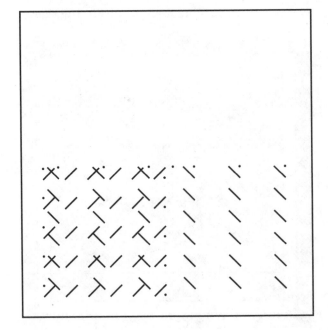

There is an alternative method if you can't tape the backing to the floor. It takes slightly longer than the process I just showed you, because you have to baste in two stages. First, spread out the backing, wrong-side-up, and then put the batting on top. Baste the backing to the batting, making sure that there are no wrinkles in this unit. Then, starting at the center, run basting stitches on the unit, parallel to the sides. Check to see that the backing is smooth. Then center the quilt top, right-side-up, on the basted unit. Pin and baste the quilt top parallel to the top edge. Start basting in the center, and form a grid with perpendicular basting stitches on the front and back of the quilt.

If you don't want to hand-baste your layers together, you can use safety pins. Quilting manufacturers have produced large nickel-plated safety pins that will not rust or tarnish on your quilt. Be careful: I once had a quilt that I was quilting at my leisure (in other words, very slowly), and when I removed the pins, they left holes in the fabric. Don't leave pins in for too long. The safety pins are great for basting projects that are machine-quilted. Sometimes the presser foot may catch on the Z basting stitches, but safety pins will make machine-quilting easier.

Get your friends to help you assemble and baste the quilt top. Have your own quilting bee! Your quilt now has body; next we will give it life by learning how to quilt.

The Least You Need to Know

➤ Prepare batting by letting wrinkles unfold and piecing similar lofts together, if necessary.

➤ Cut the batting one inch larger than the perimeter of the quilt top.

➤ Backing must be shrunk with selvages cut off, and sewn into a length of fabric that is two inches larger, all around, than the quilt top.

➤ Basting holds together all three layers with either a Z stitch or running stitch in a contrasting color thread.

➤ Small projects are basted in a sunburst design from the center out.

➤ Large projects are sewn in a four- to six-inch grid of basting stitches starting from the center and sewing horizontally and vertically.

Quilting 101

It's finally time to quilt! Your quilting stitches will add dimension to your quilt by adding shadows and subtle designs while enhancing the motifs of the printed fabric. Before taking your first stitch you need to plan where those stitches will go. That decision will affect the overall look of your completed quilt. I suggest that beginners think fewer stitches—but don't skimp. Quilting can be tedious for novices. Consider this quilt as a learning experience and don't obsess over the size of the quilting stitches.

First decide on a quilting design and where to stitch. Then transfer your design to the quilt top. There is a dilemma ahead: You need to see your markings while quilting, but then not see the markings when you are finished. Today there are many modern quilting innovations—plastic stencils and wash-out pens, to name a few—that our quilting ancestors would be in heaven over. We'll discuss equipment to make marking your designs easy and worry-free.

Lastly we will learn how to bond our three layers into one quilt. I will give detailed instructions on how I was taught to hand quilt and then explain alternative methods of tying your quilt and quilting by machine. Each has advantages and disadvantages, so you can evaluate which is best for you. So relax, pull up a chair, and let's quilt.

Choosing Quilt Designs

With modern batting choices, where you quilt will be based on artistry, not necessity. When our ancestors used fillers such as cotton or wool batting, their lines of quilting had to be only two inches apart, otherwise the fillers would shift and lump. Since most of the batting manufactured today is bonded, it will not shift, allowing us to attach the layers every six to eight inches apart.

The amount of quilting you do is up to you! You can make your designs simple or intricate. Let me suggest some ideas for quilting, ranging from the simplicity of outline quilting to the excessive echo quilting.

➤ *Traditional quilting.* The traditional method is to follow the outline of the block's design. Stitch $1/4$ inch from each seam line of your pieced or appliquéd patch. The amount of the $1/4$ inch is significant because it is just outside the pressed seam allowances.

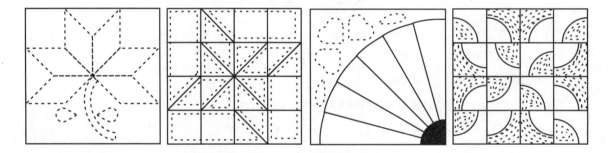

Four different ways to quilt your blocks, from left to right: stitch in the ditch, traditional, special design, or echo.

➤ *Stitching in the ditch.* Doesn't that sound strange? This is another process of quilting that follows the pieces of the block's design—only this time you stitch right into the seam. The shape of the entire design then becomes distinct. The stitches are almost invisible since the fabric on each side of the seam will puff up around the stitches.

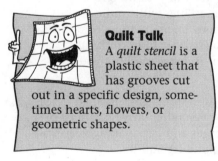

Quilt Talk
A *quilt stencil* is a plastic sheet that has grooves cut out in a specific design, sometimes hearts, flowers, or geometric shapes.

➤ *Design quilting.* You can also embellish your quilt blocks with a set design. There are many *quilt stencils* that you can purchase and simply trace onto your patch in the open spaces.

➤ *Echo design quilting.* Lines of stitching follow the outline of a block's basic design, then are repeated, like ripples in a pond, every $1/4$ inch. The concentric lines make waves of heavy quilting. This is a lot of work and not for beginners.

➤ *Overall design.* These lines of quilting ignore the block's pattern and use an overall design. You can quilt a grid of squares, diagonal lines, or a clamshell design.

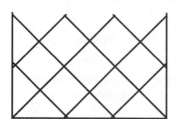 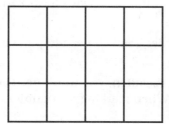 

Three overall designs. These diamond, square, or clamshell overall designs add patterning to your quilt.

For large solid spaces I suggest using a stencil of a quilt design. You can make your own with plastic sheeting and an Exacto knife, but I don't recommend it for beginners. Manufactured stencils come in a wide variety of shapes and are relatively inexpensive.

If you are determined to design your own patterns for quilting, trace common shapes and mark them in a specific order. Draw and cut out a cardboard heart or diamond or use a glass to trace a cardboard circle to style your own designs.

Look at pictures of quilts to get ideas on quilting styles that you like. Use your imagination! Decide on how you want to quilt and let's transfer your mind's creations to your quilt.

Quilting Bee
Two instances when you should quilt less: Don't waste time on an intricate design if you are quilting on a highly patterned fabric (the stitches will not show up). And, if you want a thick, puffy quilt, use less stitching since the quilting stitches compact the batting, making it flatter—goodbye, thick quilt.

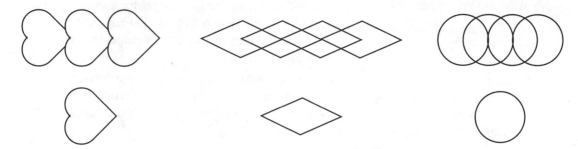

Cut out and trace shapes from cardboard to style your own designs.

Got an Idea? Mark Your Quilt!

Some quilters mark their quilt top before putting all the layers together. I prefer to mark after the quilt is assembled. My quilts are usually a work in progress, and I often change my mind as I go along.

There are certain marking supplies you will need to purchase. So let's examine the different methods of marking.

If you have chosen to stitch in the ditch, you won't need any special supplies since your seams are your sewing guides. When marking for traditional quilting, however, you have several marking options.

> **Quilting Bee**
> When marking your quilt, draw as light a line as possible that you can still see easily. Don't use a number 2 pencil—it's so soft that it may smear and make your fabric look dirty.

> **Don't Get Stuck!**
> Always test markers on your scrap fabrics first. Students have used regular markers by mistake, and then there was nothing they could do to get rid of the marks!

➤ *A number 2.5 or 3 pencil*. You'll get a fine, sharp line that won't smudge.

➤ *Wash-out markers*. You draw a line to mark the design and then, when you've completed quilting, wipe the line with a wet cloth and the marks dissolve. There are two popular brands of markers on the market: One is blue and needs water to remove it; the other is purple and evaporates on its own in a day or two— by magic, the lines disappear!

➤ *Masking tape*. This is my favorite option for marking a $1/4$-inch seam line. Buy masking tape that is $1/4$-inch wide, cut off the amount you need, and line it up to the seam you are following. Then lift and move it to another seam. You don't have to get involved with any drawing or worry about erasing.

➤ *Tailor's chalk*. These lines can be brushed off when you finish quilting. The chalk makes thicker lines as it dulls, and thin lines are better for accuracy. You can purchase powdered chalk that rolls onto the fabric and comes in a variety of colors for marking dark and light fabrics.

➤ *Soap slivers*. This is one way our ancestors marked their quilts. It is a useful technique even today, especially on dark fabrics where a pencil or marker line will not show. Save all those old soap pieces from your bathtub, but don't use deodorant soaps because they have extra chemicals.

One hint on using stencils: The grooves are cut out in the design so you can trace it with your marking tool (not masking tape). Notice that the design is not continuous but that there is an inch every so often that is not cut. Many beginners stop at each end of the grooves and then start again, making a partial design. You are supposed to bridge these spaces with stitches. The manufacturer had to stop the groove or the stencil would fall apart!

Mark your designs, then get your needle, thread, and thimble. It's time to quilt!

Place the masking tape against the straight seam you are following. Then encircle your work with a hoop.

Be sure to bridge the gaps to have continuous lines.

Hand Quilting

Quilting is short, evenly spaced running stitches that are worked through all three layers of the quilt, adding strength and decorative textures. Let's proceed with putting our quilt layers together. I find hand quilting relaxing and enjoy quilting while my husband watches sports on TV. I feel as if I'm spending time with him while I accomplish something.

Hoop or Frame?

Hoops and frames are specialized tools that help you hand quilt. Besides your quilting thread, quilting needles (sizes 8 to 10), and your thimble, you need something to hold your quilt taut. It is very important to stretch the fabric slightly to eliminate tucks on the backing.

Quilt Talk
A *quilting frame* is a free-standing rectangle that holds a quilt, allowing several people to stitch a section, then roll the quilt to another section, quilting until the whole quilt is finished.

Quilting Frames

When most people think of quilting, they picture women sitting around a *quilting frame*. I unfortunately have never had the opportunity to work my quilts on one. There just isn't enough room in my house and frames can be costly. Legs or wooden sawhorses support a large rectangular frame. The quilting frame holds your project so you can use both hands to quilt. Beginners should probably not work on a frame, since it is stationary and it takes practice to sew in the various directions of your quilting designs.

This PVC quilting frame is found in the classroom of my favorite quilting store—Acme Fabrics. Groups can work on quilt projects together with a frame like this one.

Hoops

I prefer using a hoop because I like to have my projects portable. A hoop consists of two round, oval, or square shapes that fit over one another and hold the quilt tightly between the two pieces. More basting is needed when you use a hoop because you will be moving and handling the fabric as you change the hoop's positions. Hoops come in several styles. The traditional wooden hoops have two round or oval hoops that fit into one another. The top hoop has a large screw that allows the hoop to open larger to accommodate the thickness of the batting.

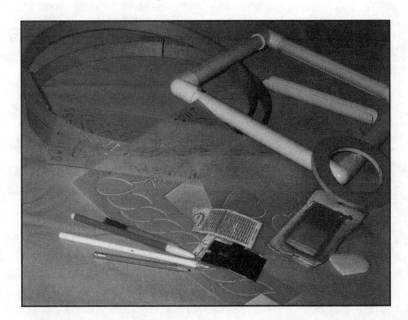

What's all the hoop-la? Here is the traditional hoop for quilting, along with other marking and quilting equipment.

There is a new type of hoop that is made out of plastic PVC piping. One of my students found that the PVC stretched and didn't hold the quilt tightly. So I suggest you don't use this type of hoop on quilts that have extra loft or thickness.

Some quilters are able to quilt without a frame or hoop, but they increase the amount of basting. Also, continually check the back of the quilt for wrinkles or tucks. Choose the best tool for you and make your quilting experience great.

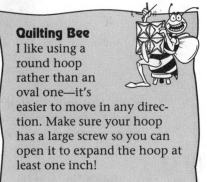

Quilting Bee

I like using a round hoop rather than an oval one—it's easier to move in any direction. Make sure your hoop has a large screw so you can open it to expand the hoop at least one inch!

Rock Your Stitches

Gather all your quilting equipment, get comfortable, and let's quilt! Although quilting simply consists of running stitches, the trick is to catch all three layers in very small uniform stitches. Making small stitches is a matter of practice. My first quilting teacher said she didn't like her stitches sewn the first 20 minutes she quilted, so she always ripped them out! Remember, this is your first project and your stitches may be large. Never fear, practice makes perfect.

Take apart your hoop and place your project over the bottom part. Take the top hoop and unscrew it as large as possible. Position the top hoop over the bottom, trapping your quilt in between.

Give your quilt a face-lift— straighten your quilt to smooth out a wrinkle here and a tuck there.

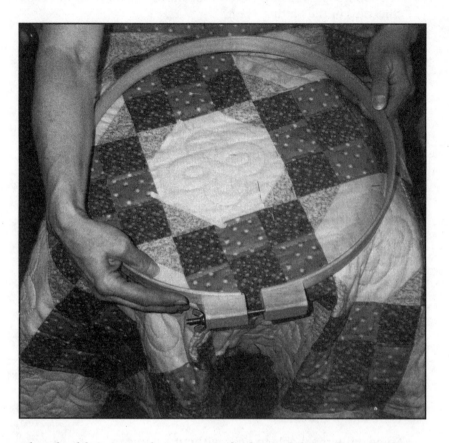

Tighten the screw so that the fabric is taut but not stretched out of shape. Turn the hoop over and check that you have no folds or tucks in the backing. Tug on the backing slightly to straighten it out.

Don't Get Stuck!
When starting to quilt, be sure the needle does not go all the way through to the backing, but keep it parallel in the batting until it reaches the quilting line. Then bring the needle up.

It's time for your first stitch. Start with about 18 inches of quilt thread, and make the small knot that you have been using for piecing. Begin working at the center of your project and quilt toward the outside edges. Your hand with the needle is on the top of the hoop and your other hand is under the hoop, pushing up the needle and guiding where the stitches go. On the top side, put your needle about a $1/2$ inch from where you want to start quilting. I call this no-man's-land. Push the needle through the batting, but don't let it go through to the backing. Then bring the needle up on the line that you want to stitch. Pull the thread through.

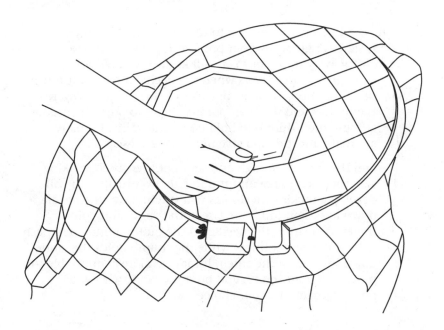

Start in no-man's-land.

Now I know you are thinking about the knot that is on the top of the quilt. Tug on the thread and the little knot will pop into the batting and be hidden. On the marked quilting line, take a backstitch and then start your running stitches, going through all three layers to secure them.

Pop goes the knot into the batting.

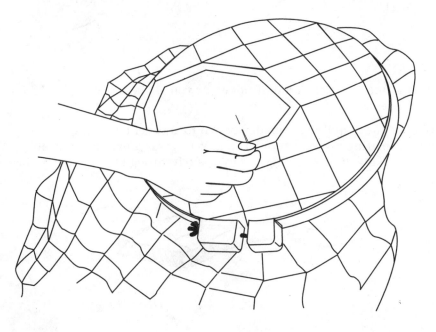

With your top hand, push the needle in perpendicular to the surface and, with your thumb, roll the needle to a 45-degree angle while your pointer finger holds down the fabric. Your stitches will be moving away from you. You will know you have gone through all three layers when the needle pricks your finger under the hoop. Ouch! Some people like to quilt toward themselves and use their pointer finger to push the needle and use their thumb to hold down the fabric. I usually alternate directions to give my fingers a rest.

> **Quilting Bee**
>
> You can use a leather thimble to protect the finger of your bottom hand, but I like to paint my finger with several coats of clear nail polish. It protects my finger but I can still feel the stitches. Don't apply nail polish if you have an open cut—that would hurt.

Pull the thread through and start another stitch, making sure the stitches are uniform in size. Eventually you will develop a rocking motion as you stitch. Move the needle down and then roll it up. Use both thumb and pointer finger to position the needle on the quilting line, then push with your pointer finger while the thumb holds the fabric down in front of the stitch. It may be more comfortable to push with your thumb and hold the fabric with your pointer finger. It's your choice.

Rock your stitches.

a   b

Take only one stitch at a time, especially around curves. As you get better you can take several stitches on your needle.

It's possible to move your line of quilting from one design to another by having the needle travel through the batting to get to another spot. When traveling, do not go all the way through to the backing. It's like taking one long stitch through the middle of the quilt.

Pack your thread and let your needle travel through the batting.

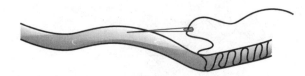

Stabbing Is a No-No

Try not to *stab* your quilt by pushing the needle into the top and pulling it out underneath with your other hand. The stitches may look right on the top of the quilt, but the stitches on the underside may be uneven and crooked. Use this method only when stitching is so hard that normal quilting is impossible—for example, when many seam allowances intersect or the quilt is too stiff to put your needle through with a running stitch.

Securing Your Stitching

Now you are at the point where there are only a few inches of thread left on your needle. What do you do to secure and knot off the line of quilting stitches? Through the years I have learned from my students several ways of finishing these quilting seams. The easiest way for beginners is this: Take a large stitch in the batting and then backstitch into the last two stitches of the seam. Bring the needle through the batting into no-man's-land and out the top of the quilt. Cut this thread so $1/4$ inch is showing. Insert the needle in the batting near the thread parallel to the top and move it back and forth catching the thread, making it disappear into the batting.

> **Quilt Talk**
> You are *stabbing* when you insert the needle into your quilt with your top hand and pull it out the bottom with your other hand under the hoop. Then, with your bottom hand, you push the needle from the bottom to the top. When you stab, you are use both hands to quilt your stitches.

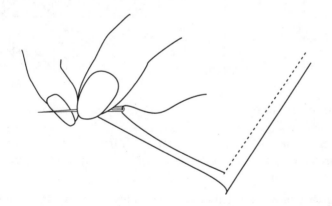

Don't be at the end of your rope— backstitch and make your thread disappear into the batting.

Tie Your Quilt Into Knots

Sometimes you may want your quilt to be thick and fluffy. You may also be short on time. Since traditional quilting is time-consuming and does compact the batting, you may want an alternative. I have found the answer to both problems: Secure your layers with knots. Yarn or embroidery floss can be used to prevent your quilt from shifting. These quilts are called tied or tufted quilts.

Don't Get Stuck!
When you tie your quilt, you must use a bonded batting so the batting won't shift.

Here are some pointers for tying your quilt.

1. Pin and baste together the quilt top, batting, and backing.

2. Thread the embroidery needle with floss or yarn in a color that blends or contrasts with your color scheme, depending on your taste.

3. Decide on the arrangement of the knots. You can choose an overall pattern (such as every five inches in a grid) or follow the block's designs.

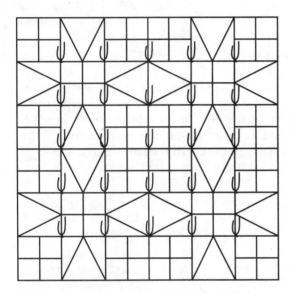
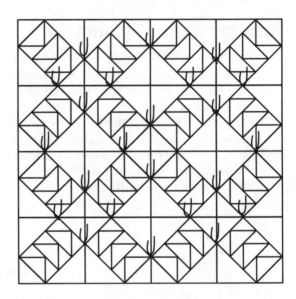

Where to tie or not to tie? Use an overall design or follow the design your blocks make.

4. Starting from the center of the quilt, take a $1/4$-inch stitch from the top to the bottom through all three layers and up to the top. Don't pull all the way through but leave a three-inch tail. Be sure you have caught all three layers.

5. With the ends, tie a square knot. Remember your scout lessons? Put the right end over the left end and under; then put the left end over the right end and under.

6. Pull the knot tight to secure it, and trim the ends to the desired length.

7. Repeat tying the knots in the designated design working to the outside edges.

Our quilting ancestors did not have all their covers quilted with complex designs. Many of their quilts were tied. For modern quilters, tying a quilt is great when you have to get a project done quickly; but make sure you use enough ties to hold your quilt together and that your knots are secure. Do get yourself tied up in knots!

> **Quilting Bee**
> When tying their quilts, some people like to leave a $1/2$-inch tuft, while others leave longer ends and tie a bow.

Machine Quilting

Machine quilting calls for advanced knowledge of your sewing machine. It is a quick way to quilt but, unfortunately, several problems may develop when quilting. You may need to find solutions by tinkering with your machine. Here are some problems and, I hope, some useful solutions. Practice on a small square of your three layers to get your stitches perfect.

Problem	Solution
The presser foot may push the top fabric along, making the top stretch and pucker.	Use a "walking foot" (a special attachment to the presser foot that has rollers to move the fabric); drop the feed dogs so you can maneuver the quilt though the seam; or loosen the top tension slightly.
You may quilt in tucks on the backing.	Baste more closely or use a hoop.
The stitches may be uneven and tension too loose.	Experiment with stitching through all three layers. Your machine may not be up to quilting, or you may have to choose a thinner batting.
There is too much fabric and bulk when you stitch a large-size quilt.	Try to roll up each end and secure it with safety pins. As you finish quilting an area, unpin and reroll to another section.
The basting stitches get caught on the presser foot while you sew.	Sew smaller basting stitches on the quilt top, or if using a hoop, remove the basting inside the hoop area.

Thread, Bobbins, and Presser Feet

Use a straight or narrow zigzag stitch of 100 percent cotton or cotton-covered polyester thread. Choose a color that compliments your color scheme. You can even choose a different color for the bobbin to give your quilt reversibility. Slide your quilt and the hoop under the needle. It can be difficult to accomplish this, and depending on your machine, you may have to remove the presser foot. Turn the hand wheel to lower the needle and start your first stitch. Hold onto the top thread, making the lower bobbin thread come up to the top of the quilt top. Make sure you lower the presser foot down. Don't forget because you would have nothing to move your quilt through the machine. Then sew on your marked lines. There is no need to backstitch, but sew slowly and carefully. Clip threads at the end of quilting.

Support and Seams

Set up your workspace for your convenience. Keep the bulk of the quilt laying on a table behind your machine, so the weight of the quilt won't pull and cause puckers or uneven stitches. The best way for beginners to machine quilt is to use the stitch in the ditch method; remember that you sew right on the seam line following the block's pattern. The seams add strength to the quilt seam and the fabric won't shift as much. Please practice on a small project, like a pillow or crib quilt. Using your sewing machine can make your quilting quick, and if you are really interested, look in Appendix B, "Suggested Reading: Books That I Love to Look At and Read," where you can find several books that explain all this in detail.

The Least You Need to Know

➤ The three layers of the quilt must be held together with hand or machine quilting or knots.

➤ Quilting designs can follow the outline of your block's pattern, be an overall design, or be a specific design drawn from a quilting stencil.

➤ Mark your quilt with as light a marker as possible, but make sure you can still see the lines.

➤ Start quilting or tying from the center and work to the outside edge.

➤ Be experienced on handling your machine if you want to do machine quilting.

Part 6
Your Finished Quilt

Now for the finishing touches! Your quilt looks beautiful, except for those ragged and frayed edges: Add a binding to finish it off. You can purchase or make your own bias tape or use a simple method of turning the backing to the front. Then sign and date your work of art.

Quilts are meant to be used and loved for a lifetime and longer. When your quilt needs to be laundered, there are special considerations before giving your quilt a bath. You'll learn the best method for cleaning and storing your quilts.

Sometimes a beginner is not ready to tackle a large bed-size quilt. The last chapter is dedicated to step-by-step instructions for creating a pillow or wall hanging. A variety of options will make your project an individual work of art.

Chapter 20

Your Finished Quilt

In This Chapter

➤ Finishing the edges of your quilt

➤ Making your own bias binding

➤ Signing your quilt

Your quilt is beautiful! We're down to the last leg of the race. It's almost time to put it on your bed. I bet you can't wait to finish off those raveling edges with batting sticking out. There are several strategies for binding off the edges. Some methods use the quilt top border fabric, the backing, or a separate bias binding. Bindings can be purchased in a multitude of colors, or you can make them using a fabric from your color scheme.

Making your own bias tape can be confusing, but I'll show you the "molar" method that one of my first quilting teachers taught me. Follow the directions step by step, and you won't get into a "bind."

Every artist signs his or her work of art and you should too. Whether with quilting thread, floss, or indelible ink pens, you can write your name, date of completion, the name of the quilt, and perhaps the occasion for giving it as a gift. Let's get started—I know you can't wait to use your quilt!

Finally Get Rid of Those Frayed Edges

Quilt Talk
Binding is a strip of fabric, usually cut on the bias so that it can stretch, that covers the outer edge of your quilt.

You are probably tired of getting everything, especially your rings, caught on the ragged outer edge of your quilt. As soon as I finish quilting—and celebrating—the *binding* that encloses those ragged edges comes soon after.

There are four ways to bind the edge of your quilt, and each gives a different look. There are advantages and disadvantages to each method. Read through this chapter and determine how you want to end your ends.

There are some last-minute preparations you must make before neatly finishing the ends. Take out all the basting threads. Cut off all errant threads from throughout your quilt top. I don't know where they all come from—they just appear. Spread your layered quilt out and cut the excess batting to ¹/₂ inch all the way around the quilt top.

Quilting Bee
Some people like to cut the batting flush with the quilt top, but I like to leave an extra half inch, to give the binding body and thickness.

The backing will be cut off differently depending on the binding technique you use, so don't do anything until you decide how to bind the edge.

The first two methods I call the cheater's way, because they really are the easiest.

Turning the Border Fabric to the Back

This finish binds your edges so that the quilt border is the last color that frames the outside of the quilt top. The batting and the backing fabric are cut to one inch less than the border all around the quilt. Turn the border fabric under ¹/₂ inch; then fold about ¹/₂ inch of it around the quilt to the backing side. The back of the quilt will have ¹/₂ inch of the border fabric folded and sewn to it. Pin about two feet at a time of the border fabric folded to the backing. Use an appliqué stitch or a catch stitch. If you don't remember, check out Chapter 14, "Combination Pieced and Appliqué Blocks," on how to sew invisibly.

Don't Get Stuck!
Binding your quilt with a border fabric or the backing is often looked down on because the methods do not produce a binding that can be replaced. As a quilt is used, the binding is usually the first part to get worn. If that happens, the quilt top will be damaged—sometimes irreparably.

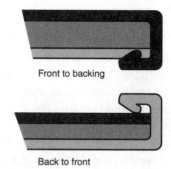

Front to backing

Back to front

You can fold the border from the front to the back or roll the backing to the front. Which way should you go?

Turning the Backing Fabric to the Front

This finish is very similar to finishing with a border fabric, just reversed. This time cut the batting about $^1/_2$ inch larger than the quilt top. Then the backing should be an inch larger all the way around. Turn the backing fabric under $^1/_4$ inch so wrong sides are together. Then turn it over to the front, making sure the $^1/_4$-inch fold covers the edge. Pin so that the binding is even, about $^1/_2$ inch, and sew with an invisible stitch. You have to make sure that the backing fabric coordinates with the quilt top since the binding forms a small frame on the front.

Attached Bias Binding

There are several steps to this method. Follow these step-by-step directions carefully.

1. Cut the batting and backing $^1/_2$-inch larger than the quilt top. With a contrasting color, baste all around the outer raw edge of the quilt top at $^1/_4$ inch.

2. Purchase or make a bias binding. Open up one $^1/_4$-inch folded edge, and place the right side of the binding to the quilt top with the raw edge facing the outer edge.

3. Pin into the $^1/_4$-inch fold, turning the short end of the binding under to finish it off.

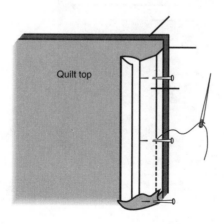

Quilt top

Doesn't this procedure look backward? Pin and align the raw edges of the quilt top to finish off the end.

Don't Get Stuck!
If you sew by machine, take care not to pull the bias binding—it has a tendency to stretch and pucker.

4. Stitch the bias binding to the quilt top in the ¹/₄-inch fold, either by hand or machine.

5. Sew to within ¹/₄ inch from the end of the seam, backstitch, stop the seam, and cut the threads. Now miter the corner. Make about a ¹/₂-inch pleat at the corner before turning. Pin the bias binding so that ¹/₂ inch is sticking up, and on the adjacent side put your needle where the other line of stitching ended and start sewing a new line of stitching.

Now this really looks wrong, but it's right. Pivot the binding and start stitching where the other line ended.

Quilt top

6. Stitch all around the perimeter of the quilt. Overlap the binding, ending where you began.

7. Fold the bias binding over the edge of the quilt and pin, making sure that the binding is turned evenly.

8. Sew with an invisible stitch until you get to the corner.

Be a magician and make your stitches in the binding disappear!

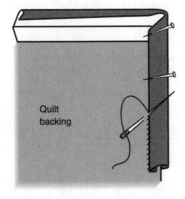

Quilt backing

264

9. Now for the part of the binding that is sticking up—fold the right side of the binding up and then the top side down to form an accurate, mitered 45-degree angle.

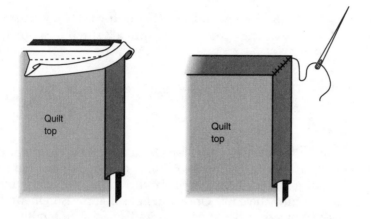

Fold under and miter the corner by turning the binding to the back and making a 45-degree angle at the corner.

10. Stitch to hold down the folded corner.

A bias binding adds a small border of color that can contrast with your quilt top, creating a frame.

Pillow Technique

One of my students uses this method regularly and it is very nice for baby quilts because you can insert lace into the edging. This finishing technique actually has to be done before the project is quilted. That's okay since I do not recommend this method for beginners—it is very difficult to sew and manipulate the fabric. It is a problem to get the quilt to lay flat and it may look bunchy. If you use this procedure for your next quilt, here are the instructions.

1. Cut the batting and the backing even with the quilt top.
2. Place the quilt top right sides together with the backing. Sew by machine all along the perimeter of the quilt leaving about two feet open to turn it right-side-out.
3. Pin the batting evenly all around the outside edge. Hand-stitch this down on top of the same seam line. I know that the two steps seem repetitive, but it prevents the batting from stretching

> **Quilting Bee**
> If you use the pillow technique, you can insert lace before you sew the backing. Place the tape end of the lace against the raw outer edges of your quilt. You can check out Chapter 22, "Projects from Start to Finish," to see how to insert lace, piping, and ruffles.

265

out of shape and getting caught on the presser foot as you sew.

4. Very carefully, reach your hand inside the quilt and turn it right-side out.

5. Flatten and smooth out the three layers, pushing out the corners. Baste with a Z stitch in six-inch grids.

6. Quilt.

The edges are finished and are inside the quilt.

Do Get Into a Bind

Quilters have found that a bias binding or a bias tape is more durable than fabric cut on the straight of grain and it can also bend to make finished rounded or mitered corners with 45-degree angles. Measure the perimeter of your quilt, adding about five inches for mitering the corners and finishing the ends. Once you have that measurement, you can plan the amount you need to buy or make. If you can find a packaged binding in a color that coordinates with the quilt top, buy it! A great deal of time will be saved. The rectangular packages come in a variety of sizes and widths, but the best to purchase is a double-folded quilt binding.

Making Bias Strips

Bias strips can be cut from the diagonal of one of your fabrics used in your quilt. It is great being able to have a coordinating fabric frame your quilt. The strips can be $1^1/_2$ inches wide for a regular tape size or $2^1/_2$ inches wide if you want to double-fold your binding. Cut the strips as long as possible. Remember to draw the diagonal and measure the width of each strip. Cut the strips carefully, and don't stretch them. Pin right sides together at a right angle; it doesn't look right, but it works. Open the binding to check if you pinned it correctly. Sew a $^1/_2$-inch seam; then press it open. Sew the ends together with a $^1/_2$-inch seam allowance.

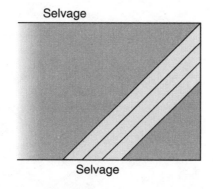

Selvage

Selvage

Angle your strips so they will stretch, and yes, I'm certain that's how to pin them.

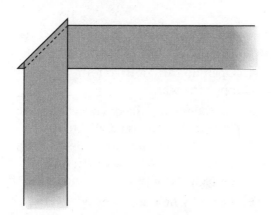

Molar Method of Making Bias

There is another method of cutting the bias strips that is faster and easier, especially if you are cutting large amounts of binding. I call it the molar method, but its true name is the continuous-roll technique. One 36-inch square of fabric will make approximately 15 yards of $1^1/_2$-inch binding or 12 yards of $2^1/_2$-inch binding. If you use the entire width of your fabric, 43 inches, you will make 22 yards of $1^1/_2$-inch binding or 15 yards of $2^1/_2$-inch binding. Isn't that amazing? The directions may seem puzzling, but I will describe them step by step.

1. Cut a square of fabric either 36 or 43 inches square, depending on how much binding you need.

2. Cut the square in half on the diagonal to form two triangles. If you want, pin a paper with letters to each of the sides so you can figure out which ones are sewn together. Follow figure a. Side A is opposite side B, C is across from D.

Cut apart the square into two triangles. (b) Pin and sew sides A and B to make a big tooth—hence the molar!

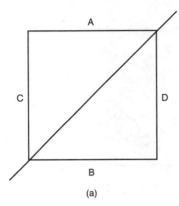

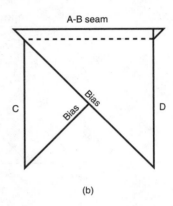

(a)

(b)

3. Sew sides A and B right sides together to form the molar shape. Make a ¹/₂-inch seam down the AB side (see figure b).

Don't Get Stuck!
When sewing by the molar technique, check to be sure that the seam is on the straight of grain and does not stretch. Pull the roots of the molar and make sure they *do* stretch. Look at figure b. I can't tell you how many times my bias did not stretch because I didn't sew the seams correctly.

4. Open up this tooth to form a parallelogram. Press open the seam.

5. On the wrong side of your fabric, use a see-through ruler to draw lines parallel to the bias sides. If you are using the binding for a full-size quilt, the width should be between 2 to 2¹/₂ inches; for a smaller project, measure 1¹/₂ to 2 inches (see figure c).

6. Carefully hold together sides C to D; they are the straight-of-grain and will not stretch. This may seem backward because the seams are going in opposite directions. You will form a tube or sleeve, but shift the right side down one bias line so the top left side has formed a tail sticking up (see figure d). Pin to match the drawn lines.

(c) Draw parallel lines from side C to D.

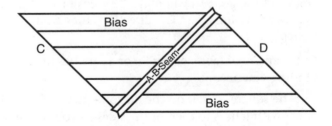

268

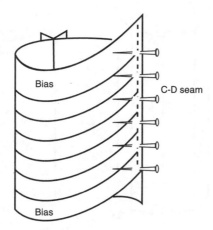

(d) Be the boss of your fabric—form a tube or sleeve with a tail off the top the size of the bias width.

7. Pin and sew a $1/2$-inch seam and be certain there is a tail on each end. Press this seam open.

8. Begin cutting at the top tail on the drawn line and spiral around the tube in one long cut (see figure e).

9. As I cut each yard of binding, I press it immediately and wrap it around a cardboard square. Can you imagine 20 yards of stretchy strips! It is so much easier to do a yard or two at a time. For a regular bias, press both sides under $1/4$ inch, then the entire strip in half down the center. When making a double bias, where the fabric is doubled, just fold the bias tape in half (see figure f).

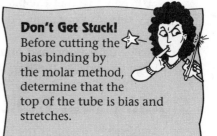

Don't Get Stuck!
Before cutting the bias binding by the molar method, determine that the top of the tube is bias and stretches.

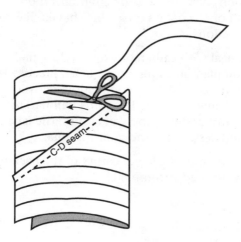

(e) This is one long cutting line. Just start at the top and cut in a spiral around and around and around.

(f) Don't get into a bind. Press as you go.

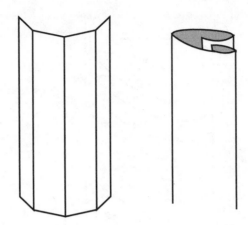

10. Sew together the bias tape right sides to the quilt top right sides, around the perimeter of your quilt. Fold over and whipstitch or use an appliqué stitch to secure.

I told you this method of making binding was tricky, but it is so efficient when making large amounts of binding that it's worth the effort.

Signing Your Quilt

Signing your quilt is the finishing touch to your quilting experience. Your work of art should be signed and dated. A running stitch of quilting thread signing your name can be sewn on the front or back of your quilt. If you want your name and date to stand out more, you can use embroidery floss and a decorative embroidery stitch.

Many of my students sign their quilts with labels placed on the back. One class assembled a wall hanging of different storybook characters for the children's room of a library. We signed the back of the quilt with all of our names on a label shaped like an open book. See this photo in the color photo section.

There are many terrific books that deal with calligraphy and styling memorable labels. Wash and shrink the fabric that you plan on using for the label. Practice writing with an indelible fine-point pen. Record your name, date of completion, occasion for making the quilt, and who you are giving it to. Some quilts are like cards hallmarking events and including memorable quotations. Turn under $1/4$ inch all around the label. You can hand- or machine-embroider the edges and designs around your insignia.

Attach your label with an invisible stitch to the lower corner of the backing. Sign your quilt and shout to the world that your quilt is complete!

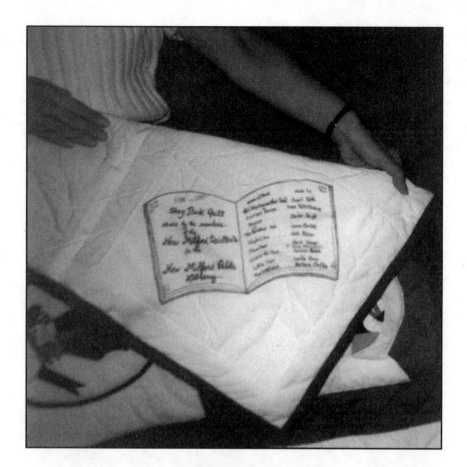

Hallmark events with your labels.

Scraps and Pieces

Those who collect quilts can date and follow a quilt's history with the information found from the signing. Many quilts were found with names signed on the front of special blocks. These were called Album quilts. Album quilts were often group projects that had each block signed by the designer. Blocks were even developed with a special space for signing your name. Our quilting ancestors took this signing seriously and developed special ink, quill pens, and patterned metal stencil plates. Calligraphy was practiced until their handwriting was perfected.

The Least You Need to Know

➤ Folding fabric over the quilt ends will enclose the raveling edges.

➤ Bias binding is the most durable technique for finishing ends.

➤ Bias binding can be made in one continuous roll.

➤ Signing and dating your quilt is the final step to the completion of your quilt.

➤ When making a label, wash and shrink the fabric and use a permanent ink pen.

Chapter 21

How to Take Care of Your Quilt

In This Chapter

➤ Elements that can destroy your quilt

➤ The best strategy for cleaning your quilt

➤ How to wash your quilt

➤ Where to store your quilt

I hope by now you are admiring and using your quilt. If you understand how and what affects fibers and batting you can add to your quilt's longevity. As you use your quilt, sometimes bad things happen. If you do need to clean your quilt, there are certain considerations you must keep in mind. Knowing the type of fiber your quilt is made of is extremely important. When cleaning, the choices range from dry cleaning to hand-washing your quilt in your bathtub to even vacuuming. We'll explore all these methods.

Throughout its lifetime, your quilt occasionally will need a rest, so where and how to store it is important. You would feel horrible taking your quilt out of storage and discovering that it has faded, stretched out of shape, or has a musty smell. We want our children and their children to treasure your workmanship. As my husband says, "Don't jilt your quilt; take care of it to the hilt!"

Drying and Dry Cleaning

I hate to even think about your quilt getting dirty, but the time will come when you will need to launder it. Before you choose how to clean your quilt, you need to know how different factors will affect it. Textiles are sensitive to light, humidity, and stretching or breaking of the fibers. In general, the less cleaning the better for your quilt. If your quilt is just dusty, you can air it outdoors when the humidity is low—but not in direct sunlight. You can hang the quilt on a line as long as the quilt is dry. For airing out my quilts, I'm lucky because I have a neighbor with three parallel clothes-lines that I can drape my quilts over so they don't stretch. A quilt that is just dusty could also be placed in the dryer on "air" setting for 10 or 15 minutes.

I hope your quilt never gets stained, but accidents do happen. Try to treat stains as soon as possible before they set. Examine the stain and spot clean it with an appropriate cleaner. There are charts that deal with specific types of stains on the cleaner bottle or packaging. Try not to rub too hard as you may destroy the fibers. If your quilt is made of silk or wool or if you don't know the origin of the stain, seek professional help. Check out several dry cleaners and choose one that is knowledgeable in quilt cleaning. If your fabric is colorfast, it is better to wash it by hand than to have it dry cleaned. Those chemicals and the way they affect the fibers always worry me.

Quilting Bee
If your quilt is just dusty and has no stains, you can vacuum it. Place a clean screen or netting over your quilt to protect it. Then use a brush attachment to carefully go over the quilt, removing the dust. The screening keeps the fabric from being sucked up into the vacuum. Wouldn't that be a horrible sight?

Give Your Quilt a Bath

Always know the fiber content of the quilts you create. It should be 100 percent cotton or a cotton-polyester blend. Because you washed your fabrics before you assembled your quilt, you already know they won't shrink or run. I usually wash my fabrics in the washing machine and then throw them in the dryer. You can treat your quilt *almost* the same way. You can use the washing machine but I would not use the dryer, as it will weaken the quilting stitches and stretch the quilt out of shape. Place your quilt in the washer carefully and use a gentle cycle with cold water. Add Woolite or a mild detergent developed especially for quilt cleaning. If your quilt is an antique or is valuable, never use a machine washer.

Quilting Bee
Don't pick up a wet quilt from one end! Gently lift under it to remove it from the sink or tub. When the quilt is wet it weighs so much that the quilting stitches may break and the fibers can stretch out of shape.

For those of you who are too timid to throw your quilts in the washer, you can launder them in a large sink or the bathtub. Use lukewarm water with a mild detergent and gently press the water through the quilt—do not squeeze. Empty the tub of water and rinse out the soap. You may have to change the rinse water several times to assure that all the cleanser is removed. Carefully pick up the wet quilt and support its weight from underneath.

Dry your quilt on a flat surface if possible. Go outside on a day with low humidity and spread out a sheet with towels over it to soak up the water. Place the wet quilt on top. Remember, do not put the quilt in direct sunlight; you don't want the colors to fade.

Fold Your Quilt the Acid-Free Way

Care for your quilt today and it will become tomorrow's heirloom. Sooner or later you will start accumulating quilts. It's great fun to be able to switch them around once in a while, so storing them properly is essential. Beware of dirt, creases, dampness, and sunlight. Find a cool, dry place to stash them. Don't use a basement or attic where your quilts may get water damaged or develop mildew or a musty smell. Fold them in a drawer or chest lined with *acid-free tissue paper* or a clean cotton sheet.

Occasionally refold your quilt in a different manner so that crease marks will not develop. I have discovered it is not a good idea to fold a Lone Star quilt (one large eight-point star composed of diamonds) down the center of the star. It stretches the center where all the points come together. I like to fold that quilt into thirds. To remove wrinkles from incorrect folding or just from storing, you could put in the dryer with a damp cloth for several minutes. This is also a good way to fluff up the batting.

> **Quilt Talk**
> *Acid-free tissue paper* is a tissue paper made without chemicals that would destroy fibers. It can be purchased from craft catalogues or from dry cleaners.

Here are two more last-minute thoughts. This first one is very important—don't iron your quilts. The heat of the iron will compact the batting and may even melt it into a gluey mess. If your quilt is wrinkled, don't worry, all the antique quilts have that wonderful rumpled, used look. Second, don't store quilts in plastic bags, especially garbage bags. The plastic traps any dampness and the fabric may mildew.

I'd like to tell you a frightening story (for a quilter, that is). One of my quilting ladies was storing this wonderful quilt she was working on in a large garbage bag. One day her husband took several bags of used clothes to the Salvation Army and deposited them in their collection bin. You can imagine what happened! Lucille made call after call to different collection agencies until luckily she found someone who had put the quilt aside. It seemed the woman was a quilter and realized that since it was a work-in-progress with pins and basting thread, it must have been put there by mistake. Lucille got her quilt back but now stores and transports her quilts in a large carryall. Please don't use plastic garbage bags!

Take care of your quilts and they will give warmth to your body and soul for your lifetime and more.

The Least You Need to Know

➤ Use a mild detergent for hand- or machine-washing your quilt.

➤ Don't hang your quilt when it is wet, since the weight will break the quilting threads and stretch the fabric out of shape.

➤ Store your quilts in a cool, dry area and wrap them in acid-free tissue paper or a clean cotton sheet.

➤ Don't iron quilts.

➤ Don't use plastic bags to store your quilts.

Chapter 22

Projects from Start to Finish

In This Chapter

➤ Preparing a pillow from a quilt block

➤ How to insert lace, piping, or a ruffle onto the edges

➤ Methods of hanging a quilt

Small projects are a good beginning for novices. Not everyone is ready to make a bed-size quilt, but you may want to make a pillow or wall hanging. Display your creation so the world can see it. Hanging quilts on the wall is very popular in decorating today. From modern geometric shapes to countrified Sampler quilts, a quilted wall hanging can enhance your room. There are different styles and methods of hanging your quilt. Decide on the look you want to achieve. Your quilt can appear to be floating on the wall, or you can make a tab top with loops of fabric, adding to your quilt's decorative value. The choice is yours.

Remember when I said not to worry if you decided not to use one of your patches? Now is the time to use it in a pillow. Your pillow can be tailored with piping, or very feminine with lace or a ruffle. Stuffing your pillow and setting it on your couch or bed is very satisfying. Let's learn how to make two small projects from start to finish.

Making a Pillow

Here are instructions for making a basic pillow. If you get really ambitious, I'll give you directions for embellishing your edges with a ruffle, lace, or *piping*.

Quilt Talk
Piping is a tiny contrasting strip of bias fabric with a cord inside. This corded fabric is sewed into a seam, forming a decorative edge.

Quilting Bee
Use an inexpensive washed muslin for the backing of the pillow top. No one will ever see it because it will be inside the pillow.

Don't Get Stuck!
When a zipper is used on the backing of the pillow, leave the zipper open for several inches before you sew the pillow backing and layered pillow top together. This way you can pull the pillowcase through the opening.

Quilting Bee
Push out the pillow corners to form a crisp point. I use the eraser end of a pencil.

Use a patch that coordinates with your quilt to make an ensemble—here goes!

1. Make the block of your choice, or use an extra one left over from your quilt. Add a border if you want to make your pillow larger than 12 inches. You can prepare a regular border and miter the corners. (Check out Chapter 17, "Setting It All Together," for instructions on borders and mitering.)

2. Press your pillow top.

3. Add batting and a muslin backing. Baste together all three layers in sunburst lines.

4. Quilt decorative stitches in your chosen design, such as the stitch in the ditch, outline, overall, or echo designs. (Look at Chapter 19, "Quilting 101.")

5. Insert any decorative edging, piping, lace, or ruffle. Each insert will be discussed later in this chapter.

6. Prepare the pillow back in a coordinating fabric. You can have one solid piece of fabric for the backing, a zippered backing, or a lapped backing held together with Velcro. I'll discuss how to prepare the backing later in this chapter.

7. To assemble the pillow, pin the layered pillow top to the pillow back, right sides together. Sew around the perimeter of the pillowcase at $1/4$ inch from the edge. If the backing is one solid piece of fabric, leave about six inches unsewn on the bottom seam so you can turn the pillowcase right-side-out. If the back is lapped with Velcro or a zipper, you can sew the seam all the way around.

8. Reach into the open seam or zipper and pull the pillowcase through, turning it right-side-out.

9. Use a pillow form or pack your pillow until firm with polyester fiberfill. Push the stuffing into the corners with a ruler or pencil and then add more if needed.

10. Fold the seam allowances over and invisibly stitch the opening at the bottom of the pillow if necessary.

Place right sides together and then sew around, leaving open about six inches on one side.

Now let's see how we can make our pillow even fancier.

Lace Insertions

Measure the perimeter of the pillow and add four more inches for finishing the corners and the ends. Purchase that amount of lace. Align the straight edge of the lace, right sides together, to the outside edge of the pillow top, with the ruffled edge facing in.

Start pinning in the middle of the bottom side of the pillow top. Make a $1/2$-inch fold at each corner and pin the lace securely all around the pillow top. When you've reached where you started, angle both ends of the lace into the edge of the seam allowance. Sew lace all around the outside edge. Continue with step 6, above—preparing the pillow backing.

This looks backward, but it's not. Sew all around the outside edge, angling the lace off the edges.

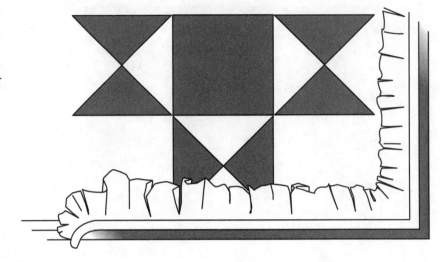

Inserting Piping

Quilt Talk

The *zipper foot* is a presser foot that can slide to one side and is used to sew in zippers. But it can also let you sew very closely to the piping cord. Use it when sewing the piping to the pillow back.

Sometimes you want to add a contrasting color but want a more tailored edge to finish your pillow. This is when you'd use piping. Measure the sides of the pillow and add about two inches more to the length. The round fabric cording can be purchased at fabric or craft stores in a variety of colors. The piping is applied in the same manner as lace, placing the piping's raw edge next to the pillow top's edges with the bulky cord facing to the center. Pin to the corner; then clip the tape up to the cord, allowing the tape to open. Turn the corner, continuing to pin up the next side. Sew along the piping's line of stitches. Use a *zipper foot* if you need to, securing the piping onto the pillow top.

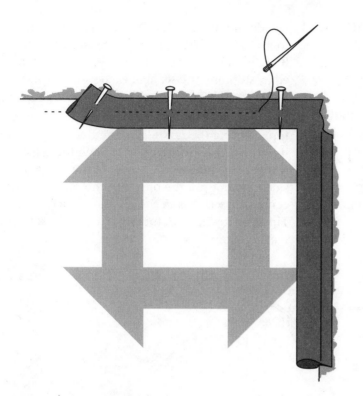

Clip into each corner to turn the piping around the pillow corner.

Applying a Ruffle

When you get really ambitious, you may want to add a ruffle to the edge of your pillow. This gets a little complicated, so I hope you are ready.

1. Cut the ruffle strips. Measure around the outside edge of the pillow; then double it to calculate the amount needed. If your pillow is 15 inches square, you need to cut a strip 120 inches (15 + 15 + 15 + 15 = 60 × 2 = 120 inches). Determine how wide you want your ruffle. Let's say two inches. Double that amount and add on $^1/_2$ inch for the seam allowance (2 + 2 + $^1/_2$ = 4$^1/_2$ inches). The ruffle should be cut 120 inches by 4$^1/_2$ inches. Cut the strips from selvage to selvage across the width of the fabric, usually three strips of 40 inches.

2. Sew each short end together; then sew the final ends together to form a circular strip. Fold the ruffle in half, wrong sides together, so the strip is 2$^1/_2$ inches wide.

3. Divide the ruffle into four equal sections and insert four pins, one to mark each section (see figure a). Baste with your sewing machine ¹/₄ inch from the edge, stopping the seam at each pin, leaving an inch-long thread between each section (see figure b).

4. Secure a pin at the middle of each side of the pillow top, aligning the raw edges together, the ruffle facing into the center (see figure c). Match the pins on the ruffle to the pins in the center of the pillow top sides. Do not pin the pins into the corners, but center the sections in the middle of each side. This way it will work for any size pillow, square or rectangular.

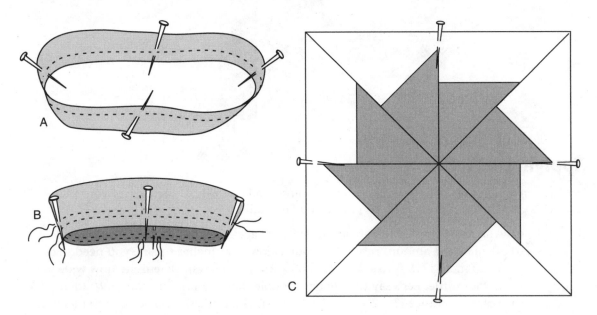

Gather ye ruffles.

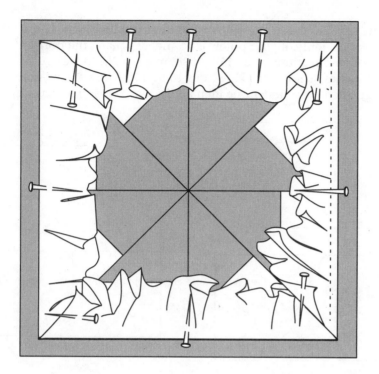

Don't get ruffled—pin the corners of the ruffle so the fabric won't shift.

5. Pull the ends of the threads between each section to gather the ruffle to fit the sides of the pillow. Pin the ruffle every few inches to secure it to the pillow top.

6. Baste the ruffle to the pillow top $1/4$ inch from the raw edges; then continue preparing the pillow back in step 6 of making a pillow, above.

Quilting Bee
Occasionally pin the finished edge of the ruffle to the pillow top, around the corners especially. There is a tendency for the ruffle to shift and get caught in the seam when you sew the pillow backing to the pillow top.

Finishing the Pillow Back

The pillow I gave you instructionsfor earlier is made with a solid square of fabric as the backing. But if you ever want to remove the pillowcase for cleaning, you will need to make a different kind of backing. In that case, divide the backing into two overlapping sections or two sections held together with a zipper. The zipper application is for experienced sewers only.

Make sure the pillow backings are large enough. There should be enough of a lap so the backing doesn't pull open when the pillow is inside. Measure the size of your pillow, and add one inch to the horizontal size. However, you must add considerably more in the other direction: Calculate half the size of the pillow, and then add four inches for a fold. Cut two of these pieces. For example, if your pillow is 15 inches square, the horizontal size is 16 inches. For the other direction divide 15 by two, making 7¹/₂ inches. Add four inches for a total of 11¹/₂ inches. Cut two backing sides 16 by 11¹/₂ inches. Fold down ¹/₄ inch to finish off the edge; then press under one inch all the way across (see figure a).

Fold ¹/₄ inch under and then fold one more inch to finish the lap. Position by overlapping these edges.

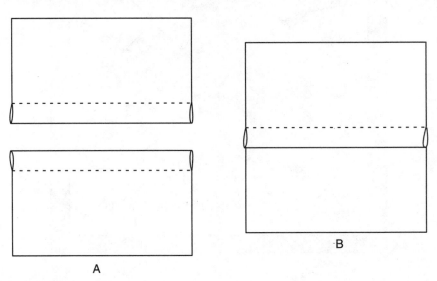

A

B

Overlap these folded edges so they are the same size as the pillow top (see figure b). Baste both ends of the lapped pieces together to hold securely. Turn this lapped backing right side to the right side of the pillow top. Pin the pillow top and backing together and sew at ¹/₄ inch all the way around the outside edges.

Add a strip of Velcro to the top and bottom of the lapped edges.

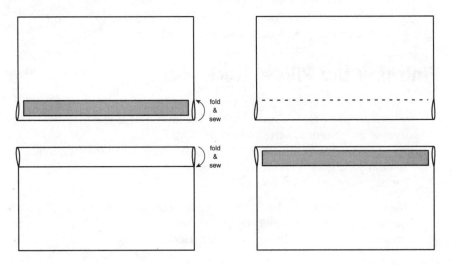

fold & sew

fold & sew

After you sew together the pieces, pull the right side of the pillowcase through the opening of the lap. Insert your pillow form, and you have a pillow.

Some people who want a professional-looking pillow insert a zipper into the backing. Beware: This is not easy. Cut two pieces of backing fabric, half the size of the backing, and then add one inch to both pieces where the zipper will be attached.

The zipper should be about two inches shorter than the width of the pillow. Read the directions on the inside of the zipper package for how to prepare the zipper placket and then stitch the zipper into the seam. Turn the backing over and center it over the pillow top, right sides together. Sew all around the outside edge. Then turn the pillow right-side-out.

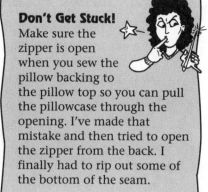

Don't Get Stuck!
Make sure the zipper is open when you sew the pillow backing to the pillow top so you can pull the pillowcase through the opening. I've made that mistake and then tried to open the zipper from the back. I finally had to rip out some of the bottom of the seam.

Zip into your pillow—calculate the size of each backing piece.

Quilts Are the New Artwork

Quilts can be found in museums and are recognized as an art form. We can hang quilts in our houses too. Make your home a gallery to display your quilts. There are several lines of thought on ways to hang quilts. You can attach a sleeve or casing to the top of the backing and push a dowel, curtain rod, or furring strip through as a hanger. The quilt in this method appears to be floating on the wall, since the casing and rod are invisible on the front. On the other hand, you can make the style of hanging a decorative part of the quilt design. Loops or tabs are sewn to the top of the quilt and hung on a fancy rod. Let's decide which you want to make. Find the wall hanging with the tab top in the color photo section.

Hidden Sleeve Method

Measure the horizontal width of your quilt, and subtract two inches from that amount. You want to have enough room at each end of the sleeve to have the rod hang on a nail. If your quilt is very wide, you may want to divide the sleeve in half, forming two pockets. Then you will be able to hang the rod on three nails, one at each end and then one in the middle. You don't want your rod to bow under the quilt's weight.

Quilting Bee
Do not sew with the tube stretched flat against the backing. Allow an excess on the top half of the tube to hang loose, making more room for the rod to slip into the sleeve.

Cut a strip three to four inches wide, depending on the size of the rod and the length of the horizontal measurement of the quilt. Finish each short end of the strip.

Then fold the length in half and sew a $1/4$-inch seam. Finger press the tube so that the seam runs down the center. Center this casing and pin it across the backing about $1/2$ inch from the top of the quilt. Invisibly stitch the top of the casing, then sew the bottom length of the sleeve.

Put your sanded dowel or rod through the sleeve and hang your work of art.

Make a long tube with both ends folded under to finish and press down.

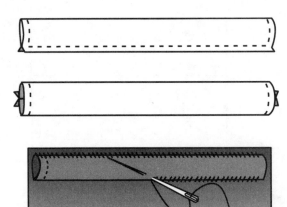

Put on your sleeves. Use an appliqué stitch or whipstitch to sew the tube into place. Sew the back of the sleeve flush against the backing, but leave the sleeve loose.

Wall hanging back

Fabric Loops

This method has visible fabric loops to hold the rod. Let's find out how to make those loops that look so beautiful.

1. Decide on the width of the loops. I like about two inches. Double that amount and add $1/2$ inch for seam allowances. I cut my strips $2 + 2 + 1/2 = 41/2$ inches wide, and from selvage to selvage for the length, making the strip $41/2$ by the fabric width.

2. Fold this strip in half lengthwise with right sides together.

3. Sew a $1/4$-inch seam down the length and press the seam down the center, forming a tube (see figure a).

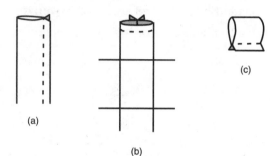

(a)

(b)

(c)

Don't get loopy! Sew and press the seam and then turn the tube right-side-out. Cut it into sections.

4. Cut the tube into sections, double the size you want for each loop, and then add $1/2$ inch seam allowance to determine the amount. If you want a two-inch loop, cut the tube into $41/2$-inch sections (see figure b).

5. Sew the ends of each section together to form a circular loop (see figure c).

6. Evenly space and attach loops to the top of the backing and whipstitch or invisible stitch.

Quilting Bee
When making loops for hanging your quilt, you can get approximately seven or eight loop sections from each 44 inch width of fabric.

This quilt hanging looks like a banner that announces your quilt artistry. If your quilt bottom ripples, you may want to put a sleeve on the bottom of the backing so that the rod will hold your quilt flush to the wall.

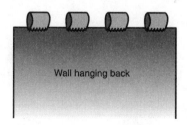

Wall hanging back

Sew loop to loop to loop to hang your quilt.

The Least You Need to Know

➤ A pillow top must be quilted with a batting and backing before the pillow back is attached.

➤ Lace, piping, and a ruffle are inserted after the pillow top is quilted but before the pillow back is attached.

➤ When cutting the pillow back for use with a zipper or lapped back, be sure to have more fabric to accommodate the finished edges and the overlapping fabric.

➤ You can hang quilts with a hidden sleeve or top loops, depending on the appearance you want.

Glossary

Acid-free tissue paper   A tissue paper made without chemicals that would destroy the fabric fibers.

Album quilts   Friendship quilts assembled from individual blocks, each executed and signed by a different person, and presented to a friend or public figure on a special occasion.

Amish quilts   Quilts made by members of the Amish or Mennonite communities. The quilts are characterized by solid dark and bright colors with intricate, beautiful hand-quilting designs.

Appliqué   Small fabric shapes placed on a background fabric and stitched on by hand or machine. Realistic motifs can include flowers, animals, houses, or almost any rendering of a picture.

Backing   The back, or bottom layer, of the quilt.

Backstitch   A stitch taken backward from the direction you are sewing to reinforce the beginning and end of each seam.

Baste   Temporarily pin together, or sew together with long stitches, one or more pieces of fabric or two or more layers.

Batting   The middle or filling layer placed between the quilt top and backing. It adds warmth and dimension to the quilt.

Bias   Any diagonal direction of a woven fabric. True bias is at a 45-degree angle to the selvage.

Binding   A long strip of fabric, usually bias, that finishes the raw edges of a quilt.

Block   A complete design unit that makes up a quilt. It can be a square that has many shapes pieced or appliquéd into the unit.

Bolt   Fabric rolled around a cardboard base. The end of the bolt includes information about fiber content, finish, and price.

Border   A long continuous piece of fabric, or series of bands of colors, that frames the outside edge of the quilt top. Borders can be as simple as solid strips of fabric or very intricate geometric patterns or appliqués.

Calico   A 100 percent cotton fabric used for quilting. The word originally meant a process of printing small floral designs using a roller.

Clipping   Cutting into the seam allowance so the fabric lays flat.

Complementary colors   The colors found across from each other on the color wheel. An example of complementary colors is red and green.

Contrasting color   A secondary color that is used in a small quilt to accent the dominant color of a color scheme. An example of a contrasting color, in a red, white, and blue color scheme if the dominant color is blue, is red.

Crazy quilts   Quilts that became popular around the time of the American Centennial and were made from random sizes and shapes of fabric (usually silks and velvets) with intricate embroidery to decorate the surface.

Crosswise grain   The grain line that runs at a right angle to the selvage.

Dominant color   The main color of a quilt.

Echo quilting   Quilting stitches that follow the outline of the blocks' basic design and are then repeated, like ripples, every $1/4$ inch in concentric lines.

Fat quarter   A $1/4$ yard of fabric cut 18" × 22".

Grain   The direction that the threads are woven in a fabric. The lengthwise grain runs the length of the fabric and parallel to the selvage. Crosswise grain is the direction that runs at a right angle to the lengthwise grain.

Hawaiian quilts   Quilts made up of one piece of fabric folded and cut into a large overall design of leaves or flowers and then appliquéd onto a background fabric.

Hue   The gradation or variety of a color, usually with a name further describing the color, such as navy blue or magenta.

Lap quilt   A small quilt usually under 60 inches square and put together with six or nine blocks.

Lattice   A strip of fabric that separates and frames each block in a quilt. It can also be called sashing.

Lengthwise grain   The direction that runs parallel to the selvage on woven fabric.

Loft   The thickness or puffiness of a quilt batting.

Log Cabin   A block that has a series of strips that are placed around a central square, which is usually red. One diagonal half of each block is colored with light fabrics and the other diagonal half with dark fabrics.

Lone Star   Also called the Star of Bethlehem, which became popular in the 1820s. This quilt pattern is composed of many small fabric diamonds assembled into eight larger diamonds that form a star.

Medallion quilt   A quilt assembled around one large central motif, with one or more borders to finish out the quilt.

Miter   To join two pieces of fabric so that the ends meet at a right angle with a diagonal seam.

Muslin   An off-white woven cotton fabric.

Nap   A quality of fabric that has its fibers brushed in one direction causing a different coloration. Velvet is an example. Patterns of any fabric with a one-way design can also be considered to have a nap.

Patchwork   A term that refers to the process of piecing or appliquéing various fabric shapes together.

Piecing   Cutting out fabric shapes and sewing them together, two pieces at a time, with small running stitches to form a larger unit, usually a block.

Piping   A tiny contrasting strip of bias fabric with a cord inside. This corded fabric is inserted into a seam, forming a decorative edge.

Quilting   The process of securing all three layers of a quilt together with small running stitches.

Quilting frame   A free-standing rectangle on legs that holds a quilt, allowing several people to stitch a section, then roll the quilt to another section until the whole quilt is finished.

Quilter's quarter   A plastic rod ($1/4" \times 1/4" \times 8"$) used to mark the $1/4$-inch seam line for quilting or cutting.

Quilt stencil   A plastic sheet with grooves cut out in a specific design, for use in marking a quilt design on a quilt top.

Quilt top   The completed patchwork design used as the right side or face of a quilt. It is the top layer of a quilt.

Sampler quilt   A quilt that combines blocks of different types of patterns, making it a perfect quilt for beginners to learn both piecing and appliqué techniques.

Sashing   Another name for lattice, or the strips that frame each block.

Selvage (or selvedge)   The two parallel finished edges of fabric that do not ravel and are more closely woven than the rest of the fabric. They run in the same direction as the lengthwise grain.

Setting the top   Arranging the completed blocks, lattices, and borders to form a quilt top. The process is also known as setting together.

Shade   A hue that has been blended with black or a darker color. Cranberry is a shade of red.

Stabbing   A stitching technique for quilting using both hands in which you insert the needle into your quilt, pull it out the bottom with your other hand under the hoop, then push it up from the bottom to the top. The stitches are uneven and crooked on the underside.

Strip piecing   A method of creating quilts by taking long strips of fabric and sewing them together in a set sequence. This newly combined material is then cut apart and resewn to form a part of a quilt. A good example is Rail Fence.

Template   A pattern shape of a quilt design made of plastic or cardboard and used to trace shapes for appliqué or piecing. Some templates include the seam allowances while others, like the ones in this book, do not.

Tint   A hue that is blended with light or white colors. Pink is a tint of red.

Value   The lightness or darkness of a color—either tints or shades.

Whipstitch   A stitch that holds together two finished edges. The needle is inserted at a right angle to the edge through both fabrics, forming a slanted stitch.

Whole cloth quilt   A quilt top for a bed covering, made of one single piece of fabric.

Yo-Yo quilt   A novelty bed covering made from small round pieces of fabric gathered to form a flat circle, many of which are then invisibly sewn together.

Suggested Reading: Books That I Love to Look At and Read

If this book has whetted your appetite for quilting, there are hundreds of wonderful books that have more challenging and creative projects. Here are just some of my favorites that I have been using for over 20 years.

Better Homes and Gardens. *American Patchwork and Quilting.* Des Moines, IA: Meredith Corporation, 1985.

Beyer, Jinny. *The Quilter's Album of Blocks and Borders.* McLean, VA: EPM Publications, 1980.

Bonesteel, Georgia. *Lap Quilting.* Birmingham, AL: Oxmoor House, 1983.

Bonesteel, Georgia. *More Lap Quilting.* Birmingham, AL: Oxmoor House, 1985.

Bonesteel, Georgia. *New Ideas for Lap Quilting.* Birmingham, AL: Oxmoor House, Inc., 1987

Bradkin, Cheryl Greider. *Basic Seminole Patchwork.* Mountain View, CA: Leone Publications, 1990.

Burns, Eleanor. *Quilt in a Day Series.* San Marcos, CA: Quilt in a Day, 1987.

Duke, Dennis and Deborah Harding. *America's Glorious Quilts.* New York, NY: Park Lane, 1989.

Donoughue, Rosemary. *Painless Patchwork.* Birchgrove, Australia: Sally Milner Publishing Pty Ltd., 1991.

Fanning, Robbie and Tony. *The Complete Book of Machine Quilting.* Radnor, PA: Chilton Book Company, 1980.

Frager, Dorothy. *The Quilting Primer, second ed*. Radnor, PA: Chilton Book Company, 1979.

Hassel, Carla J. *You Can be a Super Quilter*. Radnor, PA: Wallace-Homestead Book Co., 1980.

Hassel, Carla J. *Super Quilter II*. Des Moines, IA: Wallace-Homestead Book Company, 1982.

Hughes, Trudie. *Template-Free Quilts and Borders*. Bothell, WA: That Patchwork Place, 1990.

Ickis, Marguerite. *The Standard Book of Quilt Making and Collecting*. New York, NY: Dover Publications, 1949.

Leone, Diana. *The New Sampler Quilt Book*. Lafayette, CA: C & T Publishing, 1993.

Leone, Diana. *The Sampler Quilt*. Mountain View, CA: Leone Publications, 1980.

MacDonald, Jessie. *Let's Make More Patchwork Quilts*. Philadelphia, PA: Farm Journal, Inc., 1984.

Malone, Maggie. *1001 Patchwork Designs*. New York, NY: Sterling Publishing Co., Inc., 1982.

Malone, Maggie. *Quilting Shortcuts*. New York, NY: Sterling Publishing Co., Inc., 1986.

Martin, Judy. *Scrap Quilts*. Wheatridge, CO: Moon Over the Mountain Publishing Company, 1985.

Martin, Nancy J. *Threads of Time*. Bothell, WA: That Patchwork Place, 1990.

McKelvey, Susan. *Friendship's Offering, Techniques and Inspiration for Writing on Quilts*. Lafayette, CA: C & T Publishing, 1990.

O'Brien, Sandra L. *Great American Quilts 1990*. Birmingham, AL: Oxmoor House, 1989.

Ocvirk, Otto. *Art Fundamentals, Theory and Practice*. Dubuque, IA: Wm. C. Brown Company, Publishers, 1968.

Penders, Mary Coyne. *Color and Cloth*. San Francisco, CA: The Quilt Digest Press, 1989.

Pellman, Rachel and Kenneth. *A Treasury of Amish Quilts*. Intercourse, PA: Good Books, 1990.

Poster, Donna. *Speed-Cut Quilts*. Radnor, PA: Chilton Book Company, 1989.

Seward, Linda. *Small Quilting Projects*. New York, NY: Sterling Publications, Co., Inc., 1988.

Sienkiewicz, Elly. *Baltimore Album Quilts*. Lafayette, CA: C & T Publishing, 1990.

Wiss, Audrey and Douglas. *Folk Quilts and How to Recreate Them*. Pittstown, NJ: Main Street Press, 1983.

Index

301